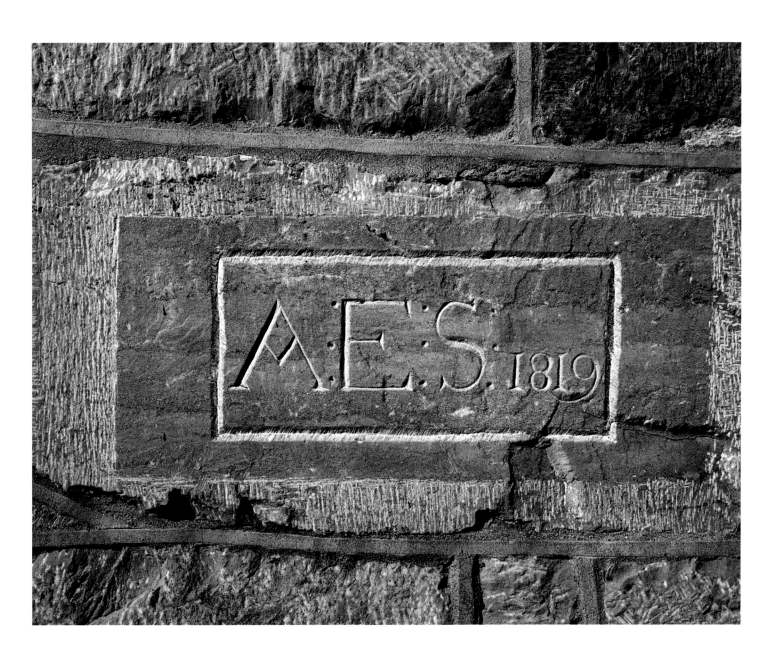

To Madeleine,

Come visit us in Jefferson County!

With best wishes.

John Allen

11·19·11

Uncommon Vernacular

The Early Houses of Jefferson County, West Virginia 1735–1835

John C. Allen, Jr.

[signature] 11·17·11

Photography by Walter Smalling, Jr.
Illustrations by Andrew Lewis, AIA

West Virginia University Press
Morgantown, West Virginia

West Virginia University Press, Morgantown 26506
© 2011 by West Virginia University Press

First edition published 2011 by West Virginia University Press
Printed in Singapore by Tien Wah Press

19   18   17   16   16   14   13   12   11   9   8   7   6   5   4   3   2   1

Library of Congress Cataloging-in-Publication Data

Allen, John C. (John Crile), Jr., 1970– author.
    Uncommon Vernacular : The Early Houses of Jefferson County,
West Virginia : 1735–1835 / by John C. Allen, Jr. ; Photography by
Walter Smalling Jr. ; Illustrations by Andrew Lewis, AIA. —
First edition.
        p.   cm.
    Includes bibliographical references and index.
    ISBN 978-1-933202-87-7 (alk. paper)
    1. Architecture, Domestic—West Virginia—Jefferson County—
History—18th century. 2. Architecture, Domestic—West Virginia—
Jefferson County—History—19th century 3. Vernacular architecture—
West Virginia—Jefferson County. I. Lewis, Andrew (Andrew Robert),
1958– illustrator. II. Smalling, Walter, photographer. III. Title.
IV. Title: Early Houses of Jefferson County, West Virginia.
    NA7235.W42J443 2011
    728.09754′9909033—dc22
                                                    2010053719

Book design by Robert L. Wiser, Silver Spring, Maryland

Composed in Monotype Bell

Page 1: Date stone, Springwood springhouse, "A.E.S. 1819"

Pages 2–3: Rees-Daniels House, ca. 1775, view of summer kitchen
in foreground sited to the side of the main house

Page 5: Limestone outcroppings in farm field, Harewood

Page 6: Jacob Homar bank barn, 1832, Leetown vicinity, decorative
brick ventilator

The West Virginia University Press
gratefully acknowledges the financial assistance
provided for this book by

Furthermore: a program of the J. M. Kaplan Fund

Historic Shepherdstown Commission, Inc.

Jefferson County Historical Society

Donald E. and Deborah A. Watts, to honor Alissa M. Watts

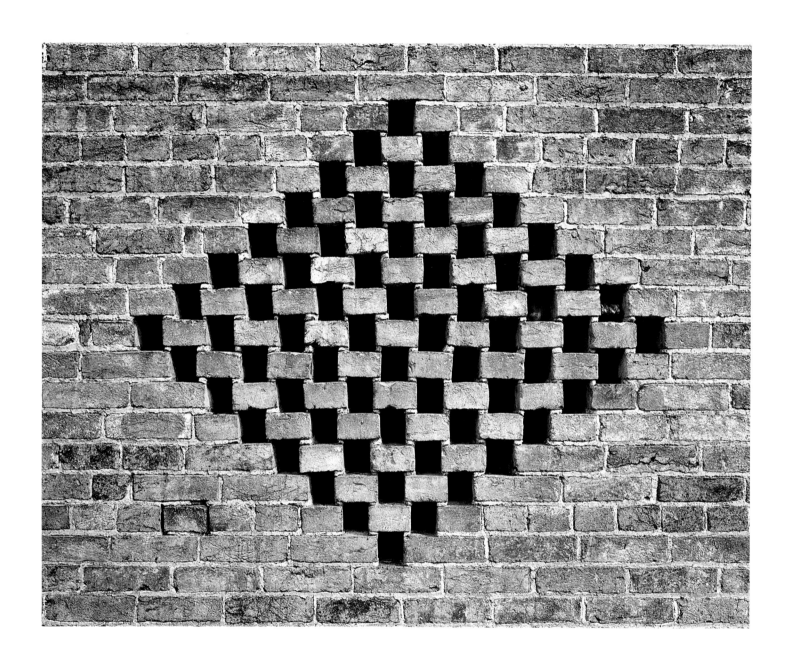

This book is dedicated
to my beloved son, Grady;
my parents for their boundless love and support;
and to the people who have lived
in Jefferson County and called it home.

Contents

Preface

View of the Blue Ridge Mountains
in southern Jefferson County

Uncommon Vernacular

The term "vernacular" means different things to different people. This modifier has caused a great deal of handwringing in the field of architectural history, where it is sometimes seen as a vague catch-all category for common buildings. Yet I contend that vernacular is the best descriptor for the early residential architecture of Jefferson County, West Virginia. The overwhelming majority of historic houses in the county do not adhere to formal archetypes, so, in that sense, the dwellings are vernacular. Even more importantly, though, vernacular can be used to describe buildings specific to an area, as in "the local vernacular." Neighboring counties have some similar building types but the group of early houses that stand today in Jefferson County is unique. The specific combinations of materials, construction techniques, detailing, and plan assortment that are common here are

absent just a few miles over the county borders. These qualities are what make the county's architecture notable, and they are what inspired the seemingly dichotomous title of this book, *Uncommon Vernacular.*

The landscape of Jefferson County is just as remarkable as its buildings. The undulating countryside, distant mountains, and winding rivers provide the dramatic setting for the county's historic farms and towns. The poetic siting and graceful forms of the county's oldest farmhouses draw frequent attention, while the houses of the small towns also resonate with history and beauty.

The county's historic town houses and farmhouses have roused the pride and curiosity of generations of residents. Despite their veneration, these homes have not been explained within their proper historical context. With their designs varied and

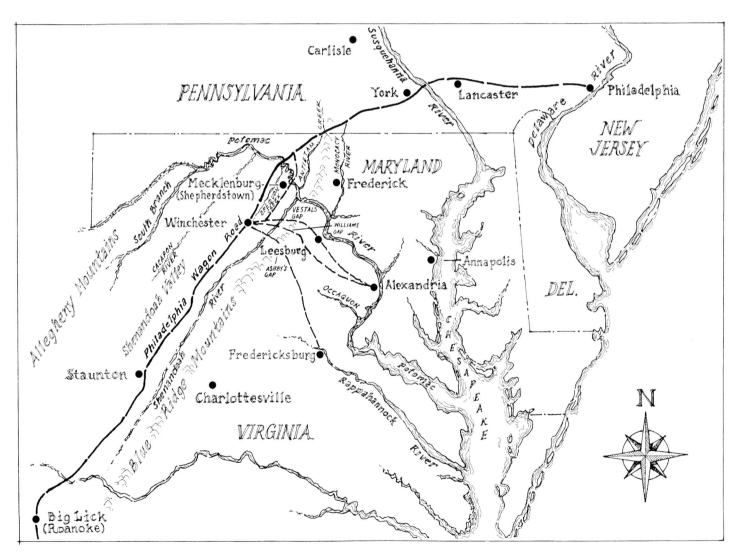

Mid-Atlantic region, ca. 1765, showing the path of the Philadelphia Wagon Road and routes over mountain passes

ages uncertain, the buildings appear to many as enigmatic relics of a murky and bygone era. They are referred to in generalized—sometimes inapt—terms such as "colonial" or "antebellum," and are often considered without any relation to neighboring houses, as if each were an alien encampment.

This study clarifies and illuminates the history of the county's early houses by tracing their development and categorizing the buildings by age and form, establishing patterns of construction, plan, and style. The book presents this work in a format that makes sense of the early residential vernacular, the type of construction and design particular to the county. Analyzing and placing these buildings in their historical context contributes to a more complex and rich understanding of the past and the people of Jefferson County, West Virginia.

Allstadt House and Ordinary

Purpose

This architectural study has three objectives: to document the physical features of Jefferson County's early houses, to accurately contextualize and understand the development of the house designs and details, and to promote the preservation of the county's historic structures and landscape.

The book is based on exhaustive documentation of two hundred and fifty houses and their associated outbuildings, which allows for in-depth examination of individual buildings as well as groups of buildings. It is important to record Jefferson County's unique architectural history not only for academic purposes but also because these houses are a finite—and dwindling—resource. Each year several of the county's historic buildings are lost to fire, neglect, or demolition. During the course of this study, six documented houses were reduced to rubble, and roughly ten percent of the houses stand unoccupied or in ruins. Documenting these irreplaceable artifacts thus becomes an increasingly urgent task. This publication catalogs and preserves the details of the county's extant historic houses and provides a framework for further study.

Second, this book assesses the collected information to provide a better understanding of how local architecture evolved in context. Discussions of the local history parallel the development of varying building practices, siting choices, material selections, ornamentation patterns, and other preferences of the county's eighteenth- and nineteenth-century builders and residents. Presented here is the wealth of cultural information contained in the early buildings of the small enclave of Jefferson County, readily available to scholars and other interested individuals.

Third, I hope that this book will inspire people to preserve these historic structures and landscapes. As the county's population grows in the twenty-first century, its rich architectural history and agricultural heritage must not be lost in the process. Many communities in this country have successfully protected their historic resources while fostering economic growth. Historic resources can, in fact, become a foundation for economic vitality. This study is intended to help identify and prioritize particular restoration and stabilization projects and aid in the long-term planning of the county and its municipalities.

Harewood interior (Samuel Washington House)

Opposite: Hurston (James Hurst House)

Methodology

From 2002 through 2004, I undertook a systematic survey of the entire county to identify historic farmhouses. I visited likely sites and searched for standing and ruined buildings; interviewed owners regarding occupied, abandoned, or destroyed houses on their property or on neighboring parcels; and made preliminary estimates of buildings' ages by exterior examination. I located two hundred and twenty farmhouses built before 1850 during this process.

Documentation of the compiled study group continued through 2010. Originally, I had planned to limit my efforts solely to eighteenth-century farmhouses. But after surveying a number of early buildings, I settled on 1835 as a more logical end-date for the study. Both stylistic and programmatic changes to the local residential architecture occur around this year, due in part to the arrival of the Chesapeake and Ohio Canal in 1834 and the Baltimore and Ohio Railroad in 1836. Roughly one hundred and fifty extant farmhouses were built before the cut-off date. I made every effort to include all farmhouses predating 1836 and by the end of the survey had documented 90 percent of them.

After identifying all of the farmhouses, I added town houses. Early extant town houses were less numerous than farmhouses—about one hundred—so this expanded the eligible pool of structures to roughly two hundred and fifty. The more significant remodeling that occurred in towns as residential buildings were adapted to commercial use left fewer town houses with intact floor plans and detailing. So I included and documented only half of the town houses built before 1836: those that retained enough original material to be conclusively understood.

In addition to the pre-railroad and -canal group, this study includes fifty houses from the period 1836 to 1850 in order to make informed conclusions regarding how local styles changed following the introduction of the new transportation systems. This sampling of later farmhouses and town houses provides a snapshot of how these buildings differed from those that were built before.

If a house plan had been radically altered within the study period, I sometimes placed the structure in two categories for the sake of statistical inquiry. Each dwelling built before 1836 was counted as a single house. However, houses that were altered before 1836 to another studied plan type were counted as two separate houses. For example, a 1790 side-hall house that became a center-hall house by addition in 1820 was counted twice. This example shows the later preference for the center-hall plan, and such statistical analysis reveals clear patterns of local building.

Traveler's Rest interior (General Horatio Gates House)

Detail at Piedmont (Dr. John Briscoe House)

Cold Spring (Robert Lucas III House)

Fieldwork

During the first site visit to a property, I examined the house and any outbuildings, recording my observations about exterior and interior features as well as the siting and orientation of each. I noted construction techniques, building materials and stylistic features, and any changes to the original fabric or plan of the house, such as additions and remodeling. I measured each house for floor plan rendering and took 35mm color photographs of the construction and details.

Architectural photographer Walter Smalling accompanied me on the second site visit. Smalling documented exterior and interior features using four-by-five-inch black-and-white film. The large-format negatives capture more detail than smaller negatives and were chosen to match the standards of the Historic American Buildings Survey (HABS) collection at the Library of Congress, with which they will ultimately be catalogued. During the seven years of documentation more than 3,000 black-and-white and 14,000 color images were taken. In addition to photograph documentation, the second visit was used to verify previous field measurements.

La Grange (John Hurst IV House)

Illustrations and Floor Plans

While some houses remained much as they had been created, others had been significantly altered. For the modified houses, illustrator Andrew Lewis created restored drawings from the field measurements and photographs. These restored views remove later alterations and return original features to the rendering, giving a clear view of the original appearance of a house. Lewis and I took care to use physical evidence and old photographs to identify missing features and minimize conjecture. We collaborated to develop floor plans for each house. The plans are coded to show the original arrangement in solid black, alterations made before 1836 in hatched forms, and original elements that have been removed as dashed outlines.

Property Research

Once the physical documentation, was complete, the historic resource firm Paula Reed and Associates researched the subject property. Most of this work, such as searching estate inventories, will records, and tax records, was done by Reed historian Edie Wallace. Wallace compiled a chain of title for each property from the current owner back to the original purchase. In most cases, it was possible to identify the owner who commissioned a particular building by using the documentary record in conjunction with the physical features of each house. Independent research by Donald Watts collected specific information for the project, such as data on the county's enslaved populations, wheat production, and early brickyards.

Peter Burr House, restored view

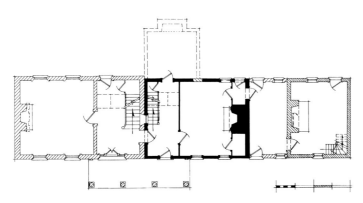

House plan showing the original section in black, later additions in hatch, and removed features in dashed outline

Property deed with boundary description

House Dating and Naming

This book is organized chronologically and thematically, grouping farmhouses and town houses by date ranges and exploring construction techniques, exterior and interior detailing, and outbuildings. Dating houses in Jefferson County can be difficult, especially for vernacular buildings with few dateable features. However elusive, the approximate time of construction is an essential piece of the historical puzzle. Many of the houses in this survey were commonly believed to have been built earlier or later than they actually were. Inaccurate dating caused confusion about craftsmen, owners, and subsequent occupants of the house. More importantly, precise dating made accurate

grouping possible, after which the similarities between houses of certain periods shifted sharply into focus.

Tax records were especially helpful in fixing construction dates, many noting the year of construction and materials used. These specific records along with physical evidence allowed me to date the surveyed houses. The study employs approximate dates when an exact year of construction cannot be pinpointed. In this book, a circa date refers to a bracket of ten years, five years before and five years after the given date.

Since most local houses have had several names over their lifetimes and because many different houses share names, it

was necessary to establish a naming convention for the houses in the study group. To avoid confusion, the name of the owner of the property for whom the dwelling was constructed is also used to identify the house. For houses that were altered into a different plan by a subsequent owner, hyphenated names are used: Bellevue (Swearingen-Shepherd House).

In Jefferson County, the earliest houses, those built between 1735 and 1815, shared more features of plan, scale, and detailing than those built after that date. The local houses built between 1815 and 1835 had great similarities as well, so they have been grouped in their own separate chapter.

An Open Door

Why study a group of houses located in Jefferson County? Because focusing on this limited geographic zone and particular historical period provides insights and understanding that more general or broader studies cannot. Limiting the study area to the county also allowed us to be more exacting and to document humble houses as carefully as grand mansions. With two hundred and fifty houses measured, drawn, notated, researched, and photographed, this thorough documentation reveals patterns of building practices and uses. The study information, as a whole, places each house in context. Though the book includes many of the county's historic structures, there are others that have yet to be examined. Therefore, this study is a starting point for further research, a threshold, and the door is open to new avenues of inquiry into the county's history and its role within the larger region and our developing nation.

William Hendricks House interior

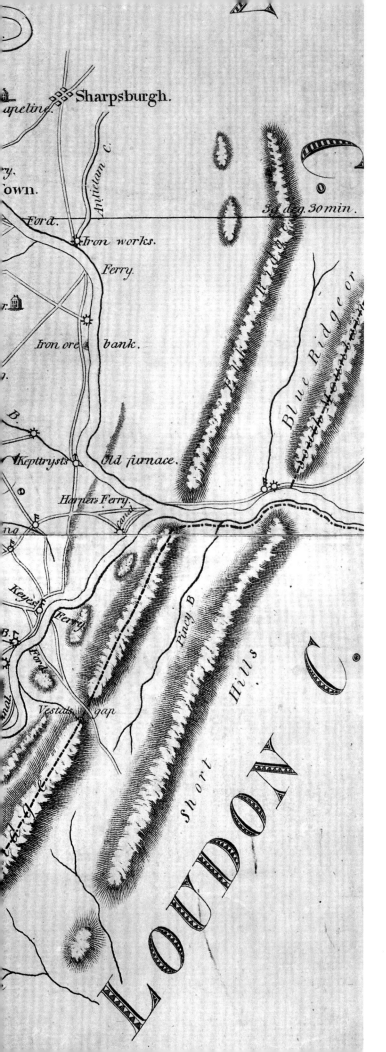

Chapter One

From Settlement to Refinement

Houses in Context

Detail from "Map of Frederick, Berkeley, & Jefferson
Counties in the State of Virginia" by Charles Varle, 1809,
Geography and Map Division, Library of Congress

Jefferson County

The area now known as Jefferson County, West Virginia, is nestled between Maryland and Virginia and contains stretches of both the Potomac and Shenandoah rivers. This verdant land lies in the northern end of the Shenandoah Valley, known as the lower valley. The county encompasses just over two hundred square miles, established partly by topography and partly by political districting. Bounded by the Potomac River and Blue Ridge Mountains on the north and east, Opequon Creek to the west, and the West Virginia and Virginia line on the south, Jefferson County consists of fertile valley bottom and the steep western slope of the Blue Ridge. Part of Virginia at the time of our study period, the county was formed in 1801 from Berkeley County, which had been separated from Frederick County in 1772. It was added to West Virginia after the new state was formed in 1863.

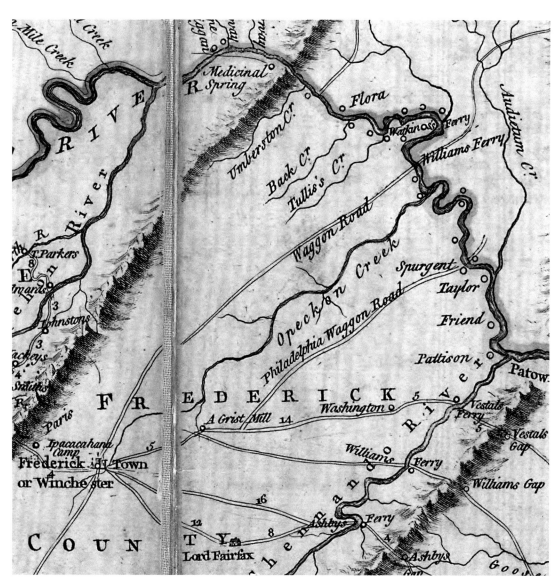

Detail showing present-day Jefferson County from "Map of the most inhabited part of Virginia containing the whole province of Maryland with part of Pensilvania, New Jersey and North Carolina." Fry-Jefferson, 1755, Geography and Map Division, Library of Congress

Early History

A growing number of books, articles, and academic papers catalog such varied subjects as the rich political and social history of Jefferson County. Research continues on the industrial history of Harpers Ferry, Washington family interests in the area, events surrounding John Brown's Raid, the ethnic characteristics of the area's early settlers, and regional military activities of the Civil War. Yet studies of the county's architecture are all but absent from the record. Where they do exist, they examine individual buildings. These narrowly defined reports shed little light on a particular building's place among its contemporaries. Through these scattered accounts the reader holds little prospect of ascertaining if a building typifies the local architectural vernacular or stands as an aberration. This lack of contextual analysis is puzzling given the number of architecturally significant structures in Jefferson County. Scores of early houses dot the rolling countryside and crowd its small towns. The number and diversity of these buildings make for a vibrant and unique architectural landscape. The object of this book is to fill this documentary and historical void, allowing informed conclusions to be drawn about the county's early domestic architecture.

A house, like any other historic artifact, has the ability to convey meaning. The parts and design of each house have intended purposes. Some of these elements are obvious, while others hide their rationales from the modern eye. Without a sense of context, however, the design or function of a particular building and its parts can be distorted or completely obscured. Context is the key to understanding historic buildings, and by extension, the people who built and used them over time. This chapter outlines the early history of Jefferson County in order to provide this crucial historical context.

Harper's Ferry by Rembrandt Peale, ca. 1812, courtesy of Maryland Historical Society

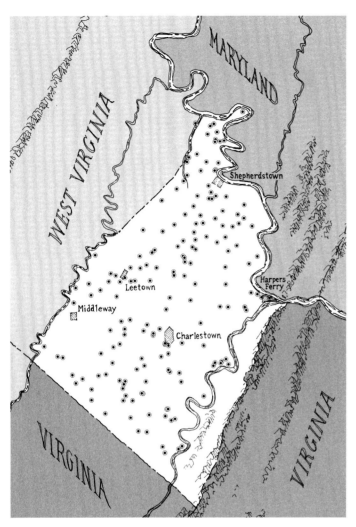

Map of Jefferson County showing farmhouses surveyed

Frontier Period: 1720–1762

In his book *The Planting of New Virginia*, historian Warren Hofstra outlines the events that led to the opening of the Shenandoah Valley and its subsequent settlement. Hofstra concludes that in the first two decades of the eighteenth century, coinciding interests, opportunities, and fears brought about the political will to populate the valley.[1] Increasing Native American incursions into the Virginia Piedmont heightened tension and uncertainty in the colony. Anxieties regarding runaway slave enclaves in the mountains exacerbated feelings of colonial peril. Meanwhile, the far-reaching goals of the British Empire converged with these fearful sentiments to compel Virginia's colonial government to grant lands on the western side of the Blue Ridge Mountains. In 1728, the Virginia Council, along with Governor William Gooch, granted the first lands in the valley.[2] Before this time, the colonies forged a tenuous peace with the Iroquois Nations, ending the westward movement of Virginia settlers at the eastern slope of the mountains. Colonial governments discouraged European presence in the valley, as it inevitably resulted in conflicts with Native Americans. These disturbances in turn brought problems to neighboring colonies, notably Pennsylvania. Governor Gooch, however, understood the benefits to the colony and the Crown of pushing westward, as well as the dangers of not doing so.

By the time Europeans explored the Shenandoah Valley, the forces of "disease, warfare, and migrations" pushed the native inhabitants from the area.[3] While few native peoples lived in the Shenandoah Valley at this time, it was frequently used as a north-south transportation route by the Iroquois, Cherokee, Catawba, Tuscarora, Shawnee, and Delaware Indians.[4] Peace with the native inhabitants was precious to those most vulnerable to attack: settlers in the sparsely populated fringes of the colony. The aid of native tribes against the French was also necessary to keep England's ancient enemy from encroaching on the vast Virginia wilderness.[5] The new strategy of peopling the valley adopted by the government in Williamsburg made large land grants available to speculators, who in turn sold smaller parcels to migrating families. Title to these lands required they be improved within two years. Thus, cheap lands would be the bait to lure immigrants to the unprotected backcountry of Virginia. If successful, these new communities would form the buffer that the colonial government desired as protection from French-orchestrated attacks toward the Virginia Piedmont. The French and Native Americans would be dissuaded from venturing east by a valley thickly settled with the small farms of Protestant families. And such settlement would advance the colonial supply line to the west, aiding Virginia's progress toward the Mississippi River.

The demand for affordable lands grew as the coastal regions of Virginia, Maryland, Delaware, and Pennsylvania became increasingly populated in the early eighteenth century. While eastern populations rose, so did the cost of nearby agricultural lands. By the second decade of the eighteenth century, for example, little if any farmland was available near Philadelphia.[6] Meanwhile, the tradition of primogeniture inheritance, especially in places like the Virginia Tidewater, further compounded the need for new lands. When the colonial government officially opened the valley for settlement, this reservoir of pent-up demand was released. A wave of people from all over the eastern seaboard, Europe, and Africa would eventually populate this empty, fertile land. By the 1730s, the first European settlers carved their homesteads into the Virginia backcountry. One of the first of these was a German immigrant named Jost Hite, who brought sixteen families into the valley in 1731. Hite and his companions crossed the Potomac near present day Shepherdstown and traveled south along what is now Flowing Springs Road, crossing the uninhabited valley bottom. After forging across the Opequon, this band of travelers headed west

to settle near Winchester, Virginia. The path that Hite's wagons cut through the wilderness is still used today by those who travel through Jefferson County.

No known buildings exist in Jefferson County from the first decades of settlement. However, the archaeological remains of a small earthfast dwelling—a house built on wooden pilings—dating to the frontier period has recently been discovered. The WILLIAM GREEN HOUSE SITE is located in the northern part of the county near the Potomac River. William Green migrated to the area with his family from coastal Maryland, where earthfast housing was common in the seventeenth and early eighteenth centuries. Unlike later houses in the area that utilized limestone foundations, the Green House was built on a series of wooden supports driven into the ground. The modest structure could have been erected quickly to provide immediate shelter for the family. Archaeological evidence dates this house to the 1740s, earlier than any other standing structure in the county. This unique site is important because it gives a rare glimpse into the humble

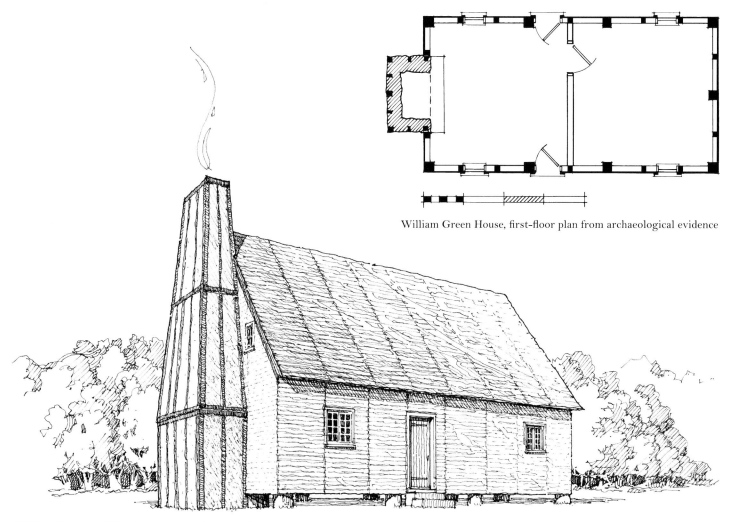

William Green House, first-floor plan from archaeological evidence

William Green earthfast house, restored perspective view

frontier life in the valley. The remains also reveal a direct architectural link to coastal forms of housing. Further archaeological research may shed more light on this formative period.[7]

The area that now composes Jefferson County was the gateway to the lower Shenandoah Valley. Immigration took place across the mountain passes and river fords. Peace with the Iroquois League in 1744 resolved the disputes over colonial occupation of the valley, which increased the flow of travelers in search of available lands. The valley, in turn, served as an important portal to settlement in the south and west during the colonial era and later into the nineteenth century. Immigrants passed through the valley on their way to emerging transmontane communities in Ohio, Kentucky, Tennessee, and North Carolina. Some of these early settlers first made their homes in the lower valley, in present-day Jefferson County. Because of its strategic location and the quality of its land, Jefferson County was among the earliest settled

areas in the valley.[8] Diverse peoples were drawn to the area beginning in the 1730s: English Quakers from New Jersey, Pennsylvania Germans, Tidewater English, Protestant Marylanders from Prince George's County, and newly immigrated Scots-Irish. These groups brought their distinct cultures and building practices with them to the frontier.

Though local houses reflected the broad diversity of the immigrating peoples, the manner of their residential construction was dictated by the availability of local materials and craftsmen. Limestone and timber, the most plentiful building materials, were used widely. One early immigrant to the valley, Samuel Washington, built his home of native limestone, a material unfamiliar to the builders of his native Tidewater Virginia. Most of the new residents, however, put up small log and frame houses.[9] Very few mid-eighteenth-century structures have survived, and those that have are generally built of more durable masonry materials.

Harewood (Samuel Washington House), Historic American Buildings Survey photograph, 1937

In the years leading up to the Revolutionary War, the population in the lower valley continued to grow. The end of the French and Indian War in 1763 brought stability and increased economic possibility to the valley. The three dominant cultures of the area began to intermingle through marriage, proximity, and commerce. Jefferson County's Germanic settlers, Virginians of English background, and Scots-Irish each represented about a third of its population in the eighteenth century.[10] The equal proportions of these parts made for unique cultural characteristics, and their assimilation over the intervening generations can be seen clearly in the local architecture. Africans, brought forcibly to the area, likely contributed their labor and talents to the erecting of buildings, further blending disparate building traditions into a rich vernacular.

The struggles of the frontier period gradually gave way to increased economic prosperity in the backcountry. Towns such as Winchester and Shepherdstown became commercial centers, trading with the eastern ports. Unlike the Tidewater areas of Virginia and Maryland with their dependence on tobacco, farmers in the lower valley produced a wide range of items for sale or trade. Wheat brought significant material wealth to the area. The climate and soils in the valley were ideal for wheat production, while the spring-fed streams and sloping terrain lent themselves to milling. The rich limestone soils were capable of producing enormous quantities of wheat, which, after being milled locally, were transported to towns like Alexandria, Fredericksburg, and Philadelphia in the form of flour.

By the latter half of the eighteenth century, the demand for Shenandoah Valley flour was trans-Atlantic. Due in part to Great Britain's population explosion in the eighteenth century, London and other cities imported substantial amounts of flour from the valley. Local flour also found markets in the West Indies and Southern Europe.[11] Visitors to the valley wrote dramatic reports of the lush and fertile land. While passing through the area in 1774, English farmer Nicholas Cresswell wrote that the place had "some of the finest land I ever saw either for the plough or pasture."[12] The commercial success of the flour trade drove more immigration to the valley and opened new markets. During the second half of the eighteenth century, both Alexandria and Philadelphia developed as primary exporters of valley flour. After inspecting the produce from the Virginia backcountry, Cresswell added that there was "as good Wheat as ever I saw in England."[13] Jefferson County's parent jurisdiction, Berkeley County, produced a million pounds of flour in 1775.[14] Much of its surplus made its way to the coastal cities and then across the ocean.

Professional soldier Horatio Gates moved to the county before the Revolutionary War to pursue farming, author's collection

Prato Rio (General Charles Lee House), ca. 1760 and 1775, Historic American Buildings Survey photograph, 1937

Close of the Eighteenth Century

The war with England brought economic hardship to the colonies. The naval blockades and restricted foreign markets stymied growth in the Shenandoah Valley. A survey of houses and barns on local farms made in 1786 by Jonathan Clark captures the humble state of the homes of the county's yeoman farmers. Most buildings were described by Clark as "worn" or "old."[15] The vast majority of these were log and frame structures. After the Revolution, however, the local economy slowly regained its footing. By the eighteenth century's last decade, wheat exports flushed the area with new wealth. The cessation of hostilities with Britain reopened European markets to valley flour. Population increases on the European continent and the French wars of this period further expanded demand.[16] Many of

Jefferson County's early houses were built with wealth derived from the period's steadily increasing wheat production and exportation. These fine homes stand as monuments to the prosperity of the period.

At the close of the eighteenth century, families that had first settled in the area were now three generations into the experience. With the economic strains of the frontier period and the Revolution behind them, and with transportation routes to urban markets improving, many residents of Jefferson County prospered. The houses built during this time reflect this increased prosperity, as well as the local population's acculturation. As in much of the United States during the early republic, agriculture served as the economic engine of the Shenandoah Valley.

Elmwood slave quarter, Historic American Buildings Survey photograph, 1937

Opposite: The Rocks (Ferdinando Fairfax House), ca. 1795, Historic American Buildings Survey photograph, 1937

Jefferson County's Eighteenth-Century Houses

From the earliest settlement to the end of the eighteenth century, the houses of Jefferson County evolved from singular, vernacular expressions into repeated and accepted types. The cultural assimilation that began during the settlement period slowly shaped the local building vernacular. Builders increasingly favored a common palette of details and plans over those from settlers' ancestral homelands, so that after a number of generations in backcountry Virginia homes built by families of Germanic ancestry differed little from those of their neighbors who descended from the Tidewater English or Scots-Irish. As succeeding generations populated the valley, their cultural identities became less European. In this way, house design gave physical form to the idea of assimilation. Through familiar building designs, neighbors signaled their similarities to one another.

Still, some cultural products continued to celebrate ethnic or religious diversity. For example, the German Reformed Church of Shepherdstown continued to keep records in German into the nineteenth century, long after Germanic influences on the local architecture had disappeared.[17] Patterns for accepted and preferred buildings had developed by the turn of the nineteenth century. Many of these would remain popular for more than a hundred years, giving Jefferson County a remarkably consistent and consolidated building language.

Piedmont (Dr. John Briscoe House), ca. 1790, Historic American Buildings Survey, photograph 1937

Opposite: Decorative escutcheon plate engraved in German, 1795, St. Peter's Lutheran Church, Shepherdstown

Early Nineteenth-Century Houses

With each successive generation, the people of Jefferson County developed a more distinctive and unified culture. The material products of the inhabitants reflected the unique mixture of tastes and preferences in this corner of the valley. Changes in the forms and designs of buildings during the first quarter of the nineteenth century were gradual and restrained. House plans initially favored by the first settlers had evolved over intervening decades to fit specific social and functional needs. Several early house types nevertheless remained popular throughout the county until the mid-nineteenth century. The urge to assimilate, together with the rural nature of the community, seems to have limited the assortment of building types. Thus, a strong local building tradition had developed by 1800 and remained with limited variation until the arrival of the railroad and canal.

Wheatland (Baylor-Turner House), Historic American Buildings Survey photograph, 1937

Houses of the Railroad and Canal Era, 1836–1850

The dawning of the industrial era had a dramatic impact on Jefferson County. Both the Baltimore and Ohio Railroad and the Chesapeake and Ohio Canal reached Harpers Ferry in the mid-1830s and brought with them great changes.[18] These advancements in transportation compressed the travel time between the valley and its urban markets, especially Baltimore. They likewise made available the consumer goods and trends of American and European cities. No longer would local builders work in isolation from their urban counterparts. The latest styles and building materials from the coastal cities were less than a day's travel away. It is no coincidence that the Greek Revival style became ascendant in Jefferson County with the introduction of the railroad and canal. The year 1835, therefore, stands as the close of the period of a distinctly local architectural vernacular in Jefferson County, and marks the beginning of a regionalized style.

Scene of the Baltimore & Ohio Railroad and Chesapeake & Ohio Canal at Harper's Ferry, Virginia,
by George Harvey, ca. 1836, courtesy of Godel & Co. Fine Art, New York

Chapter Two

Early Farmhouses

1735–1815

Piedmont (Dr. John Briscoe House), ca. 1790,
Charles Town vicinity, front elevation

Basic Plan Types

The survey of houses conducted for this book includes one hundred and twenty houses built before 1815. This chapter will focus on the county's early farmhouses of that period. For the purposes of contextual similarity, farmhouses will be examined separately from town houses, and a later chapter will be devoted to urban residences. Though each of the early farmhouses is unique, nearly all of them can be categorized into one of three basic plan types: hall-and-parlor, center-hall, or side-hall. The chapter is divided into three sections, one for each plan. Examples show common arrangements for the plans and variations of each. The benefits and drawbacks of the three plan types will be discussed, as will the popularity of the different plans through the study period.

In 1798, the United States government required each state to collect a special tax, known as the U.S. Direct Tax, from property owners. Among other things, this tax evaluated improvements such as houses. The government used information about the physical features of these improvements—their size, building materials, and amount of window glass—to calculate property assessments. In Berkeley County, Virginia, houses and slaves were subject to this tax assessed by appointed commissioners. The transcript of the 1798 House Tax and Slave Tax of Berkeley County, archived at the Martinsburg courthouse, is a rare Virginia survivor. It contains a detailed list of owners, tenants, and rates of tax for all houses standing at the time, giving the researcher a broad view of the local housing stock at the close of the eighteenth century.[1] Since Jefferson County was part of Berkeley County until 1801, the tax includes the property owners of the former county. In the area that now composes Jefferson County, 655 houses were taxed. Roughly half of these are farmhouses, and half are town houses. These buildings can be broken into three categories by rate of assessment. The first grouping includes humble dwellings valued below $300. Half of the taxed structures fall into this category. These houses were generally modest log or frame cabins of one or two rooms. Only a handful of buildings in this segment of the valuation exist today, such as the REES-DANIELS HOUSE. The second category includes houses valued between $300 and $500. Roughly a quarter of the houses fit this range, representing larger and better-built two-story houses. Extant examples include the frame PETER BURR HOUSE and the

Peter Burr House, near Bardane, valued at $315 on the 1798 U.S. direct tax

log York Hill, both valued at $315 in 1798. Again, many of these houses would have been log or frame construction, though some small stone houses were included. The last quarter of the assessed houses make up the third category—those valued over $500. These substantial homes, such as Traveler's Rest, Mount Eary, and Taylor's Meadow, were generally constructed of brick or stone. The vast majority of extant eighteenth-century homes are part of this last segment of the tax.

A comprehensive evaluation of the county's early buildings cannot be made because most of those buildings have vanished from the landscape. The group of houses studied in this chapter includes only buildings that exist today. Though the 1798 tax record indicates a value for each house standing in that year, it does not elaborate on plan, material, or age. It is only with an understanding that the houses included here represent a sampling for study, not a complete inventory, do we make assessments of the local architecture. Still, Jefferson County retains a relatively large number of early houses, so comparisons can be made. General patterns of scale, construction, and form can also be determined by looking at these surviving houses.

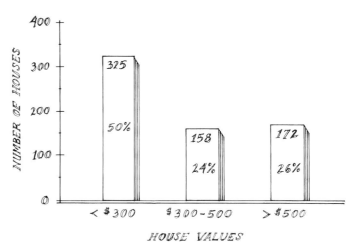

Breakdown of house valuations from the study area in the 1798 house tax

Traveler's Rest (Gen. Horatio Gates House), ca. 1760, National Historic Landmark

Hall-and-Parlor Houses

The hall-and-parlor house found in Jefferson County utilizes a two-room plan on the primary floor, a form descended from post-medieval house types in the British Isles.[2] The hall is the larger room, which serves as an everyday multipurpose living room. Although it was smaller, the early parlor was typically finished with more formal detailing than the hall. Documentary evidence suggests that the parlor had more limited uses. Estate inventories from the eighteenth century locate food preparation and storage wares in the hall, along with work implements and common furniture. The parlor, on the other hand, had objects such as books, desks, beds, and finer furniture.[3]

The plan of these hall-and-parlor houses maximizes open, usable space. The stair is tucked into a corner of the hall beside the chimney. The interior partition wall measures from one to three inches in width, taking up little room. In this way, the hall-and-parlor house was a model of efficient design.

Despite its simplicity, the hall-and-parlor plan was favored by those earliest settlers of the valley with enough means to build significant houses. Surviving examples were commonly built of stone or brick, but a few early log and frame hall-and-parlor houses also remain.

The standard elevational arrangement of the hall-and-parlor is three-bay, with centered front and rear doors. Commonly two full stories, these houses stand on raised basements. One enters the building into the larger room, or hall, where the stair is located. Chimneys in this plan are placed on the end walls, always inboard, as the masonry mass of the chimney supports the framing of the corner stair.

As with other house types, the detailing of these early buildings varies considerably. However, hall-and-parlor houses in Jefferson County usually have the most developed interior finishes like paneled end walls.

The hall-and-parlor house Taylor's Meadow is not only one of the best detailed early houses in the county, it may be its oldest brick residence. Built for John Taylor about 1775, this house has unusual exterior features, such as decorative, recessed arch chimney tops. This chimney detail can be found in some surviving mid-eighteenth-century Virginia Tidewater houses, from where Taylor's father migrated to the Shenandoah Valley. The small, thin bricks that make up the structure are unique to the county.

The fieldstone Nathan Haines House, known locally as Fairfax Grant Stock Farm, is arranged in a double-parlor plan, a variation on the two-room hall-and-parlor plan. Haines was a Quaker from New Jersey, and he had the house built before the American Revolution on a site overlooking Bullskin Run. The double-parlor plan—also called the Pennsylvania or Quaker plan—was made popular in the Delaware River Valley and the North Midlands of England.[4] William Penn dictated this plan for his fellow Quakers in 1684 when he encouraged them to build "a House . . . with a partition near the middle, and an other to divide the end of the House into two small rooms."[5] An early kitchen wing, which likely replaced a freestanding summer kitchen, was added to the side elevation later in the eighteenth century.

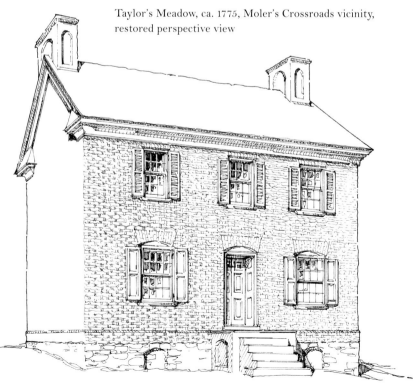

Taylor's Meadow, ca. 1775, Moler's Crossroads vicinity, restored perspective view

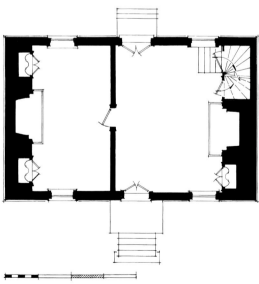

Taylor's Meadow, hall-and-parlor plan

Nathan Haines House (Fairfax Grant Stock Farm), ca. 1775, Summit Point vicinity, Historic American Buildings Survey photograph, 1937

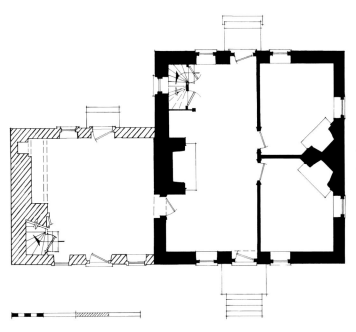

Nathan Haines House, double-parlor plan with later kitchen wing

Many hall-and-parlor houses were designed with kitchens in the basement. The RICHARD MORGAN HOUSE, also known as Springdale, one of the earliest existing buildings in the county, is an example of this arrangement. Built of rubble limestone, the house has features common to early local buildings, such as a watertable and segmental arched openings. An empty niche in the upper gable is reported to have held a date stone marked 1760. The house originally had a double-parlor plan, though an extensive renovation in the 1840s changed the room arrangement. A restored plan reveals the similarities between this house and the Nathan Haines House.

The WILLIAM GRUBB HOUSE, also known as Brook Manor, is the county's only known example of stone-end log construction, or "stone ender." Located along upper Bullskin Run, the Grubb House is one of several early houses in that watershed. Three of the four walls of the house are log while the gable end is constructed of stone. Grubb migrated to the valley from New Castle County, Delaware, where stone-end houses were common. The chimney and winder stair are housed in the stone end of the building. Other than the combination of building materials, the house employs a standard hall-and-parlor plan.

The PETER AND JACOB WILLIAMSON HOUSE, built in 1782 near Rocky Marsh Run, is a rare surviving example of the single-story hall-and-parlor house with rear chimneys. This residence was built on a raised basement that housed the kitchen. The first floor is divided into two rooms with rear corner fireplaces. The unusual placement of these chimneys can also be seen in a number of the earliest surviving buildings in the county, including TRAVELER'S REST and PRATO RIO. Precedent for the eave chimney can be found in Wales and parts of southeastern Britain.[6] Now uninhabited, this house is unique to the county and an important remnant of its early architecture.

Richard Morgan House (Springdale), ca. 1765, Shepherdstown vicinity, restored perspective view

Peter and Jacob Williamson House, 1782, Shepherdstown vicinity, restored perspective view

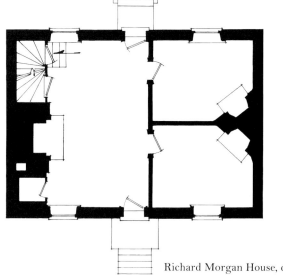

Richard Morgan House, double-parlor arrangement, restored plan

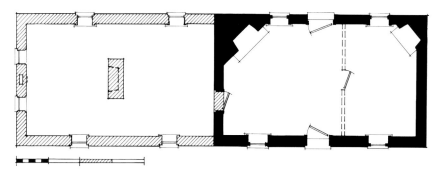

Peter and Jacob Williamson House, first-floor plan with later addition

The McPherson Mill House on Long Marsh Run was home to successful eighteenth- and nineteenth-century millers. In a variation of the standard hall-and-parlor plan, this house has a straight-run, or ramp stair, against the front wall, as opposed to the more common corner stair. The house, built about 1785 adjacent to John McPherson's flour mill, is also notable for the belt course along the second-floor sill height of the front elevation. This projecting feature was not decorative, but designed as a support for a porch roof. The rear elevation lacks the center second-floor window.

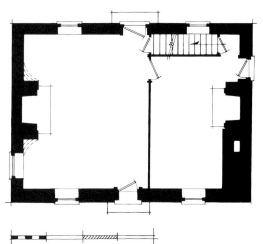

McPherson Mill House, first-floor plan

McPherson Mill House (John McPherson House), ca. 1785, Rippon vicinity, north gable

The ADAM LINK HOUSE, built about 1795, has the same arrangement of windows on both sides as the McPherson rear elevation. Like the Richard Morgan House and the Nathan Haines House, the plan of the Adam Link House is double-parlor. However, this building has the uncommon variation of a single, centered corner chimney in the front parlor only. This is the only known example of such a chimney arrangement in the county. Link's home is steeply banked into a hill so that the front door of the house is at grade and the rear door was accessed by steep stairs.

Near the Adam Link House, along Elk Run, stands another excellent example of the hall-and-parlor plan. MELVIN HILL was built around 1805 of limestone with large, decorative sandstone three-piece headers over the openings. Similar projecting keystones can be seen on a number of local buildings dating from the turn of the nineteenth century. The unusual four-bay front elevation of Melvin Hill was rarely used on the farmhouses of Jefferson County. This arrangement, however, is commonplace in eastern and central Pennsylvania and Maryland, and in fact the Melvin family moved to the area in the eighteenth century from Bucks County, Pennsylvania. The plan of this double-parlor house differs somewhat from local three-bay counterparts. At Melvin Hill, the parlors are not of equal size and are more rectangular. Here, a hierarchical bias toward the front parlor, with its extra window and better interior detailing, stands in contrast to the area's standard. The house also has the uncommon feature of a shallow root cellar under the stair.

Adam Link House, ca. 1795, Uvilla vicinity, restored perspective view

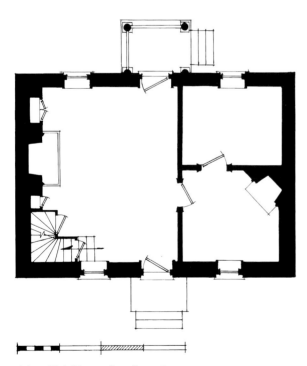

Adam Link House, first-floor plan

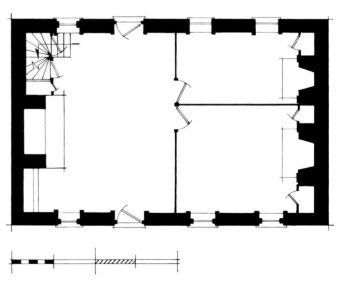

Melvin Hill, first-floor plan

Melvin Hill (Thomas Melvin House), ca. 1805, Duffields vicinity, oblique view

Both the VAN SWEARINGEN HOUSE and the THORNBOROUGH HOUSE were three-bay hall-and-parlor houses before being enlarged and renovated. Originally, each house employed the double-parlor plan. Built of native limestone, these houses feature the horizontal massing common in colonial Georgian architecture. The fine, ashlar stonework of the Van Swearingen House, built around 1790, is atypical of the county's stone farmhouses, where random rubble walls are more common. Formal ashlar stonework is found in the stone houses of valley towns, such as Sharpsburg, Maryland, and Winchester, Virginia. Swearingen, along with many settlers of the Terrapin Neck area, migrated from Prince George's County, Maryland. He may have brought his taste for more dressed stonework with him from that region.

The THOMAS CROW HOUSE, near Halltown, started off as a small stone hall-and-parlor house. Three bays wide and one room deep, this house became a rear section of the amorphous Beallair mansion in the mid-nineteenth century. Built before 1791, the house conforms to the county's standard hall-and-parlor configuration.

The original house at The Rocks, built for Ralph Wormley of Williamsburg, was also a typical hall-and-parlor arrangement. This building was later turned into a kitchen by Ferdinando Fairfax.[7] The RALPH WORMLEY HOUSE features exterior stone chimneys, which are unusual on masonry buildings locally, though common in the Virginia Piedmont and Tidewater.

MORGAN'S SPRING (Abel Morgan House) was built in about 1785 above a large spring that feeds Shepherdstown's Town Run. The plan of the diminutive house is a variation of the local hall-and-parlor type. The stair does not occupy a corner of the hall; rather, it is located between the rear door and window. This stair placement is common in the stone houses of Kentucky built for Ulster immigrants.[8] As with many homes of the county, the kitchen of this steeply banked house is in the basement. The same stair arrangement is also used in the small log BURR-MCGARRY HOUSE near Shenandoah Junction.

The ABRAHAM SHEPHERD JR. HOUSE, on Terrapin Neck, is another small log hall-and-parlor dwelling. Similar in scale to the Burr-McGarry House, the house had a finished attic sleeping loft. Built about 1800, the original section is now the rear wing of a frame house.

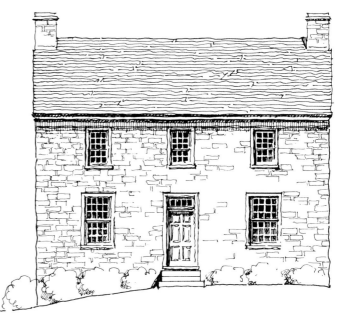

Van Swearingen House (Springwood), ca. 1790, Terrapin Neck vicinity, restored elevation

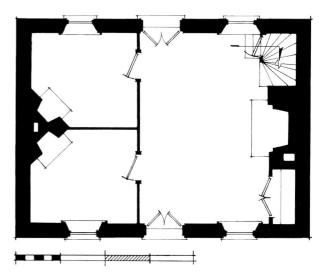

Thornborough House (Millbrook), restored first-floor floor plan before additions

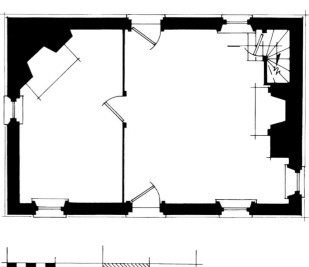

Thomas Crow House (Beallair), restored first-floor plan

Ralph Wormley House (The Rocks kitchen), view of exterior gable chimney, Historic American Buildings Survey photograph, 1937

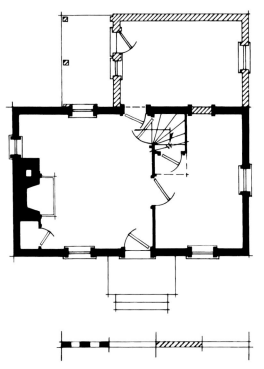

Burr-McGarry House, first-floor plan with later wing

Abraham Shepherd Jr. House, ca. 1800, Terrapin Neck, south elevation

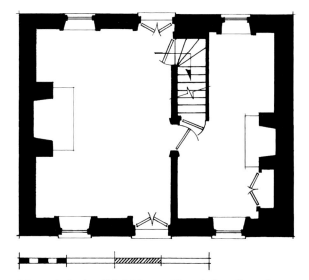

Morgan's Spring (Abel Morgan House), first-floor plan

Henry Strider House, ca. 1810, Harpers Ferry vicinity, west elevation oblique view

Henry Strider House, ca. 1810, Harpers Ferry vicinity, restored perspective view

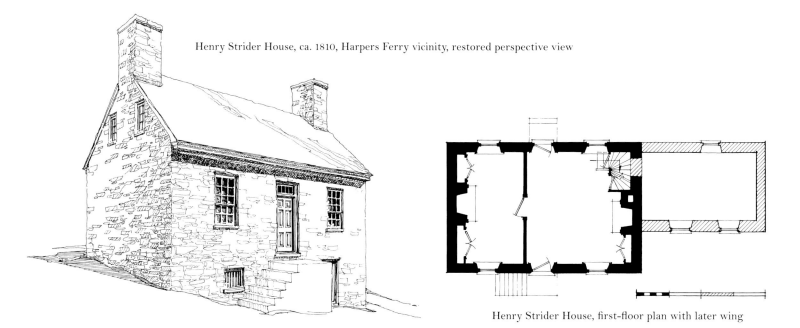

Henry Strider House, first-floor plan with later wing

The popularity of the hall-and-parlor plan diminished during the nineteenth century. Only a few examples of hall-and-parlor houses exist from that later time. One is the HENRY STRIDER HOUSE near Harpers Ferry, which dates to the first decade of the nineteenth century. This story-and-a-half stone house has an original sleeping loft in the attic and a kitchen in the basement. The compact house is banked laterally into the site, allowing basement entry at the ground level.

Built in 1812, the GEORGE REYNOLDS HOUSE is another that shows a late use of the hall-and-parlor plan. Like the Adam Link House, this dwelling is banked into a steep hill, making the rear elevation a full story taller than the front. The basement of the house has windows and a centered door matching the bays of the upper floors. The unusual use of decorative brick arches over the windows on this stone house lends visual interest to the simple composition.

George Reynolds House, cut-away view through gable wall showing corner stair and chimney arrangements

George Reynolds House, 1812, Moler's Crossroads vicinity, west elevation

Hall-and-Parlor Varietals

The oldest extant variation on the hall-and-parlor plan in the county is the PETER BURR HOUSE near Bardane. The house was built in three distinct sections over about fifty years. The original part of the house, built by Burr in the 1760s after he arrived from Connecticut, showcases the timber-frame building techniques favored in the northern colonies. Unlike the typical hall-and-parlor arrangement, the parlor of the Peter Burr House is in front of the larger hall. In this manner, the parlor is entered from the front door, and the hall is entered from the rear. Similar two-cell plans can be found in northern Pennsylvania, Connecticut, and Massachusetts.[9] The house also features a log kitchen built in the eighteenth century that was attached to the house with an intermediate room in about 1815 by David Moore. This wonderful remnant of the county's settlement period gives clues as to the possible variety of building types that may have been built in the area, which have disappeared from the landscape because of neglect, calamity, or demolition. The descendants of Peter Burr built several houses in the immediate area that more closely follow local building preferences. Taken together the building practices of this family illustrate cultural assimilation that occurred over time in the county, as a local vernacular became established.

The REES-DANIELS HOUSE, along Opequon Creek, started as a single-room plan, but became a hall-and-parlor through addition. This timber-frame house featured early details such as exposed beaded floor joists and an outboard, or external, stone chimney. In the late eighteenth century, the original vernacular house was enlarged into a hall-and-parlor plan with an unusual long rear room. This room has a gable door facing the log summer kitchen.

Built about 1785, the THOMAS CAMPBELL HOUSE stands near the southwestern edge of Jefferson County. Erected along the old "Hite Waggon Road," this house served as a tavern in the late eighteenth century. The original plan mirrors that of the Peter Burr House with its back-to-back rooms. A two-story side-hall house was added to the older section in 1829.

Peter Burr Farm, Bardane vicinity, Historic American Buildings Survey photograph, 1983

Rees-Daniels House, ca. 1775, Middleway vicinity, oblique perspective view with log kitchen

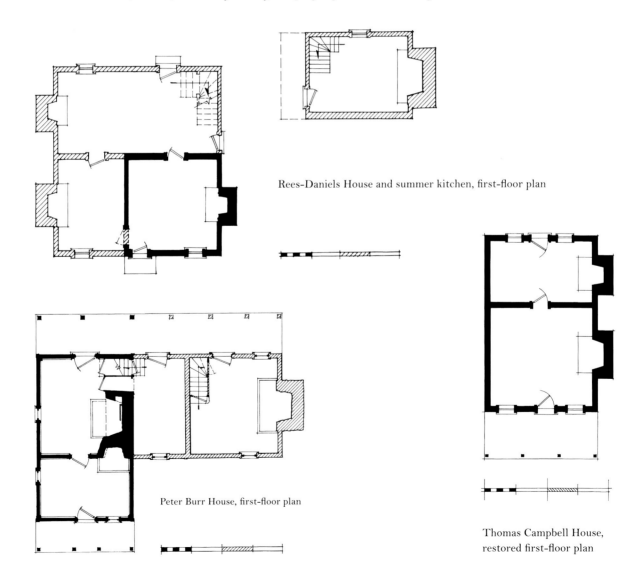

Rees-Daniels House and summer kitchen, first-floor plan

Peter Burr House, first-floor plan

Thomas Campbell House, restored first-floor plan

Prato Rio (Hite-Lee House), Leetown, ca. 1760 and 1775, east elevation

PRATO RIO, because of the eccentricities of its most famous owner, General Charles Lee, defies architectural categorization. The original section of the stone house, then known as HOPEWELL, was built by Jacob Hite in the mid-eighteenth century with a hall-and-parlor plan. After purchasing the land and house from Hite in 1774, Lee set about remodeling the place. He attached an addition to the south that matched the scale of the original. The addition, however, had no interior walls. This large open-plan house followed no known precedent. Stories persist that Lee used chalk lines to divide the open new space into rooms.[10] The British-born general was obviously not concerned with convention or appearances, as he invented his own unusual house type, which stands today as a testament to his imagination.

One plan type noticeably absent from Jefferson County's historic buildings is the German-style three-room plan, known as *flurküchenhaus*, which can be found across the river in Maryland, to the north in Pennsylvania, and to the west in Frederick County, Virginia. The standard flurküchenhaus has three rooms, the *kammer*, *stube*, and *küeche*, organized around a central chimney. The absence of this building form in Jefferson County is surprising, considering the number of German settlers in the northern half of the county in the eighteenth century.[11] Houses such as the Jonathan Hager House near Hagerstown, Maryland, the John Gray House in Berkeley County, and the Paul Froman House near Winchester, Virginia, are neighboring examples.[12] But none were known to exist within the county. Only one of the roughly 300 buildings in the 1786 Jonathan Clark notebook, which covered several valley counties, was described as having a center chimney, and that property was located well west of present-day Jefferson County.[13] The reason for the

Charles Lee Eq.er, Major Général de l´Armée Continental,
engraving ca. 1780, author's collection

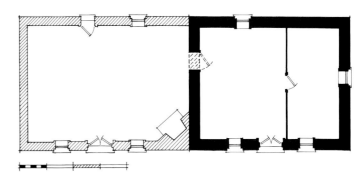

Prato Rio, first-floor plan

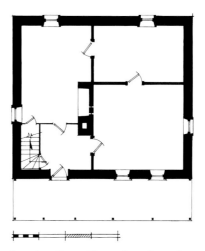

Jonathan Hager House, first-floor plan

absence of flurküchenhaus in the county is unknown, but one possible explanation is that the interior chimney telegraphs the nonconforming plan of the building from the exterior. Such buildings would signal to neighbors the "otherness" of the inhabitants, in this case German immigrants. The existing houses built by this group of immigrants suggest that they demonstrated their assimilation into the dominant English culture through architecture.

The efficient hall-and-parlor plan was popular with Jefferson County's early residents. Of the houses predating 1815 that were surveyed, nearly 40 percent are hall-and-parlor type. However, this ancient plan began to lose favor as the nineteenth century wore on. The increased desire to separate rooms and their uses doomed the hall-and-parlor plan to extinction by the 1830s.

Number of surveyed hall-and-parlor houses by decade

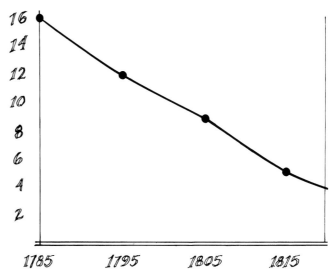

Center-Hall Houses

Through most of the late eighteenth and early nineteenth centuries, the most popular plan for farmhouses in Jefferson County was the center-hall type. Roughly 40 percent of the houses built before 1815 were center-hall houses. This was a significant increase over the pre-1790 level of center-hall residences, which was just 17 percent. With the stair hall running through the center of the house, this plan allowed for the separation of public and private spaces. The hall-and-parlor house, though a more efficient use of space, cannot accomplish the same compartmentalization of use. In Jefferson County, like much of the mid-Atlantic, center-hall houses are either single-pile or double-pile, meaning one or two rooms deep. Examples of this widespread house type can be found in single-story, story-and-half, and two-story houses. In Jefferson County, most of the early center-hall buildings rest on raised basements, which typically house their kitchens.

The popularity of the center-hall house in Jefferson County rose with the tide of prosperity that came after the end of the American Revolution. The standard was set locally before the war with the construction of Harewood. Built of limestone, this imposing house was erected for Samuel Washington, who moved his family into their new home in September 1770. George Washington wrote in his diary that, "My Brothr. Sam. and his wife set out in my Chariot for his House in Fred[eric]k [present-day Jefferson County]."[14] The choice of building material is striking, given the Washingtons' roots in Tidewater Virginia. One might have expected the house to have been built with brick, or weatherboarded frame construction, reflecting Tidewater vernacular traditions. In this case, local building materials trumped cultural familiarity. In plan, Harewood was more ambitious than most of the local center-hall examples that followed. A large, single-pile structure, Harewood incorporated a single-story kitchen wing set on axis with the main block of the house. The plan allowed for a later matching wing to the north of the house. The exterior detailing is quite austere, with traditional flourishes such as a modillioned cornice,

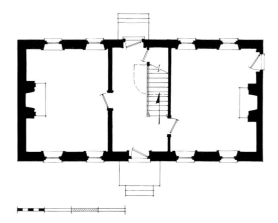

Center-hall house, single-pile plan

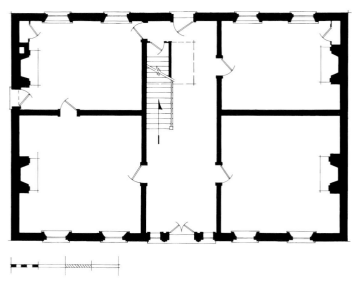

Center-hall house, double-pile plan

hipped roof, and segmental arched openings. Inside, the wide stair hall contains formal Georgian detailing. Unlike the modest exterior detailing, the interior millwork takes its cue from earlier rooms of the Tidewater. The drawing room paneling is unparalleled in the region, having Doric pilasters and a full entablature with pulvinated cushion frieze.

Harewood (Samuel Washington House), first-floor plan

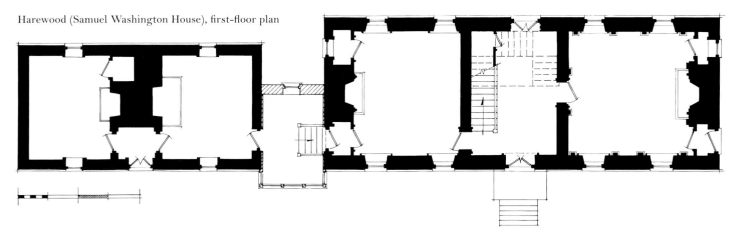

Harewood (Samuel Washington House), 1770, Charles Town vicinity, west elevation

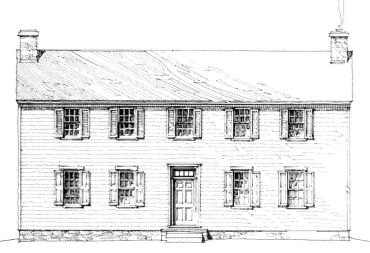

New Hopewell (Thomas Hite House), 1774, Leetown vicinity,
restored elevation

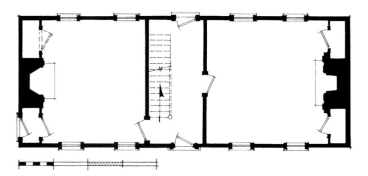

New Hopewell (Thomas Hite House), restored first-floor plan

Mount Eary (Keith-Straith House), ca. 1775, Wheatland vicinity,
restored perspective view

NEW HOPEWELL was built in 1774 for Thomas Hite of frame construction with applied clapboard weatherboarding. Located near Leetown, this house was among the grand homes of the Shenandoah Valley in the pre-Revolutionary era. Like Harewood, the residence boasted highly developed interior detailing and rigorously symmetrical elevations. Again, one would expect Hite's home to be built of stone given his German ancestry, like neighboring Prato Rio built by Hite's father. But the patron chose frame construction, a method associated more with English building traditions. This may have been an attempt by Hite, the son of a German immigrant, to assimilate into the dominant culture of the colony.

Both Harewood and New Hopewell utilize the single-pile plan, but the double-pile plan was also popular in the area during the eighteenth century. MOUNT EARY (Keith-Straith House), a frame house sited above Bullskin Run, was originally configured as a double-pile center-hall house. The frame house, now known as Locust Hill, was likely built for James Keith around 1775. In the early nineteenth century, Dr. Alexander Straith altered the floor plan of the house adding a long hall across the front. With interior paneling similar to that at Harewood and refined exterior elements, like its hipped roof, Mount Eary stands as one of the county's most sophisticated early houses.

Another example of the double-pile center-hall plan is the WILLIAM HENDRICKS HOUSE, now the Quinn Farm. The house presents itself as a story-and-a-half structure on a raised basement banked into a hill above Lucas Run. Built in 1794, this building hints at the coming popularity of brick construction in the county.

The watershed of Lucas Run, now known as Rattlesnake Run, a tributary of the Potomac in the northeast part of the county, contains a large number of early houses. Like the William Hendricks House, many of these dwellings feature double-pile center-hall plans. The most formal of these early houses is ELMWOOD, built for Edward Lucas III in 1797. With walls laid in Flemish-bond brick on all four sides, this house is two stories with a raised basement. The rear and side elevations utilize glazed or vitrified headers, giving the brickwork a checkerboard effect. The cornice boasts a Wall-of-Troy band below the bed mold. An unusual gable-end door allows access to the dining room of the house from the side yard. This feature, part of the original plan, was found in only two other houses surveyed. All three of these were large brick dwellings. Though the portico and entry door date from the mid-nineteenth century, the rest of the house remains unchanged. Even Elmwood's shutters and their hardware are original.

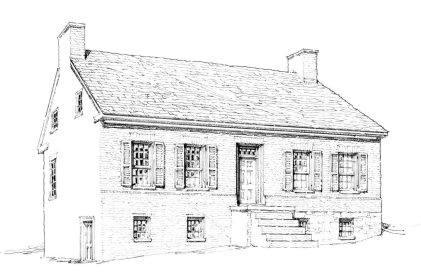

William Hendricks House, 1794, Moler's Crossroads vicinity, restored perspective view

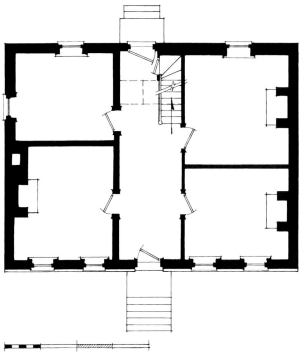

William Hendricks House, first-floor plan

Elmwood (Edward Lucas III House), 1797, Shepherdstown vicinity, Historic American Building Survey photograph, 1937

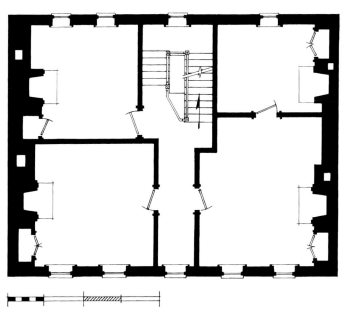

Elmwood, second-floor plan

Sojourner's Inn (William Buckles House), ca. 1790, Ridge Road vicinity, restored perspective view

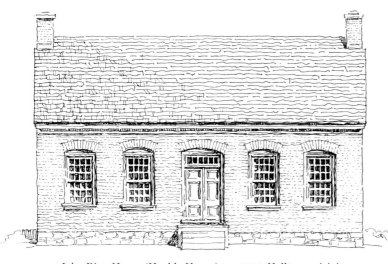

John Rion House (Henkle House), ca. 1785, Halltown vicinity, restored elevation

Not far from Elmwood stands the house known as COLD SPRING. Built of rubble limestone for Edward Lucas's younger brother Robert Lucas III, this five-bay center-hall house also utilizes the double-pile plan. Cold Spring, though not as formal as Elmwood, has many of the same features, including first-floor twelve-over-twelve window sashes and an interesting variation of a jogged hall on the second floor. This innovation was undoubtedly used to gain more room in the upper bedchambers.

Both Elmwood and Cold Spring contain a basement kitchen that has exterior access. Such basement entries were typical for the area. Produce, water, firewood and other necessities could be brought into the house through this basement door. At Cold Spring, massive stones were used to form a porch and stairs to the rear of the house in the nineteenth century.

Another example of the double-pile center-hall house stands in the neighborhood of the Lucas houses. Built about 1795 for William Buckles, the SOJOURNER'S INN, now known as Locust Ridge, is a north-facing stone house with flat sandstone arches over the first-floor windows. The top of this ridge is one of the only areas in Jefferson County where sandstone could have been quarried in significant quantities, and several houses near Sandy Ridge Road incorporate sandstone detailing. The basement entrance is located on the gable end of the house. Barred windows allow ventilation to the basement kitchen and storage areas.

Along Cabbin Run near Halltown stands an early example of a double-pile center-hall house. Built of brick, the JOHN RION HOUSE was originally a story and a half structure with a separate kitchen. The house was built for John Rion who married into the neighboring Lucas family that subsequently built Elmwood, Cold Spring, and Rion Hall, all following the center-hall plan. The John Rion House has early detailing such as segmental arched brickwork over the windows and paneled wainscoting inside, and appears to be the second earliest brick farmhouse in the county, after Taylor's Meadow. A second story was added to the house in the mid-nineteenth century.

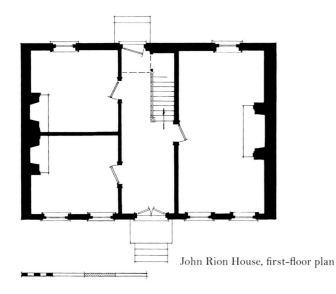

John Rion House, first-floor plan

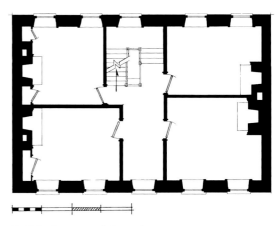

Cold Spring, second-floor plan

Opposite: Cold Spring (Robert Lucas III House), ca. 1800, Shepherdstown vicinity, rear stair

One of the most unusual examples of the double-pile center-hall house is located on what is now the USDA farm at Bardane. Built as a story-and-a-half limestone house, HURSTON possesses a very steeply pitched roof and large second-floor gable-end windows. The effect of this massing gives the house a European feel, from a century earlier. In fact, the house was built for James Hurst, who by 1792 had migrated to what is now Jefferson County from Fairfax County, Virginia. His grandfather had come to the Virginia colony from Leckhampstead between London and Bristol, England. While exemplifying a vernacular building expression, Hurston resembles earlier Maryland Tidewater antecedents like Patuxent in Calvert County.

The fine brick house at the intersection of Warm Springs Road and the Kearneysville Pike, a site known as Walper's Crossroads, was completed in 1805 for former Hessian soldier Casper Walper. Used as a tavern and residence, the CASPER WALPER HOUSE, now known as Pleasance, has highly developed detailing and a variation on the standard center-hall plan. The modillioned cornice with a Wall-of-Troy band complement the formal entry. The house uses false windows, covered by shutters, to balance the east gable elevation.

In the southern end of the county, several formal examples of the center-hall house can be seen today. THE ROCKS, a single-pile house, built of local limestone was erected circa 1795 for Ferdinando Fairfax along the Shenandoah River. Fairfax commissioned this classic five-bay house and was one of a small number of Jefferson County residents who insured their properties in the early period. In an 1803 insurance report,

The Rocks (Ferdinando Fairfax House), ca. 1795, Long Marsh Run, east elevation

Ferdinando Fairfax of The Rocks, artist unknown, ca. 1810, courtesy of the Virginia Historical Society

Hurston (James Hurst House), ca. 1795, Bardane vicinity, oblique view

The Rocks was valued at $1,800 by the Mutual Assurance Society. The house was described as: "A Stone Dwellinghouse 46 feet by 20 feet Two stories high covered with wood. a cellar underneath."[15]

Near The Rocks stands WOODBYRNE, a large brick house situated on a knoll above Long Marsh Run. Built about 1810 in accordance with the will of Battaille Muse for his son George, the house has formal detailing, including a modillioned cornice, paneled end walls, and other ornate millwork. Also single-pile, the building was expanded at the rear with a kitchen and dining wing. A decorative recessed circle was laid into the western gable end near the roof peak. This unusual feature was plastered; because of weathering it is unknown what flourishes the design entailed.

Woodbyrne (George Muse House), ca. 1810, Long Marsh Run, restored perspective view

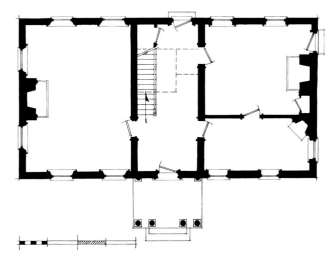

Casper Walper House (Pleasance), first-floor plan

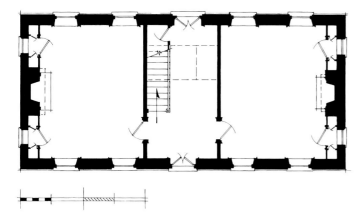

Beverly (Beverly Whiting House), restored first-floor plan

Beverly (Beverly Whiting House), ca. 1800, Wheatland vicinity, south elevation

Prospect Hall (Peter Hunsiker House), ca. 1810, Middleway vicinity, restored perspective view

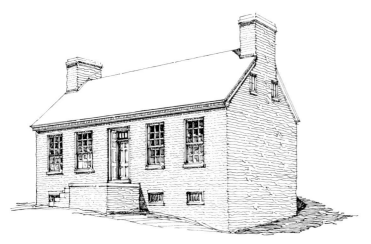

Rock Springs (Hendricks-Snyder House), ca. 1810, Ridge Road, restored perspective view

Adam Stephen Dandridge Sr. of The Bower, by Charles Peale Polk, 1799–1800, Colonial Williamsburg Foundation

Built about 1800, BEVERLY presents another formal example of the single-pile center-hall type. The windows were enlarged and the entry changed in the nineteenth century, but its classical cornice and fine brickwork remain. As with Elmwood, the house originally had twelve-light sashes. Built for Beverly Whiting, the house utilized narrow gable-end windows like those at Harewood and the JOHN WARE HOUSE in Charles Town.

The largest of Jefferson County's early center-hall houses is THE BOWER. This enormous brick mansion overlooking Opequon Creek was completed in 1806 for Adam Stephen Dandridge. Conceived on an impressive scale, compared to its more modest country neighbors, the house is over sixty feet long and forty feet deep, and boasts twelve-foot ceilings. Dandridge sited the house to face west, toward his vast holdings inherited from his grandfather, General Adam Stephen. The interior of the house burned and was rebuilt in a Gothic Revival style in the late nineteenth century.

Near Summit Point, Samuel Mendenhall built a stone dwelling utilizing the single-pile center-hall plan. Now known as Aylmere, the house has paneled end walls and stair detailing similar to that of Woodbyrne. A dining room wing was added to the rear of the SAMUEL MENDENHALL HOUSE in order to attach the once freestanding kitchen.

Built about 1810 by Peter Hunsiker, PROSPECT HALL also stands on a rise above Opequon Creek in the southwestern corner of the county. Another single-pile center-hall house, Prospect Hall had a kitchen in an outbuilding rather than in the basement. The roofline of this brick structure was altered in the nineteenth century to accommodate a two-story portico. A restored drawing illustrates the original arrangement.

The log center-hall house HOPEWELL was built for William Little Jr. around 1810. This one-and-a-half-story five-bay house is steeply banked into a hill overlooking Little's Falls. Just below the house stands the MICHAEL DORSEY MILL HOUSE, named for the owner of the adjacent mill. These two houses were likely built contemporaneously by the same craftsmen. The lower house may have been built for lockkeeper, John Grove, who manned the nearby lenticular lock at Little's Falls on the Shenandoah River. In addition to sharing the same plan, both log houses have plank interior walls.

Along Sandy Ridge Road, the Hendricks-Snyder House, also known as ROCK SPRINGS, is an example of a center-hall plan where the dining room is located in the basement. The upper floor housed the parlor with a bedroom across the hall. Greatly enlarged in the mid-nineteenth century, the original front elevation of this brick house is now covered by an addition. The drawing of a restored view shows the front elevation as it stood before 1850.

The Bower (Adam Stephen Dandridge House), 1806 with later alterations, Opequon Creek area, west elevation

Lansdale (Thomas Lafferty House), ca. 1810, Ridge Road, restored perspective view

Mount Hammond (James Hammond House), ca. 1790, Bloomery vicinity, restored perspective view

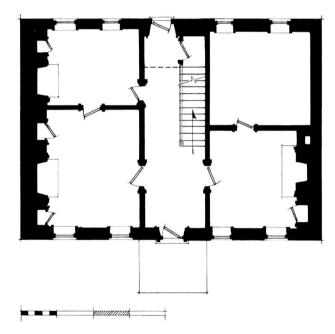

Lansdale (Thomas Lafferty House), first-floor plan

Simeon Shunk House (Calico Cottage), ca. 1813, Kearneysville vicinity

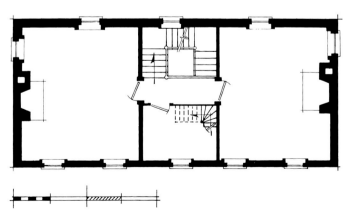

Snow Hill (John Hurst House), second-floor plan

Snow Hill (John Hurst House), 1813, Leetown vicinity

Rockland (James Verdier House), 1812, Walper's Crossroads vicinity

Within sight of Rock Springs stands the county's only sandstone house, LANSDALE. Built about 1810 for Thomas Lafferty, this double-pile house shows the relative ease with which sandstone can be cut. In sharp contrast to the rubble limestone work in the area, the front elevation of Lansdale has neatly coursed ashlar stonework. The house is also unusual among most local double-pile houses in that it does not have gable-end windows for cross-ventilation. The oversize projecting keystones may have been inspired by one of the plates of Palladio's rustic work, which were widely available in builders' guides during this time.[16]

Perched atop a steep rise overlooking the Shenandoah River, MOUNT HAMMOND enjoys one of the most dramatic settings in Jefferson County. This five-bay stone house was built about 1790 for Scots-Irish immigrant James Hammond. Though it was gutted by fire, the house clearly conveys the standard center-hall plan.

Built in 1812 for James Verdier Jr., the son of a French Huguenot, ROCKLAND is another limestone house that makes use of the nearby sandstone for decorative effect. Flat sandstone jack arches are incised to simulate a soldiered course above the windows. The house also has rare sandstone date stones in each of the upper gables. Like neighboring Cold Spring and Sojourner's Inn, this house employs a first-floor plan broken into two rooms on one side and one large room on the other. By banking the house laterally, like Sojourner's Inn, access to the basement kitchen is

granted by a gable-end door. The entry surround with its long transom and sidelights was altered in the mid-nineteenth century. At the same time, the interior was given a Greek Revival makeover. On lower ground behind the house stand the log slave quarter, brick meat house, and stone springhouse.

Standing one-and-a-half stories, the SIMEON SHUNK HOUSE was built about 1813 of limestone. This single-pile house, known now as Calico Cottage, has masonry and millwork detailing similar to Cold Spring and was likely constructed by the same builders. The wide band below the eave and above the first-floor windows hints at the low-ceilinged sleeping loft. Having a south-facing five-bay front, the single-depth rooms are well lit. The north elevation has only three bays—allowing ventilation through the house but reducing heat loss in the winter.

SNOW HILL was built of brick in 1813 for John Hurst near his father's home, Hurston. The house features a formal paired-door entry, a developed box cornice, and Flemish-bond brickwork. The gable ends of the house have patterns formed by burnt brick headers. Like the Simeon Shunk House, the front elevation has five bays while the rear has only three. This house became the Jefferson County Alms House in 1857. The rear wing, with its numerous bedrooms, dates to that time. The interior of the center-hall house has exceptional detailing for the period, including molded panel doors, an overpaneled chimney wall, and elegant stair.

Atop Sandy Ridge and at the headspring of Lucas Run stands GLENBURNIE, built about 1815 for James Glenn. The drawing of a restored view shows the center-hall house with its original window sash arrangement. This house—single-pile in plan—features north-facing gable-end windows. Typically, single-pile houses of the period did not have gable windows, especially with northern exposure. These openings, however, give a view of Ridge Road from the formal parlor. The solid construction of this large house features brick partition walls.

Some of the county's early houses were later altered to become center-hall types, as seen in the THORNBOROUGH-BILLMYER HOUSE, now known as Millbrook. Originally hall-and-parlor, the house was enlarged and the plan changed in a dramatic renovation around 1815 by Martin Billmyer. The corner chimney was removed and replaced with a rectangular stack. The other stack,

however, was allowed to remain in the new hallway. Billmyer approximated symmetry on the front elevation, though it is clear the house was built in stages.

Only two double-crib log houses, also known as "dogtrot houses," were found in the county. These houses are amalgams of two freestanding, parallel single-cell log cribs attached by a breezeway. In other parts of the south, this connecting breeze-way is usually enclosed to form a central hall. Although very popular in areas of Kentucky and Tennessee, the dogtrot appears not to have been favored in Jefferson County.[17] In cases where a single crib had been added to, usually a frame or masonry addition is placed against the crib wall. The JOHN COWAN HOUSE along Cat-tail Run is the sole early example of a dogtrot house in the county. Over fifty feet long, the house is made up of two standard log cabins and a wide hallway con-

necting them. One log section dates to the late eighteenth century, while the second crib and hall are nineteenth-century additions.

Located between Shepherdstown and Kearneysville, the VANDERVEER-BUTLER HOUSE stands on a hill overlooking the road below. This log house has a unique layout that can be best described as a divided passage plan. The room arrangement isolates the central stair in the rear of a divided hall. The plan has no remaining contemporaries in the county. On this continent, these plans were found in grand Tidewater homes, not in the Virginia backcountry. In fact, the plan of the Vanderveer-Butler House closely resembles that of Brooke's Bank in far-removed Essex County, Virginia. Originally a story-and-a-half structure, the Butler family added the second story to the house in the nineteenth century

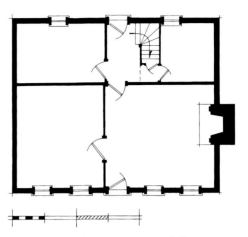

Vanderveer-Butler House, restored plan

Thornborough-Billmyer House (Millbrook), restored perspective view after ca. 1815 addition

Glenburnie (James Glenn House), ca. 1815, Ridge Road, restored perspective view

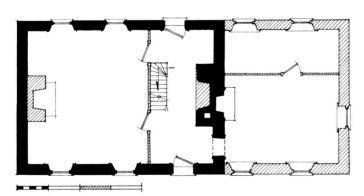

Thornborough-Billmyer House (Millbrook), first-floor plan

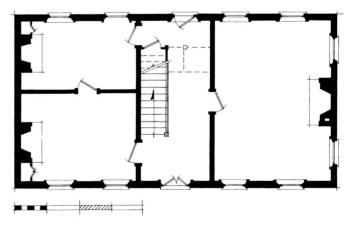

Glenburnie (James Glenn House), first-floor plan

Opposite: Thornborough-Billmyer House (Millbrook), ca. 1770 and ca. 1815, Shepherdstown vicinity, oblique view

Piedmont, central pavilion detail with modillioned cornice and oculus in the pediment

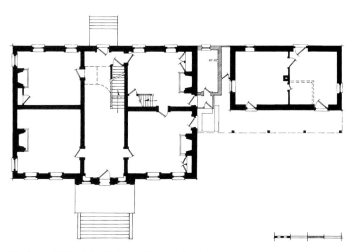

Piedmont (Dr. John Briscoe House), first-floor plan

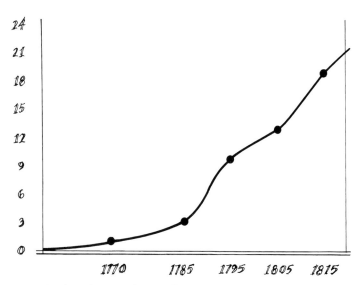

Number of surveyed center-hall houses by decade to 1815

Dr. John Briscoe of Piedmont by John Drinker, Museum of Early Southern Decorative Arts, Winston-Salem, North Carolina

Eleanor Magruder Briscoe of Piedmont by John Drinker, Museum of Early Southern Decorative Arts, Winston-Salem, North Carolina

Certainly, the most architecturally impressive of the county's early center-hall houses is Piedmont. Mixing elements of the Palladian and Adam palette, Piedmont brought a more refined building type to the region. Built about 1790 for the wealthy Pennsylvania native Dr. John Briscoe and his wife Eleanor Magruder Briscoe. The physician and his family commissioned a large and stylish residence that challenged the local vernacular with its intricate detailing. Architecturally, the house has little connection with contemporary houses in rural Virginia. The town houses of Annapolis or Philadelphia appear to have inspired the composition of this remarkable structure, which features a three-bay projecting pavilion flanked by the main block of the building.[18] The pavilion is topped by an oculus under a capping pediment, while dentil coursing runs below a modillioned cornice. The brick body of the building has a molded watertable, banded string course, and segmental flat arched openings. The formal pediment entry with fluted pilasters is the most academic example in the county. For all of its ornate millwork, one might expect a formal hipped roof to crown this structure. However, Piedmont utilizes a standard gable form.

The plan of the house is a standard double-pile form with a detached stone kitchen wing to the side. Due to its unusually elaborate construction, the house was the highest assessed structure in the 1798 house tax, with a value of $2,625—exactly twenty times that of a single-cell log cabin.[19] The quality of the exterior detailing of Piedmont surpasses any brick house of the period in the Shenandoah Valley. Piedmont's ornament would not have a significant influence on the conservative farmhouses that would follow. Only one of the county's subsequent houses would attempt such sophisticated exteriors.

As this section has illustrated, the center-hall house was a popular early plan in Jefferson County. In this survey, center-hall plans make up 36 percent of farmhouses predating 1815. Though each of these houses has unique characteristics, the underlying elements of the center passage and five-bay front are shared by all.

Side-Hall Houses

The third basic plan typical of Jefferson County's early houses is the side-hall. The hall in these houses is used as a passage, as in the center-hall arrangement. The plan is found more commonly in towns, although the earliest uses of the side-hall are seen in smaller farmhouses. Typically arranged with three bays on the front elevation, this plan had several benefits compared to the competing plans of the day—the hall-and-parlor or center-hall types. Having the stair in the narrow side hall allows for physical separation of the entry from the common rooms. In this way, the side-hall plan improves upon the hall-and-parlor, acting much like the center-hall. In contrast to the center-hall plan, a window can be placed on the gable end to light the hall. This increased illumination is not possible in the center-hall house—one of the few detractions of that plan. The side-hall plan also allows for simple shed additions to the rear. Two examples of just such arrangements follow.

The MICHAEL BURKETT HOUSE, near Shepherdstown, was built over a spring with the kitchen in the basement. Flooding may have caused the family to abandon the basement kitchen and build an attached cooking room soon after completing the main house. Now part of Fruit Hill Farm, this limestone house features decorative sandstone-topped openings. The stack of the parlor chimney is hidden from the front elevation. This unusual type of eave chimney is found locally in such early houses as Prato Rio, Peter and Jacob Williamson House, and Traveler's Rest.

Another of the county's pre-Revolutionary side-hall structures is AVON HILL. This property was advertised for sale by Ralph Wormley in 1776. The advertisement speaks at length of the improvements that had been made to the property, which include "a good stone house, 2 stories high, with 2 rooms on a floor."[20] This compact, side-hall house was built above Bullskin Run, near what is now Kabletown. John Gantt, who settled in the valley from Prince George's County, Maryland, purchased the farm from Wormley. Like the Burkett family, Gantt added a kitchen to the rear of the house. The house has small stonework, typical of local early houses, and features a watertable on all four sides. Before its demolition in 2009, Avon Hill was the only surviving early example of a gambrel roof house in Jefferson County.

Another of the county's early side-hall houses was the JOSIAH SWEARINGEN HOUSE, also known as Willowdale. Built in several stages, the house was constructed of diamond-notched logs. A nineteenth-century log addition altered the plan to a center-hall house. It stood on the east side of Shepherd Grade about two miles north of Shepherdstown. Although the house was demolished in the 1980s, National Park Service conservator Alan Levitan had documented it, and provided measured drawings for this survey.

Michael Burkett House, ca. 1770, Shepherdstown vicinity, restored perspective view

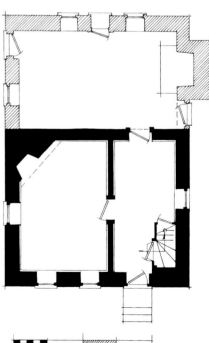

Michael Burkett House, first-floor plan with later rear addition

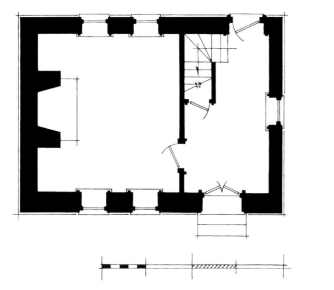

Avon Hill, restored first-floor plan

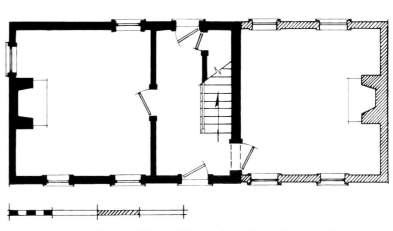

Josiah Swearingen House (Willowdale), first-floor plan with later addition

Avon Hill, ca. 1770, Kabletown vicinity, gable view showing gambrel roofline and later shed addition to rear

The ROBERT HARPER HOUSE in present-day Harpers Ferry was constructed long before the town that now surrounds it. Originally, this stone house utilized a simple side-hall plan. Like the landscape around it, the dwelling was dramatically altered in the nineteenth century. The drawing of a restored view shows the house as originally constructed.

Built along Evitt's Run, THE HERMITAGE is a rambling farmhouse that began as a humble side-hall dwelling. The clapboard-covered log structure has been enlarged to the side and rear with additions and wings—a development that is common throughout the county.

Located near Lake Louisa on Turkey Run, the MOSES SMITH HOUSE is another early log house built in the side-hall plan. Erected in about 1805, this compact house employed an extra rear window to light the stair hall. A later addition turned the house into a rear service wing.

The stone side-entry section of WHITE HOUSE TAVERN, near Summit Point, was built by Andrew McCormick in about 1800.

Robert Harper House, ca. 1780, Harpers Ferry, restored perspective view

White House Tavern (Dr. John McCormick House), ca. 1765 and ca. 1800, Historic American Buildings Survey photograph, 1937

York Hill (John Snyder House), ca. 1798, Ridge Road, restored perspective view before additions

Medley Springs (Carver Willis House), ca. 1815, Opequon Creek area, restored perspective view

He added this single-pile side-hall section to his father's hall-and-parlor house. Banked into the site, the basement is accessed on the gable end. The stonework features three-piece headers over the principal openings.

Along Ridge Road, a side-hall house stands between later additions. Known as York Hill, this log house was built just before 1800 by John Snyder, who moved to Jefferson County from neighboring Washington County, Maryland. The original configuration of the house utilized the single-pile side-hall plan. A single-bay frame addition was attached to one side and then a two-bay stone addition followed.

Medley Springs, built for Carver Willis about 1815, was sited adjacent to Opequon Creek near the village of Middleway. The dwelling utilized a two-story wing that housed the kitchen. This lateral wing arrangement became popular in the nineteenth century as a way to make the kitchen more accessible while still separate from the main living areas.

The Daniel Staley House along Engle Moler Road near Shepherdstown shares many similarities with Medley Springs. Both stone houses employ the side-hall plan, have similar scale, and utilize service wings. They also have comparable stone detailing over the openings, with multi-piece flat jack arches with large flanking shoulder stones.

About 1815 Hezakiah Beall made a frame addition to an earlier log house built by Adam Wever. Beall's enlargement is an unusual example of a side-hall house arranged perpendicular to an earlier building. The alignment of these two pieces required

Vinemont (Wever-Beall House), ca. 1815, Leetown vicinity, side-hall house addition

an alteration to the typical side-hall plan; the stair was shifted inboard to allow access to the earlier portion. The house, now known as Vinemont, has an exterior stone chimney that is topped with brick. This combination of masonry materials on outboard chimneys occurred commonly around Leetown and Middleway.

Standing near Bardane, the WILLIAM BURR HOUSE exemplifies the compact nature of the side-hall cabin. As with Willowdale, a two-bay addition in the 1830s turned this log building into a center-hall house. However, the original section has the typical side-hall plan. The house has deep closets flanking the chimney. The center window of the second floor was left off the elevation, which is a typical treatment locally.

Adjacent to the Haines Mill on Bullskin Run stands the FEAGAN'S MILL HOUSE. This small log side-hall house, built about 1820, was home to the miller. Again, a later addition transformed the house into a center-hall plan. The original, single-pile cabin was built adjacent to a low, single-story kitchen. In this case, a second rear door allowed a convenient access to the kitchen.

James McCurdy completed his single-pile side-hall house sometime around 1813. Since then, the house has come to be known as MOUNTAIN VIEW. Because of its overscale, twelve-over-twelve windows, this large brick house reminds the visitor of the Daniel Morgan House twelve miles north, near Shepherdstown. Similar twenty-four-light windows were also originally used at The Bower. The front entry of Mountain View is flanked by a pair of hall windows like those at THE HILL, PIEDMONT, and RICHWOOD HALL. Inside, the placement of a rear-facing stair allows access to an earlier part of the house.

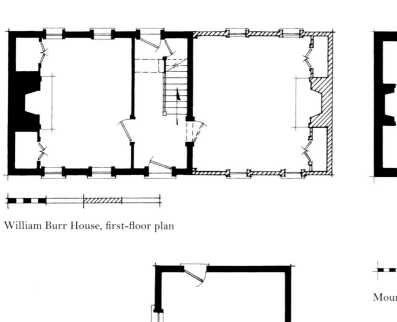

William Burr House, first-floor plan

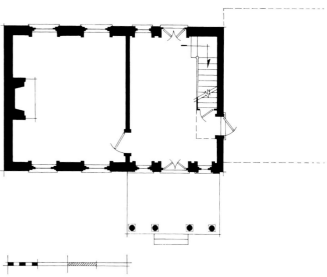

Mountain View, first-floor plan

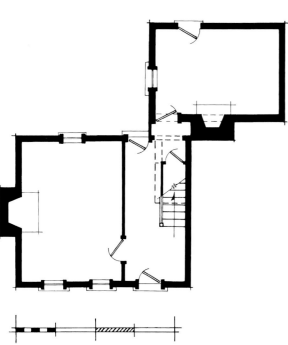

Feagan's Mill House, first-floor plan

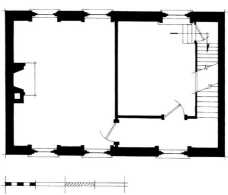

Mountain View, second-floor plan

Opposite: Mountain View (James McCurdy House), ca. 1813, Kabletown vicinity, south gable

William Burr House, ca. 1815, Bardane vicinity, side-hall house with addition

Side-Hall Varietals

The study includes two houses that utilize modified side-hall plans. These two structures are among the oldest in Jefferson County and the plans of both were altered by early renovations. The first of these side-hall plan varietals is the pre-Revolutionary-era VAN DEEVER-ORNDORFF HOUSE, sited along Rocky Marsh Run near Shepherdstown. Although this house was incorporated into a larger nineteenth-century building, two sides of the original stone structure are still clearly visible. With a most unusual two-bay front, the house was likely originally arranged in single-pile side-hall plan. A conjectural plan of the house shows a possible layout. With features such as radiused, segmental arched openings, the Van Deever-Orndorff House is an obvious example of early local construction.

TRAVELER'S REST was originally arranged as a variation on the side-hall plan. This first section of the house was built at the headspring of Spaw Run by the Hyatt family, who were early settlers of the area. By truncating the hall to only half the depth of the building the builders were able to place an extra chamber at the back of the house. Back-to-back corner fireplaces heated the pair of rear rooms. The chimney for these openings was located at the rear eave, so it was not visible from the front of the house.

In 1773, colonial architect John Ariss remodeled the house for its new owner, Horatio Gates, who would later become a general in the Continental Army. Ariss, who lived a few miles to the south, near present-day Rippon, was probably the most prominent architect in the region and Traveler's Rest is the only house that can be definitively attributed to him. Ariss's first interventions on the house, which was about fifteen years old, were to make it more befitting Gates and his wife, who had recently moved to Virginia from England. As the architect wrote to his client, he changed the size of the parlor, or drawing room, so that "the Room as its now Drawn is a better proportion." The architect added in the same letter that he had widened the hallway to "allow for a Better Staircase."[21] In 1781, Ariss returned to design an addition for General and Mrs. Gates.[22] At this time, a large flanking room was constructed to the west, balancing the

Van Deever-Orndorff House, ca. 1775, Shepherdstown vicinity, restored perspective view

facade. The addition expanded the front elevation to seven-bays, an arrangement unique in Jefferson County. Remarkably, the house stands much as Gates and his wife left it in 1790.

In this survey, side-hall farmhouses made up nearly a quarter of all extant rural houses built before 1815. They were popular throughout the survey period, with numerous examples constructed of log, frame, brick, and stone. With one exception, the front elevations of these houses are three bays. Whether single-pile or double-pile, side-hall houses shared the same passage placement. The utility and practicality of this simple plan accounted for its frequent construction. Center-hall houses became widely used only after the Revolution. The five-bay arrangement could also be built one or two rooms deep, depending on the wealth of the owner and the size of his family. The symmetry of the plan and the ease of addition appealed to many of the county's affluent farmers, whose ranks expanded each year. The center-hall's ascendency contrasted the precipitous decline of the hall-and-parlor house, which lost favor with all but a few patrons by 1815. Because fashionable families desired plans with a dedicated hallway that separated household activities, the hall-and-parlor came to be considered antiquated. This perception spread to the yeoman farmers and eventually relegated this once time-honored plan to accommodate work-force housing. The rising and falling popularity of these plan types reflects the cultural and economic dynamics in the county at this time. With their increasing prosperity in the coming years, residents would demand other house forms to take the places of the outmoded and serve their rising aspirations.

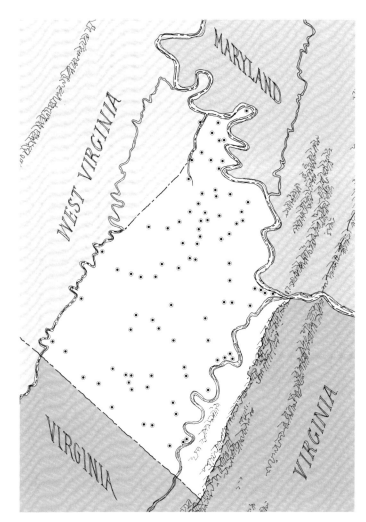

Pre-1815 farmhouses surveyed

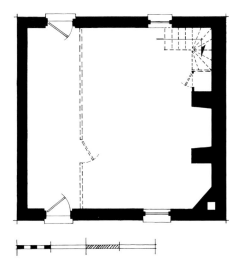

Van Deever-Orndorff House,
conjectural first-floor plan

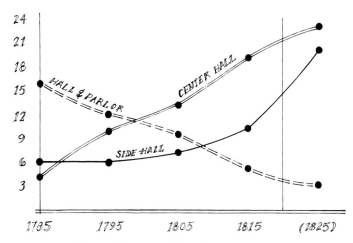

Surveyed houses by type and decade

General Horatio Gates, by Gilbert Stuart, ca. 1793, courtesy of
The Metropolitan Museum of Art, image copyright The Metropolitan
Museum of Art/Art Resource, NY

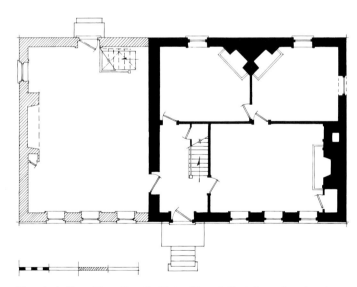
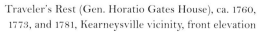

Traveler's Rest (Gen. Horatio Gates House), first-floor plan showing
addition to original section

Traveler's Rest (Gen. Horatio Gates House), ca. 1760,
1773, and 1781, Kearneysville vicinity, front elevation

Chapter Three

Later Farmhouses

1815–1835

Allstadt Ordinary, 1839, in foreground, and Allstadt House, ca. 1800 and ca. 1820, behind to right

New Types of Plans

By 1815, the houses of Jefferson County had become standardized into two principal forms: center-hall and side-hall. With a few exceptions, the days of the hall-and-parlor plan were over. The powerful pressures of assimilation had squeezed plan variation out of the local building vocabulary and successive generations of residents narrowed the idea of acceptable housing to these two common forms. Differences in material, scale, and detail kept the houses from appearing uniform, but in plan they were all country cousins. A divergent precedent, however, was to be set locally with the completion of HAZELFIELD in 1815. The appearance of this new house form would signal a coming burst of creativity and decorative energy in the county's residential architecture.

After the death of her son David in the War of 1812, Ann Stephen Dandridge Hunter looked to move to her farm in Jefferson County from Martinsburg, the town founded by her father, General Adam Stephen. Anne Hunter decided to commission a new house, so her son-in-law, Henry St. George Tucker, made arrangements to secure a loan of $2,000 from his father in Williamsburg to pay for its construction.[1] This house would be known as Hazelfield.

The building of Hazelfield was a seminal event in the area, bringing an entirely new residential plan and appearance—one that would steadily gain popularity among the county's elite. Hazelfield became the archetype for two new house forms that would define the local landscape—the transverse-hall house and the three-bay center-hall house. For members of the community with means, Hazelfield now provided a local model for differentiating their homes from those of their neighbors.

Transverse-hall houses are found in relative abundance in the later period of this survey. This unusual plan places two parlors behind the stair hall, which runs across the front of the house instead of through it. Though new to Jefferson County in 1815, the transverse-hall plan had been used in Britain and America in the eighteenth century. Architectural historian Mills Lane cites Robert Morris's *Select Architecture* (1757) and William Halfpenny's *Useful Architecture* (1752) as likely sources of the plan.[2] These earlier transverse-hall designs were rectangular forms with open room plans, such as the Semple House in Williamsburg. The transverse-hall plan provided in *Vitruvius Scoticus* by William Adam is more like the squarish houses found locally. Adam's book was published in 1812, more than sixty years after his death, but close to the time of the plan's introduction to Jefferson County. A book of Scottish house plans may have appealed to Ann Hunter, whose father was a Scottish émigré, especially if her intention was to set herself apart from locals.

Hazelfield (Ann Stephen Dandridge Hunter House), 1815, Bardane vicinity, east elevation

Built of thick limestone walls covered with stucco, Hazelfield stands two floors over a raised basement. The three-bay center-entry front is located on the gable end of the house. This arrangement must have been striking for the visitor. At this time, gable entry was reserved for public buildings such as churches or courthouses. Other impressive features are the great fanlight that adorns the pediment and the towering brick chimneys that rise from the building's sides. The house left its biggest surprise, however, for those who stepped inside. Instead of the requisite hall running darkly toward the back of the house, the great entry hall of Hazelfield filled the entire front length of the building, with a stair to the left and parlor doors ahead. The generous stair hall is twelve feet deep and thirty-seven feet long, with two large windows flanking the door. The massive light-filled hall would have been a new experience for most visitors. With its bold new plan, Hazelfield had turned local convention on its head.

For all of its daring in form, the millwork at Hazelfield is restrained and traditional. The combination of this locally unique plan with the conservative detailing might seem incongruous. However, it appears that the leading families would only stray so far from local building traditions. Time-honored appointments were retained inside, lending a familiar feel to the unusual layout.

To the southeast in Fauquier County, the transverse-hall plan was imported by renowned jurist John Marshall, who built Oak Hill in 1819.[3] Justice Marshall may have been inspired by *Vitruvius Scoticus* as well when designing his country home, since his mother had family connections to Scotland. Though built later, the other transverse-hall houses of Fauquier County, namely Clover Hill, Oakwood, and Woodbourne, are similar to Hazelfield. With the exception of their chimney placement, which tended toward the rear wall of the building, the plan and scale were nearly identical.[4] The real difference between Hazelfield and the Fauquier houses is the pronounced Greek Revival influence of the latter.

There are no known examples of transverse-hall houses in neighboring Frederick County, Virginia; Berkeley County, West Virginia; or Washington County, Maryland. One must stray farther south to find groups of these uncommon houses. Eastern and Piedmont North Carolina have several transverse-hall houses. Of these, Ayr Mount is the earliest, built at the same time as Hazelfield by Scottish immigrant William Kirkland.[5] The Carolina examples are generally tripartite houses with

Henry St. George Tucker (1780–1848) of Woodbury by Charles Bird King, ca. 1816, Museum of Early Southern Decorative Arts, Winston-Salem, North Carolina

Anne Evelina Hunter, daughter of Ann Stephen Dandridge Hunter of Hazelfield and wife of Henry St. George Tucker of Woodbury, by Charles Peale Polk, ca. 1800, Corcoran Gallery of Art, Washington, D.C., Gift of Mrs. Francis Washington Weeks and Miss Nancy Hunter Weeks

Transverse hall at Hazelfield with front door to the left and parlor doors to the right

matching wings to either side of the main block.[6] In Jefferson County, most transverse-hall houses followed the layout of Hazelfield, having a single wing to one side of the main block.

In the years to come, other houses associated with Henry St. George Tucker would utilize the transverse-hall plan. Tucker built Woodbury and purchased yet another transverse-hall house, Western View, for his daughter. It may well have been Tucker who brought the idea for this new plan to Jefferson County, by guiding the design of Hazelfield for his mother-in-law. Tucker was known to have been interested in architecture and likely made contributions to Hazelfield's design.[7] However the plan made its way to the county, the transverse-hall house signified status. Many of the community's most prominent families—Washington, Hunter, Hite, Tucker, Willis, Humfreys, and Douglas—would favor this plan in the coming decades. Considering the small area that constitutes Jefferson County, there is a surprising density of these rare houses.

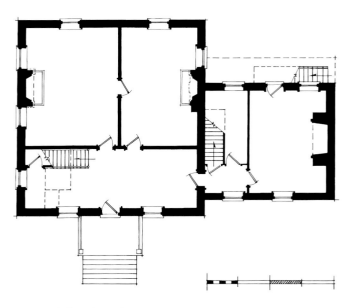

Hazelfield, first-floor plan

Transverse-Hall Houses

After the introduction of the transverse-hall house, some of the county's leading families began to utilize the plan. The Washington family built two transverse-hall houses in the county, the first of which was CLAYMONT COURT. This enormous house was built for Bushrod Corbin Washington, who may have used a plate from Robert Morris's book *Select Architecture* as his inspiration for the design. Unlike Hazelfield, the gable-roofed main block of Claymont Court was bookended by a pair of wings. In addition, square freestanding outbuildings were set to the sides. Each of these square flankers has the unusual feature of a central chimney and pyramidal roof. This design is not found elsewhere in Jefferson County, though it can be seen at Mount Airy in the Virginia Tidewater.

Some of Washington's neighbors ridiculed the great scale and cost of Claymont Court referring to his "folly in erecting such an expensive building."[8] The mansion was reported to have cost an astounding $30,000 at the time of construction. Others, such as historian Samuel Kercheval, were more generous in describing Washington's pretension. Kercheval noted in his 1833

Claymont Court, restored perspective view of original north elevation

book, *A History of the Valley of Virginia*, that Claymont Court was finished in the "most tasteful style of modern architecture." The house burned in 1838, but Washington rebuilt it using the original walls. He enlarged the plan at that time with wider flanking wings. This remarkable building was certainly one of the largest residences in the Shenandoah Valley and a monumental example of the transverse-hall plan.

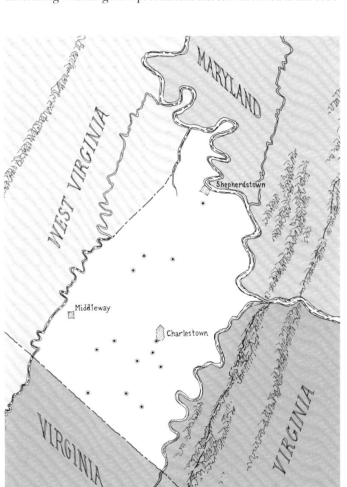

Transverse-hall houses in Jefferson County

Plates from *Select Architecture* by Robert Morris, 1757

Claymont Court (Bushrod Corbin Washington House), 1822, Charles Town vicinity, north elevation

Claymont Court, restored perspective view of post-fire south elevation

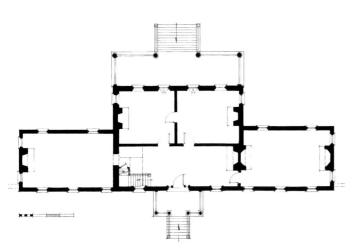

Claymont Court, original first-floor plan

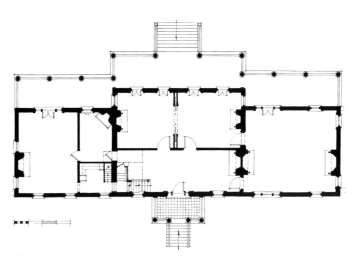

Claymont Court, first-floor plan after rebuild in 1838

Cedar Lawn (John Thornton Augustine Washington House), 1829, Charles Town vicinity, east elevation

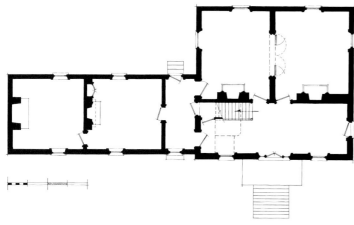

Cedar Lawn, first-floor plan

Cedar Lawn, view of original kitchen wing,
Historic American Buildings Survey photograph, 1937

The second of the Washington transverse-hall houses, Cedar Lawn, was completed in 1829. The following year the property's tax assessment reflected this improvement noting "$3,000 added for new Brick Building." The plan and fenestration pattern of Hazelfield was copied on all sides, though the chimneys were moved from the exterior to the interior walls. Owner John Thornton Augustine Washington also attached a similar service wing to the side of the main block, though his version was larger, in order to include a dining room. Like Hazelfield, the house is set on a raised basement and the core has no rear door. The main difference between the two is the roofline. Washington chose a hipped roof instead of the gable-fronted roof at Hazelfield. Likewise, the shallow-pitched entry portico is a Greek Revival element that had not been present in the county just a decade earlier.

Two houses in the county adapted a transverse-hall through remodeling. Mount Eary, originally a center-entry house, was modified to a transverse-hall plan by new owner and Scottish émigré Dr. Alexander Straith in about 1820. This significant alteration of the interior reoriented the old house to the more fashionable plan. However, the heavy paneled walls of the earlier design remain.

Springdale, the Richard Morgan House, was also changed into a transverse-hall house about 1840. Formerly a hall-and-parlor plan, this reconfiguration of the house is another example of how older layouts were modified or discarded. Though transverse-hall houses were popular around Charles Town and Leetown, Springdale remains the only example of this plan in the neighborhood of Shepherdstown.

By the mid-1830s, the transverse-hall plan had been accepted and embraced by the prominent families of the area. Modifications, however, would have to be made. Because the plan as built at Hazelfield and Cedar Lawn had only two rear bays, and neither were doors, those houses had only a single entrance. At Western View in 1831, James Hite expanded the rear elevation to four bays, making two of these doors, as would be worked later at Claymont Court. In this way, one could exit either of the formal parlors to enjoy the long east-facing porch. This useful modification would stick, and it would even be used locally on some center-hall houses. In addition to the novel plan, Western View has some of the most refined interiors of the period.

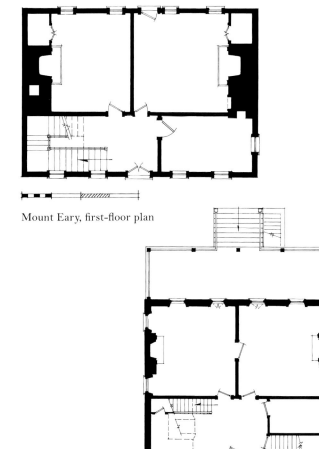

Mount Eary, first-floor plan

Western View (James Hite House), 1831, Kearneysville vicinity, restored perspective view

Western View, first-floor plan

An unusual variation of the transverse-hall plan was built in 1830 for Samuel Howell. At LITTLE ELMINGTON he managed to modify the layout for a story-and-a-half structure with a gable roof. Howell's plan also altered the balance of the room arrangement, giving more weight to the front room adjacent to the stair hall. This house is the only local transverse-hall design to utilize a four-bay front.

Very near Little Elmington stands SPRINGLAND, built in 1835 by Samuel Lackland. This handsome structure is the quintessential Jefferson County transverse-hall house, built of brick with a hipped roof. The chimneys are set on the interior partition wall like those at Cedar Lawn. And like other transverse-hall houses in the county, Springland has large rooms with high ceilings and fine detailing.

On the farm adjacent to Western View, Henry St. George Tucker completed WOODBURY in 1833. This became the grandest, and in some ways the most unusual, of the local transverse-hall houses. Tucker employed stucco-covered stone, as had been used for his mother-in-law's house, Hazelfield. In the nearly twenty years since the completion of Hazelfield, Tucker had developed some new ideas for his retirement home. In 1829 Tucker advertised that he would purchase 11,000 feet of plank of varying thicknesses to be delivered to the "farm I lately purchased . . . three miles north of Leetown." Clearly, the scale of the structure had been decided. In addition to its great size, Woodbury represented the accumulation of all of the best in the form, unsurpassed locally in detailing. The most interesting twist that Tucker would employ was to go back to a five-bay front and gable roof. In this arrangement, the stair presents a planning difficulty since it takes up one end of the hall. In a five-bay plan the stair would have to pass across the end bay of windows. This awkward issue was resolved by making a false window on the stair bay, permanently covered by shutters from the outside. With this simple solution, a handsome five-bay transverse-hall house was achieved. At roughly 10,000 square feet, the scale of Woodbury dwarfed its neighbors. Tucker expanded the rear elevation to six bays, four of which gave access to the vast rear porch. Samuel Kercheval wrote in 1833: "Judge Henry St. George Tucker has erected in the neighborhood of Leetown a most splendid stone building, rough cast, finished in beautiful style, three stories high; the writer does not recollect the exact size of the edifice, but it is a very large building."

The interior of Tucker's home was also rich and inventive by local standards. The elliptical stair, basement dining room, servant's stair, and finished attic with dormer windows were all unusual features for that time in Jefferson County. These interesting components would be incorporated into many of the large houses that followed the construction of Woodbury.

Springland (Samuel Lackland House), 1835, Charles Town vicinity, west elevation

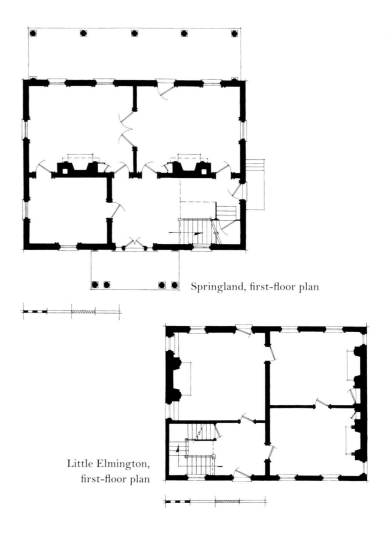

Springland, first-floor plan

Little Elmington, first-floor plan

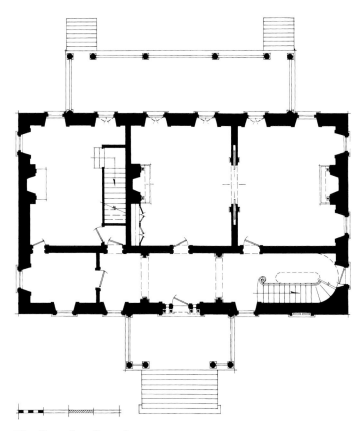

Woodbury, first-floor plan

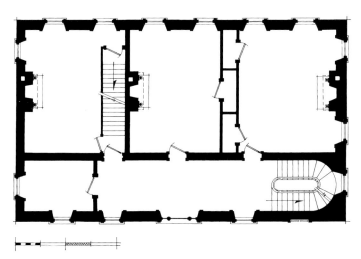

Woodbury, second-floor plan

Woodbury (Henry St. George Tucker House), 1833, Leetown vicinity, west elevation

Woodbury, rear elevation

Three-Bay Center-Hall Houses

Though the five-bay center-hall house continued to be popular in Jefferson County during this later period, a new variation came into use after 1815. This new form utilized the same interior plan of the five-bay center-hall, but with only three bays on the front. This elevational change presented the contemporary look as defined by plate 36 in Owen Biddle's widely used book, *The Young Carpenter's Assistant*. The three-bay front was easily adaptable to the austere Greek Revival detailing that would appear locally in the 1820s. The function of the center-hall floor plan was retained with an updated facade. More formal examples were topped with hipped roofs, and expanded windows were employed as larger glass panes became available in the valley. As estate inventories of the first quarter of the nineteenth century suggest, material wealth had greatly increased from the preceding century. In correlation, more furniture and decorative items appear in these records, and the new three-bay center-hall plan provided generous expanses of unbroken wall space for the use and display of these furnishings. As with the five-bay version, chimneys were kept inboard on the gable ends, with less formal houses having outboard stacks.

One of the earliest examples of this new form is Belvedere, near Charles Town. Built by the Tate family around 1818, this brick house boasts a decorative transom and sidelights around the front door. A tripartite central window on the second story balances the elevation. Such upper sidelights would become a recurring and defining feature of Jefferson County's three-bay houses built during the second quarter of the nineteenth century. The expanded glazing around the door not only added emphasis to the central bay, but also improved conditions in the otherwise dark entry hall.

Now a five-bay house, Blakeley was originally a three-bay structure. Built in 1821 by John Augustine Washington II, this formal house mirrored the arrangement of Belvedere. The house had a center-hall main block with detached service wing, and a large rear wing was added in the late nineteenth century. Blakeley faces the grander south elevation of Claymont Court across the north Fork of Bullskin Run. Though not as large as the latter, Blakely was a formidable house in its day.

The three-bay center-hall house was far more popular in the central and southern parts of the county, but a few formal examples were nevertheless found in other areas. The Daniel Morgan House near Shepherdstown, for example, was completed in 1828. This brick house, now known as Rose Brake, has large twelve-light windows, as at earlier houses like Elmwood, Wynkoop Tavern, and Beverly.

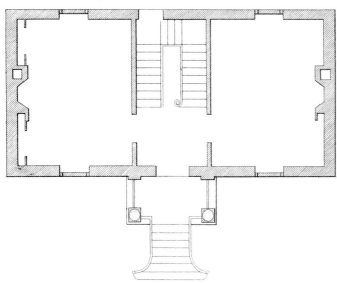

Elevation and plan of three-bay center-hall house,
The Young Carpenter's Assistant, plate 36, by Owen Biddle, 1805

Opposite: Daniel Morgan House (Rose Brake), 1828, Shepherdstown vicinity, rear elevation, Historic American Building Survey photograph, 1937

Belvedere (William Tate Heirs House), ca. 1818, Charles Town vicinity, east elevation, photograph ca. 1910, courtesy of Nancy Wilson

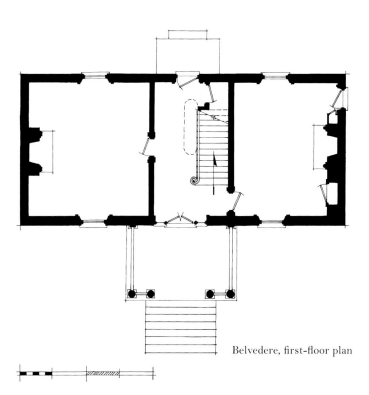

Belvedere, first-floor plan

Cool Spring (Thomas Griggs House), 1832, Summit Point vicinity, east elevation

Allemont (William Craighill House), ca. 1825, Bloomery vicinity, east elevation

Mantipike (Thomas G. Baylor House), 1833, Leetown vicinity, west elevation

Falling Spring (Jacob Morgan House), 1834, Shepherdstown vicinity, restored perspective view

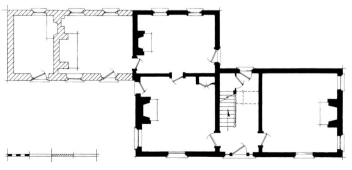

Rosemont (James Wysong House), restored first-floor plan

Ripon Lodge (William F. Turner House), ca. 1835, Rippon vicinity, east elevation

By the 1830s, the three-bay house was prolific in both refined and vernacular forms. A number of less formal houses dating to this decade are found around the county. Cool Spring built for Thomas Griggs in 1832, utilized outboard brick chimneys and thin gable windows, unusual on local single-pile houses. Thomas G. Baylor commissioned Mantipike in 1833 along the Leetown Road. This house, like the Morrison House, Kensley Ordinary, and Tulip Hill, is a log three-bay building with a central stair hall.

A frame example of the three-bay type, Fenton Hill, overlooks the Shenandoah River. Now known as Allemont, this clapboard-covered house was built by William Craighill in about 1825 on the foundation of the hall-and-parlor residence of William Little. The newer house was bound by the dimensions of

the predecessor, but the plan was changed by Craighill to center-hall. A second story was added later to the kitchen wing.

The large brick house known as Rosemont was built near Charles Town for James Wysong. This three-bay center-hall house, built in 1830, had a rear wing that was later enlarged with a stone kitchen addition.

Examples of large stone three-bay center-entry houses include Ripon Lodge and Falling Spring. The center stair at Ripon Lodge was moved to a later wing, though the original arrangement was typical for the county. Built in 1834, Falling Spring is one of the largest houses of the period. This double-pile center-hall house features paired gable-end windows—a novel window arrangement that would be copied later on several Greek Revival houses along Washington Street in Charles Town.

George W. Moler House, 1834, Bakerton vicinity, east elevation

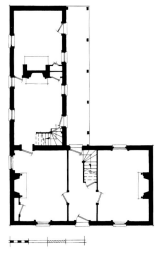

George W. Moler House,
first-floor plan

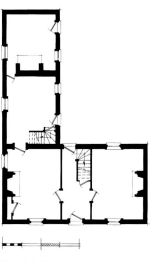

Rawleigh Moler House,
first-floor plan

Gap View (Walter Baker Jr. House), ca. 1817, showing modified
center-entry arrangement, Historic American Building Survey
photograph, 1937

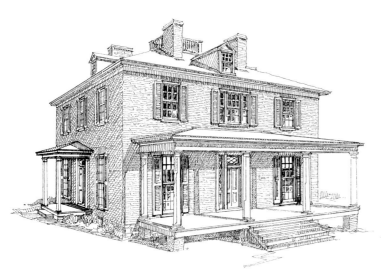

Cassilis (Andrew Kennedy House), 1834, Charles Town vicinity, restored perspective view

Cassilis (Andrew Kennedy House), restored perspective view of rear elevation

Two of several masonry houses built by the Moler family in the 1830s, the RAWLEIGH MOLER HOUSE and GEORGE W. MOLER HOUSE near Bakerton, use an enclosed winder stair in their center halls. This unusual variation on the three-bay form speaks to the individual preferences of the owners, who were brothers. Amazingly, these two houses are nearly identical in plan, size, and elevation.

The original side-hall plan of GAP VIEW, built before 1820, was changed to the fashionable three-bay center-hall type by James L. Ranson. After the renovation, this stone building was stuccoed to hide the signs of alteration.

One of the most formal of Jefferson County's three-bay center-hall houses is CASSILIS, along the old Berryville Pike just south of Charles Town. Cassilis also shares plan elements with the transverse-hall houses of the county. Built in 1834 by Andrew Kennedy, this formal brick house merged the center-hall and the transverse-hall plans to make a hybrid that is unique within the county. The Kennedy family had roots in Maryland, where at least two other houses with this unusual plan can be found—Woburn Manor in Washington County, Maryland, and Carrolton Manor in Frederick County, Maryland. To the west in Berkeley County another example of this plan stands at Allendale. One would expect Cassilis, with its paired interior chimneys, three bays on the west-facing front, and four bays on the rear, to have a transverse-hall plan. However, the hall is centered between two front chambers. The stair rises between the front and back rooms leaving the wide hall open. Like a transverse-hall arrangement, two large parlors join in the back of the house and open onto a wide east-facing porch.

These later houses are evidence of their owners' willingness to break from the local tradition and expand the accepted house forms. The ingenuity in layout of these houses foreshadows the appearance of new plans in the following decades.

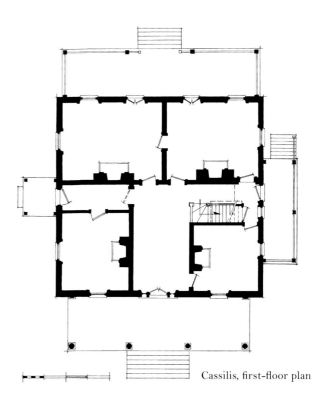

Cassilis, first-floor plan

Later Five-Bay Center-Hall Houses

The emergence of the new three-bay house types did not mean that the older five-bay center-hall plan was on the wane. To the contrary, the era between 1815 and 1835 was the heyday of the five-bay center-hall house in Jefferson County. As with the period before 1815, both single-pile and double-pile center-hall plans were used extensively. A variety of scale and formality can be found in these plentiful houses. RICHWOOD HALL (Smith Slaughter House) stands as the most elaborate example of the period. Built about 1815, this single-pile house has a projecting central pavilion, like the earlier Piedmont. The ornate pediment-topped bay features a lunette window over a pediment-topped second-story window. The paired entry door has an unusually formal surround and, like the upper story, is flanked by narrow windows. For all of its exterior pretensions, however, Richwood Hall conforms to the standard template of the five-bay center-hall plan.

A large stone house built for Michael Moler, LINDEN SPRING has flat jack-arched openings and large quoins. The L-shaped building was designed to accommodate a rear two-story porch or gallery, as the porch projection balances the gable elevation. This integral porch configuration was widespread in the decades after this house was constructed and continued to be popular locally after the Civil War. Linden Spring, therefore, is one of the earliest examples of this interesting local design.

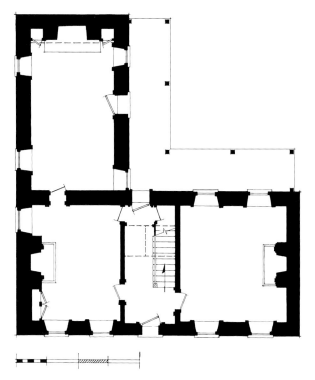

Linden Spring, first-floor plan

Linden Spring (Michael Moler House), ca. 1818, Moler's Crossroads vicinity, east elevation

Opposite: Richwood Hall (Smith Slaughter House), ca. 1815, Charles Town vicinity, central pavilion, east elevation

Michael Shaull House (Green Spring), ca. 1815, Middleway vicinity, restored perspective view

Nicholas Shaull House (Thorn Hill), 1816, Middleway vicinity restored perspective view

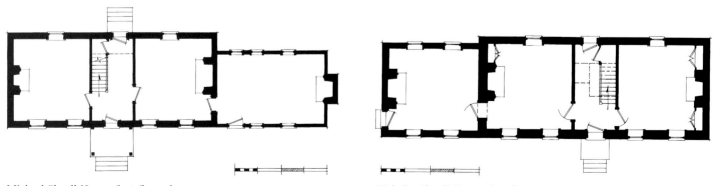

Michael Shaull House, first-floor plan

Nicholas Shaull House, first-floor plan

A cluster of stone farmhouses stands along the Opequon near Middleway, each with the center-hall plan. These include MICHAEL SHAULL HOUSE (Green Spring), NICHOLAS SHAULL HOUSE (Thorn Hill), and FREDERICK ROSENBERGER HOUSE (Round Top). It appears that all three were constructed by the same builder for different clients. The mason responsible for these houses also likely built neighboring MEDLEY SPRINGS a few years earlier, as the stonework and millwork is very similar. These three stone houses have minor variations in plan but nearly identical dimensions.

The enclosed winder stair in the center-hall of Round Top was seen in Shepherdstown two decades earlier.

One of the last stone five-bay center-hall houses built in the county, the CHRISTIAN ALLEMONG HOUSE, was completed in 1830 near Summit Point. In his mid-sixties at the time, Allemong built in the older style, with a standard plan. Although some of the largest houses in the county to be built of stone were erected after 1825, its general popularity as a building material faded in favor of brick.

Frederick Rosenberger House (Round Top), ca. 1815, Middleway vicinity, restored perspective view

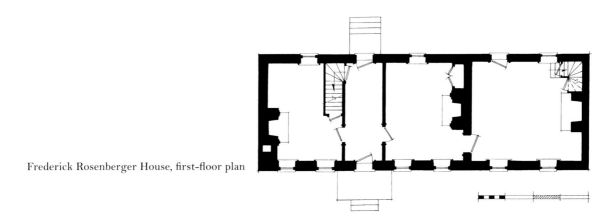

Frederick Rosenberger House, first-floor plan

Hawthorne (John Thomson House), ca. 1832, Summit Point vicinity, east elevation

Pleasant Valley (Abraham Snyder House), 1825, Duffields vicinity, east elevation

Fertile Plain (Samuel Harris House), ca. 1818, Moler's Crossroads vicinity, rear elevation

Shenstone (Harfield Timberlake House), 1820, Summit Point vicinity

HAWTHORNE is an excellent example of a single-pile center-hall log house. Constructed in 1832, this building was stuccoed when the stone rear wing was added in the 1840s. The house has generous rooms and handsome millwork.

Another center-hall log house of the period is PLEASANT VALLEY. Built in 1825 for Abraham Snyder, this double-crib house presented five bays to the east and three to the west. Two free-standing log cribs were erected and then a hallway was framed between them. Pleasant Valley has two exterior chimneys with stone bases and brick stacks.

Five-bay center-hall houses such as MOUNT ELLEN and FERTILE PLAIN, both built in about 1818, show the rising popularity of brick in the construction of farmhouses in Jefferson County.

SHENSTONE, built for Harfield Timberlake in 1820, stands as a finely executed local brick house. Similar in scale to Fertile Plain, the house has a five-bay front with center-hall plan. The single-pile structure boasts high ceilings and excellent detailing. An early half-round fanlight crowns the formal entry and a molded brick cornice adds decorative flair to the front elevation.

Built for county farmer Thomas Abell in 1829, CLEARLAND is located to the south of Duffields. The five-bay brick house stands two stories on a raised basement, typical massing for local residential structures. Clearland differs from most county houses in its unusual orientation. The front elevation faces due north, an arrangement rarely seen in the area.

Clearland (Thomas Abell House), 1829, Duffields vicinity

Opposite: Mount Ellen (Benjamin Davenport House), ca. 1818, Summit Point vicinity, east elevation

Straithmore (John Myers House), 1830, Wheatland vicinity, south gable, Historic American Building Survey photograph, 1937

Martin Billmyer House (Rock Spring), 1831, Shepherdstown vicinity, south elevation

Clay Hill (John Hurst III House), 1835, Ranson vicinity, south elevation

Jacob Moler House (Bel-Mar), 1834, Zoar vicinity, east elevation

Jacob Moler House, first-floor plan

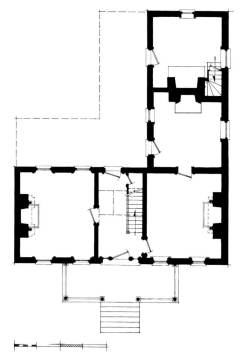

Altona (Abraham and Braxton Davenport House), ca. 1795 and 1834, Charles Town vicinity, south elevation

By the 1830s, brick center-hall houses covered the county. STRAITHMORE, completed in 1830 by John Myers, was built along the Bullskin adjacent Arc Mill. This brick structure was steeply banked into a hill to allow gable end access to the house and kitchen wing.

The MARTIN BILLMYER HOUSE, now known as Rock Spring, was finished the following year. Situated on Rocky Marsh Run, near the county's northern border, this double-pile house has exceptional detailing for the period, including a fine fanlight entry.

The late eighteenth-century frame house, ALTONA, had a brick five-bay front added in 1834. Owner Braxton Davenport transformed the old building into a spacious double pile home for his family. Davenport included a fanlight entry and a hipped roof with stylish dormer windows.

That same year, Jacob Moler completed his stately five-bay home, now known as Bel-Mar. Like relatives Michael, George, and Rawleigh Moler, Jacob built an L-shaped masonry house. The attached rear wing housed the kitchen and dining areas. Along with handsome exterior finishes, the JACOB MOLER HOUSE has refined interior detailing.

Another family of prolific builders in Jefferson County were the Hursts. They also preferred center-hall houses. The earliest of their family houses, Hurston and Snow Hill, used this plan. Later generations added a string of fine buildings to the area north of Charles Town in the 1830s and 1840s. Beginning with Snow Hill, their preference in building material was brick. In 1835, the L-shaped CLAY HILL (John Hurst III House) was erected on a large scale. The house had a rear wing for dining and a summer dining room in the basement, like its contemporaries Woodbury, Western View, and Springland. Later Hurst houses include the five-bay LA GRANGE, built for John Hurst IV, three-bay ASPEN HILL, the home of James G. Hurst, and Minor Hurst's home, QUINCE HILL, a three-bay residence.

Later Side-Hall Houses

As with center-hall house plans, the side-hall continued to be popular in Jefferson County after 1815. The use of this plan in towns was especially prevalent. In the country, the side-hall plan became more common during this time, and more formal examples were built as well. As discussed in the previous chapter, the side-hall plan had many benefits. One attractive advantage was the ease of balancing the front elevation with a later addition. This section shows several examples of side-hall houses that later became center-hall houses through just such additions. However, many side-hall houses built between 1815 and 1835 were not conceived for later additions. Side-hall farmhouses of this period were generally larger and more ornate than their eighteenth-century antecedents, which made additions less necessary. These houses were typically composed as two-story residences, unlike the earlier story-and-a-half types.

One of the best examples of this scale difference of later side-hall houses is the house known as THE HILL near Charles Town. Matthew Frame added the side-hall section on to an earlier house. The size of the main block makes the former house appear as a minor wing. Completed about 1815, The Hill has several unique features. In addition to its large scale, the house has a pair of inboard end chimneys that are unattached above the peak and a highly developed cornice for the period. Also unusual is the four-bay front, a town house feature that is exceedingly rare in rural Jefferson County. The larger scale of The Hill portends changes that would be embodied in side-hall houses in the coming decades.

Constructed about 1818, CLAREMONT was built for Thomas Beall, a wealthy merchant. This well-built limestone house is

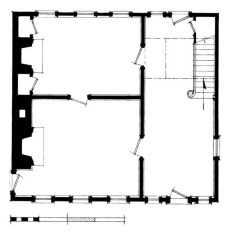

The Hill, first-floor plan without earlier wing

double-pile in plan. A gable window lights the hall, as with most side-hall houses. The stair is pushed to the rear of the hall allowing access to the back room. Flat sandstone arches accent the window and door openings. Set on a steep hill, this large house holds a commanding view of the creek and turnpike below.

Another large side-hall residence of the period is the WILLIAM GROVE HOUSE near Duffields. Built of brick in 1826, this double-pile structure used the novel arrangement of an offset kitchen wing to bed a rear porch. The house has a molded brick cornice and an excellent stair.

Two neighboring side-hall examples of this era are the original section of GAP VIEW, built for Walter Baker around 1817, mentioned earlier, and MOUNT PLEASANT, which was the home of Charles Yates-Aglionby. The two stone houses are similar in scale, plan, and detailing. The houses, on adjacent farms, were built with a vertical aspect and a rough-cast plaster finish over their limestone exterior walls.

The Hill (Matthew Frame House), ca. 1815, Charles Town vicinity, restored perspective view

Mount Pleasant (Charles Yates–Aglionby House), ca. 1825, Ranson vicinity, east elevation, demolished

Claremont (Thomas Beall House), ca. 1818, Halltown, south elevation

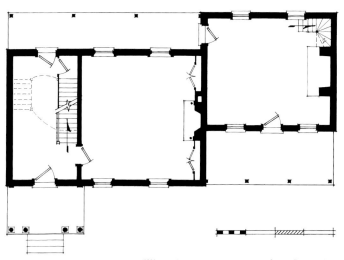

William Grove House, 1826, first-floor plan

Built near Rocky Marsh Run in about 1825, the GEORGE FULK HOUSE is another stone side-hall house. Featuring a wide hall, the house has a standard double-pile plan. Later, the stair was removed from the hall to the unheated rear room when a log wing was added.

Built in 1826, the DR. JOHN R. HAYDEN HOUSE is now enveloped by the town of Bolivar. The Federal detailing of the exterior is unusually refined for the area. The entry has a half-round fanlight transom topped by a projecting brick key.

Across the road, the VALENTINE DUST HOUSE mirrors the plan and detailing of its neighbor. The house is a good example of the smaller scale of town buildings. Built around 1815, the brick structure was raised to two full stories in 1829 by Susan Downing.

The THOMAS CAMPBELL JR. HOUSE, completed in 1829, was a side-hall addition to Campbell's father's earlier house. The single-pile log house boasts a wide stair hall and an outboard stone chimney. The original beaded siding was later covered with stucco.

Brick was used widely in the construction of side-hall houses during this period as well. The compact plan of the DANIEL HAINES HOUSE restricts the hall width to gain more spacious living areas. In this regard, the house has the scale and feel of an earlier period or a town house. Built with a narrow double-pile layout, the structure is much deeper than wide, like many town houses. The Haines House, completed before 1820, features an early example of a decorative brick cornice.

The YATES-BEALL HOUSE, near Flowing Springs, utilized a slightly modified side-hall plan. Built about 1825, this brick house divided the hall into the stair room and a rear chamber. This truncated-hall plan is similar to the earlier Traveler's Rest, though the chimney placement differs. A mid-nineteenth-century addition enlarged the Yates-Beall House, providing a large parlor.

One of the most architecturally interesting side-hall houses in the county, CALEDONIA, stands as a model of vernacular building.

Dr. John R. Hayden House, 1826, Bolivar, north elevation

After moving to Jefferson County from Lancaster County, Pennsylvania, William Cameron Sr. completed his new home in 1816. Cameron must have brought strong ideas for the house with him because Caledonia defied the local building traditions of the time. The door placement alone—located in the second bay from the right, not on the end—shows the Pennsylvania influence. Caledonia is the only extant side-hall farmhouse in Jefferson County with such an arrangement. Cameron designed the interior to be just as novel. The wide side hall has a handsome stair pushed to the very back, leaving the expansive hall as a usable chamber. Unlike all of the other double-pile side-hall houses in the county, the gable-end of this mammoth hall was unfenestrated. Taking an additional swipe at local convention, the house faces due west into the weather. Cameron, however, did make plans for the elements by constructing a full-length porch on the front. The west-facing orientation was embraced by the builders of the county's great houses almost twenty years later, when it became popular for grand homes.

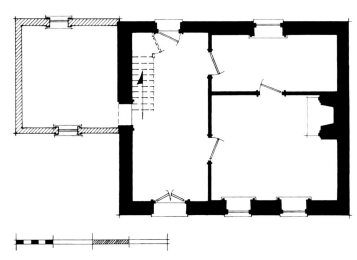

George Fulk House, ca. 1825, first-floor plan

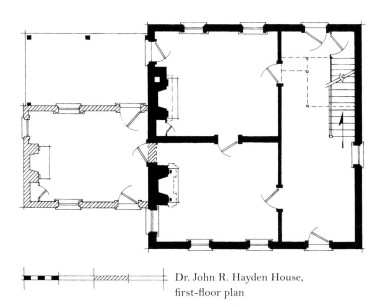

Dr. John R. Hayden House, first-floor plan

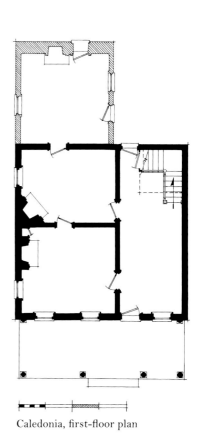

Daniel Haines House, first-floor plan

Daniel Haines House, ca. 1818, Summit Point vicinity south elevation

Caledonia (William Cameron Sr. House), 1816, Cameron's Depot, west elevation

Caledonia, first-floor plan

The DANIEL HEFFLEBOWER JR. HOUSE, built in 1828, stands near Kabletown on Bullskin Run. Like the Camerons, the Hefflebower family moved to the area from Pennsylvania, but their home had been farther west in Franklin County. New ideas in architecture traveled with these transplants to Jefferson County as well. Daniel Hefflebower built a brick side-hall house, but altered the local form to create a new form, creating a subjugated two-story wing to house the kitchen and an additional bedroom above. In the local vernacular, the first-floor area would have been halved to provide parlor and dining area. Hefflebower chose instead to divide the space into a large front room and a

Southwood (Edward Southwood House), 1833, Kearneysville vicinity, Historic American Building Survey photograph, 1937

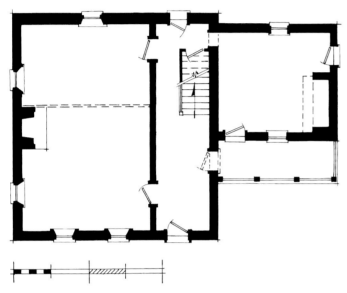

Daniel Hefflebower Jr. House, 1828, first-floor plan

Abraham Hefflebower House, 1826, Kabletown vicinity, rear elevation

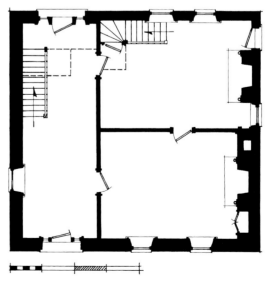

Southwood, first-floor plan

smaller keeping room in the rear. By being economical, he was able to carve four bedchambers out of the second-floor space.

Two years earlier, Daniel's brother, Abraham, built a similar brick side-hall house just to the north. Though larger, the ABRAHAM HEFFLEBOWER HOUSE differs little from his brother's. These houses are unique in Jefferson County for their plan and massing.

SOUTHWOOD, a large house built of stucco-covered stone, has an expansive entry hall with high ceilings. Built for Edward Southwood in 1833, this is one of the largest side-hall houses in the county. The house also has a service stair in the rear room, which is uncommon in the area.

High on a hill above the Shenandoah River, the aptly named RIVERSIDE faces the water and the Blue Ridge Mountains. Built in 1822 by Samuel Lackland, this single-pile side-hall house has a large outboard stone chimney. The wide stair hall at Riverside accesses the large open parlor, which like The Hill has three bays. A few years later, Lackland would build the transverse-hall house Springland, mentioned earlier.

The frame house known as BOIDESTONE'S PLACE was moved to its current site by Charles M. Shepherd in 1835. The house, originally built on the adjacent farm for Marcus Alder, may have originally employed a transverse-hall plan. The structure was reoriented by Shepherd, and arranged as a side-hall plan on the location of the earlier Boidestone house, of which, the earlier kitchen wing remains.

Riverside (Samuel Lackland House), 1822, Bloomery vicinity, east elevation

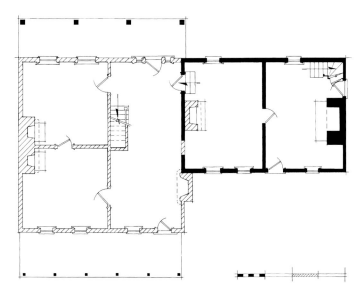

Boidestone's Place, first-floor plan showing earlier kitchen wing

Boidestone's Place (Alder-Shepherd House), ca. 1822 and moved in 1835, Terrapin Neck area, west elevation

Retirement (Richard McSherry House), log house ca. 1795, stone addition ca. 1817, Leetown vicinity, restored perspective view

Several side-hall additions have outlived the original house to which they were added. This scenario is more likely where masonry additions were added to log houses. Two such survivors are RETIREMENT and ASPEN POOL. These stone additions have become freestanding side-hall houses through attrition. Built for Richard McSherry, the addition to Retirement was a single room on the first floor with one bedchamber above. The stair remained in the log house until it burned in the mid-1800s. The main block of the house and its attached kitchen wing have

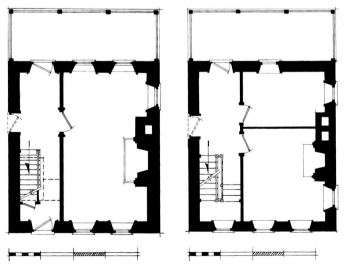

Aspen Pool (John Unseld House), 1827, Moler's Crossroads vicinity, first- and second-floor plans

typical stone detailing of the early nineteenth century. Aspen Pool, like neighboring Linden Spring, was built to employ a two-story porch. A second-story door in the stair hall gives access to the upper gallery. The east end of the gable is clipped allowing the upper porch to complete the roof angle. This stone side-hall section was added to an earlier log house, which was removed in the 1970s.

At the SWEARINGEN-SHEPHERD HOUSE (Springwood), the side-hall addition was attached to the earlier hall-and-parlor house about 1820 by Abraham Shepherd. In this combination, one can see the obvious difference between the horizontal massing of local eighteenth-century buildings and the verticality of those of the early nineteenth century. The addition was built with a story-and-a-half kitchen wing to the rear. After 1815 service wings became common throughout Jefferson County.

The asymmetrical elevation of the PETER SHARFF HOUSE is due to a sequence of building events. A side-hall addition was added to the earlier center section of the house making for a locally rare example of four-bay farmhouse. The lopsided plan shows the combination of individual buildings, a common practice throughout the county.

By the mid-1830s, the Greek Revival influence was widespread, and that taste prized symmetry. As a result, the offset entry of the side-hall house became less desirable to county farmers intent on showcasing the style of the moment. Though the side-hall house would continue to be used in towns, its days as a preferred farmhouse were waning in Jefferson County.

Swearingen-Shepherd House (Springwood), ca. 1820, side-hall addition by Abraham Shepherd, Terrapin Neck

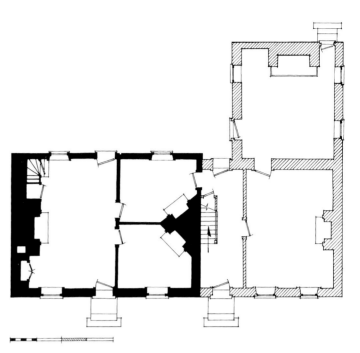

Swearingen-Shepherd House, first-floor plan showing side-hall addition to original hall-and-parlor house

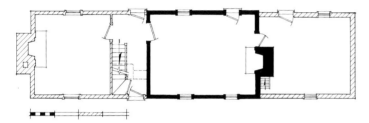

Peter Sharff House, first-floor plan

Peter Sharff House, ca. 1820, Leetown vicinity, west elevation

The Last Hall-and-Parlor Houses

Though the hall-and-parlor plan lost popularity after the close of the eighteenth century in Jefferson County, a few late examples exist. Most of these buildings were small log tenant houses or work-force housing. The humble TOOLE-VAN SANT HOUSE was built overlooking the Potomac River in about 1830. The structure was home to farm families with modest acreage and rocky land. A kitchen wing was added in the 1850s, followed by a full second story in the 1890s, giving the house an asymmetrical facade. Three compact hall-and-parlor cabins near Shepherdstown share simplicity and scale, ISABELLA ENGLE HOUSE (ca. 1830), the WILLIAM ORNDORFF HOUSE (ca. 1835), and JAMES WALKER HOUSE (1839).

One later brick house, the HEFFLEBOWER MILL HOUSE, followed the hall-and-parlor plan. This house was completed in 1826 for Daniel Hefflebower Sr., who was nearly sixty years old at the time of construction. The antiquated plan may have been more familiar to the elder Hefflebower. Though built of brick, the diminutive scale of this house is similar to the later log and stone hall-and-parlor houses.

Samuel Cameron House, 1829, Cameron's Depot, restored perspective view

Toole-Van Sant House, ca. 1830, Terrapin Neck area, oblique view of south elevation

William Orndorff House, ca. 1835, Shepherdstown vicinity, demolished

A handful of stone houses built during this period use the old hall-and-parlor plan but exude a distinct Greek Revival presentation. Their many similarities, such as small size, large stonework, and brick-topped chimneys, suggest these stone houses were built by the same masons. This group includes the REVEREND JAMES BLACK HOUSE, built in 1823 near Shepherdstown, the BEALL HEIRS' HOUSE, which was completed in 1828 south of Leetown, and the SAMUEL CAMERON HOUSE, finished in 1829 along Evitt's Run. The OLIVER CROMWELL HOUSE near Kabletown, erected in 1833, is another modest hall-and-parlor house. The unbalanced three-bay front elevation has more in common with the houses of Middle Virginia than those of the lower valley.

Another group of late small stone hall-and-parlor houses are located near Bakerton. Several of these houses were built by the Engle family, including HOMESTEAD (John Engle House), SALLIE MELVIN HOUSE, both in 1834, and the ISAAC CLYMER HOUSE. These houses are similar in scale, material, and plan. Built in 1835, the Isaac Clymer House is steeply banked into a hillside, like the neighboring George Reynolds house. The large cornerstones are typical of local stonework of this period.

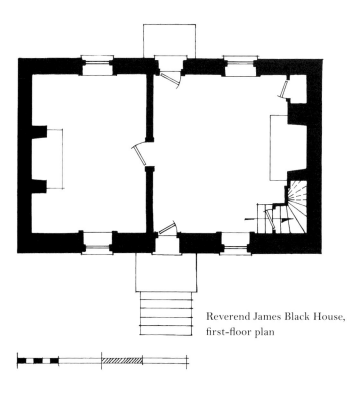

Reverend James Black House, first-floor plan

113

Hefflebower Mill House, 1826, Kabletown vicinity, west elevation

Hefflebower Mill House,
first-floor plan

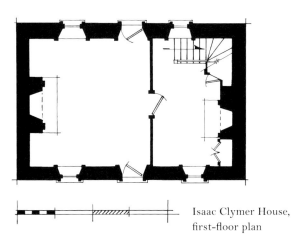

Isaac Clymer House,
first-floor plan

Opposite: Isaac Clymer House, 1835, Bakerton vicinity, east gable oblique view

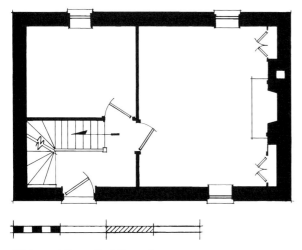

Richwood Farm (Thomas B. Washington House), 1831, Charles Town vicinity, front elevation

Richwood Farm, first-floor plan

Nonconforming Houses

Just a handful of farmhouses of the 1815–1835 period were found during the survey of early houses that did not conform to the three primary plan types. The scarcity of nonconforming houses argues for the powerful pressures of assimilation in the culture of the time.

One interesting plan variation is used at RICHWOOD FARM, which was built in 1831 for Thomas B. Washington. The two-bay front elevation hints at the unusual nature of the interior arrangement. This plan is a modified side-hall, having an offset entry with a small stair hall. Unlike most other examples, this hall does not go through the house; rather, it sits side-saddle allowing for a room behind it. The two-bay rear elevation has the additional novelty of lacking a back door. Because of its plan and fenestration, Richwood Farm is one of the most unusual houses of the period in Jefferson County.

The original nonresidential nature of some buildings account for their divergent plans. ELMWOOD-ON-OPEQUON, built about 1835, appears to have been built for use as a kitchen. The single-room building was enlarged by Anthony Kennedy, who added a second story and a wing in 1842, transforming it into a primary residence. As will be discussed in the chapter on outbuildings, the original plan of this building fits with the standard summer-kitchen type: two bays on the long axis with a gable entry.

The ALLSTADT HOUSE is another such kitchen-to-residence renovation. The structure was built in about 1800, and altered around 1820 to serve as a residence by Jacob Allstadt, a Pennsylvania native. This frame building near Harpers Ferry has a standard two-room kitchen plan with central chimney and corner stair. Two features in particular telegraph its former use as a kitchen building—the central chimney and the gable entry. Allstadt's heirs added a stone ordinary adjacent to the house in 1839. Built as an inn, the ALLSTADT ORDINARY utilizes a modified hall-and-parlor plan. The stair of this stone building, however, is located on the porch rather than inside the house. This unique arrangement allows for individual privacy, while maximizing the number of guest rooms.

The changes in residential architecture during the brief time between 1815 and 1835 in Jefferson County, reflect the cultural and economic prosperity of that era. This twenty-year period saw new house types blossom and old ones wither. Antiquated houses were modernized to current tastes with contemporary plans and service additions. Kitchens moved out of the cellar and became part of the living area. Earlier houses of the settlement period took a defensive posture in the landscape, hunkered down with small windows and reinforced doors. The houses after 1815 became more welcoming with natural light spilling through larger windows and decorative entryways. This period shows the local architecture at its most creative and abundant. As farms prospered throughout the county, their owners fashioned homes befitting their success. This was truly Jefferson County's architectural golden age.

Elmwood-on-Opequon (Anthony Kennedy House), ca. 1835 and 1842, Leetown vicinity, oblique view

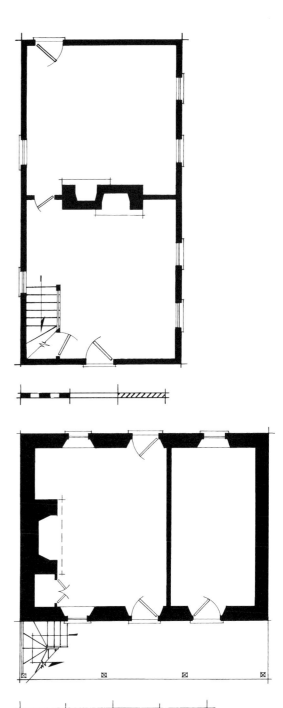

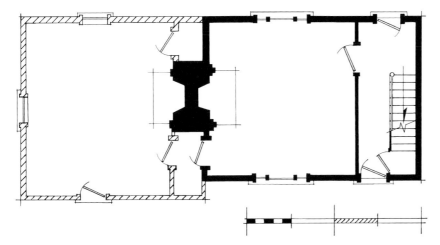

Elmwood-on-Opequon, first-floor plan showing conversion to central chimney residence

Allstadt's House and Ordinary, first-floor plans

117

Chapter Four

Outbuildings

Farm Structures
Serve the House

Adam Link farm, Uvilla vicinity, assemblage
of historic farm buildings clustered around the residence

Beyond the Farmhouse

The farmhouse was only one of several buildings on the typical Jefferson County farmstead. Various satellite structures were sited near the house, each playing a particular role in the working farm. Outbuildings facilitated the production of materials and housed the farm's workforce. Most of these buildings have vanished, but enough survive to give a contextual sense of the local eighteenth- and nineteenth-century farm. A few of the county's farms, such as ELMWOOD, NEW HOPEWELL, ALTONA, and SPRINGWOOD, retain these varied outbuildings. In most cases, though, only one or two ancillary structures remain in what were once farmyards crowded with unique buildings and features: kitchens, meat houses, wash houses, springhouses, dairies, quarters, blacksmith shops, offices, privies, cemeteries, stone fences, and barns. This chapter will explore each of these building types and elements in detail.

Altona outbuildings

Joe Crane's Barn, Jefferson Co. Virginia 1847/1850 by David Hunter Strother, courtesy of West Virginia and Regional Collection, West Virginia University Libraries

Rockland quarter, springhouse, and meat house, Shepherdstown vicinity

Kitchens

Freestanding kitchens, known locally as summer kitchens, were common outbuildings on the farms of the county. But most houses predating 1815 had kitchens in their raised basements, or cellars as they were known at the time. Large cooking fireplaces were used to prepare the food below the living area. The opening of the basement cooking fireplace was usually topped by a large wooden lintel, and the back of this piece was chamfered to facilitate the draw of the firebox. Cooking fireboxes measured up to twelve feet in width, as seen in the kitchen of THE HILL. These large openings allowed cooking and other domestic chores to be done simultaneously with several fires.

Some of the early houses with cellar kitchens also had freestanding summer kitchens. By placing the much-used cooking fireplace in a separate building, the main house was protected from fire. It also provided comfort to the farm family by reducing the amount of heat and odors introduced to the main house in the warmer months. Messy food preparation, such as butchering, could be performed in the summer kitchen rather than the residence. On farms with slave labor, the summer kitchen also "established a clearer separation between those who served and those who were served."[1]

After 1815, basement kitchens were rarely built locally, as attached service wings became more popular. These additions, which contained the kitchen and dining room, had become common by 1825, especially on masonry buildings. The convenience of having the kitchen attached to the house at ground level probably drove this change of arrangement. So, by 1830, most of the houses surveyed employed a rear or side service wing. Also

during the mid-nineteenth century, wings were added to many earlier houses that previously had freestanding kitchens. Often, the basement kitchens were then abandoned in favor of the attached ground-level cooking room.

Summer kitchens were generally sited back from the front plane of the house, or placed behind the house. This hierarchical arrangement obscured the business of food preparation from the formal front of the residence. At Claymont Court and Blakeley, brick colonnade walls attach the service wings to the main house. These walls screened exterior work areas from view at the front of the houses. In less formal houses, this basic effect was achieved by siting the kitchen away from the front elevation. In a lease agreement between Lydia Henderson and Samuel Russell in 1812, Henderson required the tenant to build a kitchen "twenty two feet by twenty in the clear with a passage between the dwelling house and said kitchen" behind her house in Charles Town.[2]

Summer kitchens appear locally in two basic forms: single-room and two-room. The single-room kitchen typically utilizes a chimney on the rear gable wall. The door is usually located on the opposite gable, toward the main house. To maximize the working area in these kitchens, the stairs used to reach the attic were tucked into corners, either on the entry end of the building or beside the chimney. The attic was used as a storage area or as living quarters for servants. With one or two windows on the log axis and a single door on the short side, the kitchen is a rare gable-entry building in Jefferson County. Examples of one-room kitchens were found at Hawthorne, Elmwood-on-Opequon, Locust Grove, Wayside, Rose Hill, Mountain View, Mount Eary, and other farms.

Hawthorne summer kitchen, Historic American Buildings Survey photograph, 1937

Wayside summer kitchen, Rippon vicinity, east gable

Rose Hill summer kitchen, oblique view

Opposite: The Hill, interior view of cooking fireplace

The two-room kitchen was a longer version of the single-room form, with the main difference being the location of the chimney. A chimney was placed in the center of the two-room kitchen, and it vented fireboxes in each room. The large cooking fireplace was located in the room closest to the house, while a smaller fireplace warmed the rear room. The room at the back provided a bedchamber for servants or an additional work room. The space to either side of the chimney was used for stairs, storage cupboards, or passage between the rooms. The long walls of the two-room kitchen are usually arranged into two bays. This form is repeated all over the county—from the earliest kitchens, such as those at Harewood and Piedmont, to mid-nineteenth-century kitchens at Avon Bend and the George W. Moler House. The kitchen at Harewood and the ruin at Cedar Lawn are likely the earliest examples of summer kitchens in the county. It is remarkable how little the forms changed after those examples were constructed.

Formal houses such as Belvedere, Happy Retreat, the Swearingen-Baker House, and Richwood Hall had brick two-story freestanding kitchens. In addition to the kitchen, these ancillary buildings have formal dining rooms with well-appointed bedchambers above. Houses like Rosemont, Samuel Mendenhall House, and Jacob Moler House have one-and-a-half-story kitchen wings. The plan of these wings is identical to that of the two-room summer kitchen. The upper story here houses sleeping areas for servants. The Allstadt House probably started as a typical two-room kitchen, but was converted into a two-story residence, and it is now the only early central-chimney house in the county.

A few kitchens that broke with the tradition of gable entry were surveyed, such as those at Cool Spring, Ripon Lodge, Aspen Hill, George Reynolds House, and Rees-Daniels House. All of these buildings, however, also served as quarters or living space, so the rooms were not arranged solely for food preparation. Several of these buildings predated the houses that they served, which likely explains their residential arrangement.

Baking ovens were common additions to summer kitchens, with the oven placed on the exterior of the gable end adjacent to the chimney. The body of the oven was built outside the structure but opened into the firebox for easy access. An example of this oven placement can be found in Shepherdstown at the Wynkoop Tavern. Here a brick oven is attached to the exterior wall of the stone summer kitchen. The oven was enclosed by a brick bakehouse to protect it from the elements. A single interior oven was discovered during the survey. The kitchen at Happy Retreat has a small side-mounted brick oven between the wall and fireplace. Though unique locally, this type of interior oven was common in the Tidewater of Virginia.[3] Few baking ovens survive today, though the outlines of their forms can be found at many summer kitchens.

Central chimney from former kitchen on Cedar Lawn property

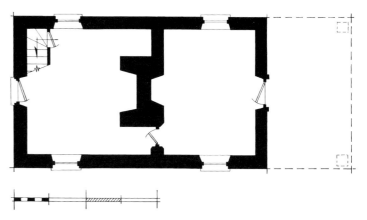

Avon Bend kitchen, Kabletown vicinity, first-floor plan, gable entry with central chimney

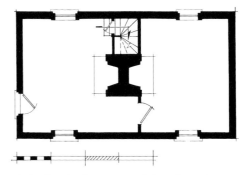

Belvedere kitchen, restored first-floor plan

Harewood kitchen, east elevation

Rosemont kitchen and quarter, rear elevation

Swearingen-Shepherd House (Springwood) kitchen wing, ca. 1820

Richwood Hall, rear elevation showing the large two-story kitchen wing at right with its central chimney

Rees-Daniels House, view of summer kitchen in foreground sited to the side of the main house

Wynkoop Tavern bake oven attached to the exterior wall
of the summer kitchen, interior view

Happy Retreat summer kitchen, cooking fireplace
with side-mounted bake oven

Allstadt House, side view, arranged in the typical two-room kitchen
form with central chimney and gable entry

Cool Spring kitchen and quarter, oblique view

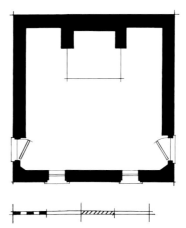

Ripon Lodge summer kitchen,
first-floor plan

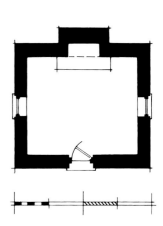

Beverly summer kitchen,
first-floor plan

Meat Houses

Meat houses, also known as smokehouses, were found in large numbers throughout the county. Most farms used these buildings for storing and curing meat. Hams were among the most valuable items produced on the farms of Jefferson County, and the meat house was used to protect that resource. These buildings were built of stone, brick, or log. In the later nineteenth and twentieth centuries, meat houses also utilized frame construction, but no early frame examples were found in this survey.

There are two basic types of meat houses in Jefferson County. The first type is the gable-roofed meat house. This building is rectangular in plan, utilizes a gable roof and a gable entry. In some cases, the roof cantilevered out several feet to give more weather protection to the entry. Most examples, however, have a roof that is flush with the end of the building. Masonry meat houses typically employ ventilation slits in the walls. Thin vertical openings were laid into the side walls to allow air movement through the building. Keeping cured meat at a controlled temperature facilitated its preservation, and this ventilation allowed smoke to pass around the meat but prevented the temperature in the room from rising high enough to spoil the produce.[4] Log meat houses did not have ventilation openings since they were more often used for storing meat than for smoking it. The oldest existing meat houses are rectangular gable-roof designs. Meat houses at Rees-Daniels farm and Lost Drake farm were among the earliest in the county. In the rectangular plan, the door is most often centered on the gable, though a number of offset entries were found, including meat houses at Shirley farm, Piedmont, Mount Pleasant, Traveler's Rest, Frederick Rosenberger farm, and Smith-Grantham farm. The entry doors, usually reinforced, open into the building and are typically mounted on large strap hinges. Locks and security bars further protected the valuable contents. The meat houses at Mountain View and Dr. Thomas Hammond House were the only rectangular forms surveyed that were not entered on the gable end.

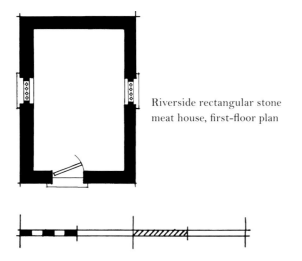

Riverside rectangular stone meat house, first-floor plan

The second meat house type, and the one most commonly found in the county, is the square form. These buildings are distinctive for their hipped, or pyramidal, roofs. This unusual roof shape may have aided the meat-curing process by concentrating smoke around the hanging hams. Eighteenth-century examples of the pyramidal roof form are rare, though a few were documented as part of this study. The meat house at Gap View farm is an early example, constructed with diamond-notched logs. As with the rectangular form, square meat houses of masonry construction also had ventilation slits. Vents splayed inward from the exterior wall. The splayed vent jamb is sometimes referred to as a "rifle slot," and many local meat houses are mistakenly called forts. These buildings were not designed to act as garrisons. All extant meat houses post-date hostilities with Native Americans in the area. If a masonry meat house did not utilize ventilation slits, barred windows vented the building. These openings can also be found locally in wash houses, barns, and other outbuildings. As with the rectangular forms, the square meat houses employed heavy doors hung on thick frames. The security of the building's contents was obviously important to each farm.

The meat house was the place where hams and beef were smoked and stored. Before storage, the meat had to be preserved by brine or dry cure.[5] In the dry-cure process, the meat is bled, butchered into cuts, and rubbed with a mixture of salt, saltpeter, and usually brown sugar. Once cured, the hams and meat were hung from nails or hooks attached to the roofing members to cure, making it more difficult for rodents to get to them. Hickory ashes were rubbed on the meat to keep insects at bay.

Some of these meat houses were used to smoke meat as well. The residue of years of fires can be seen on the walls and roof systems of these buildings. All but a handful of the meat houses surveyed originally had dirt floors. Stone and log were the most common wall materials, though several brick meat houses exist. The most elaborate houses—such as Richwood Hall, Bellevue, Dr. Thomas Hammond House, and Piedmont—had brick meat houses close by the residence. The largest and most decorative of the county's meat houses stand at The Bower and Falling Spring. Both of these buildings are made of brick and are significantly taller than the typical meat house. The Bower meat house, built about 1805, is the older of the two. The fine brickwork and developed cornice of this meat house are unusual for an outbuilding. Its proximity to the expansive mansion house may have led the owner to enhance this meat house with refined architectural elements. The structure has a double set of ceiling joists at alternating heights. This arrangement allows more hams to hang at once and is the reason for the additional height of the building. The meat house at Falling Spring, built in about 1835, is nearly identical in size, being 16 feet square. However, it

Prato Rio frame meat house, Historic American Buildings Survey photograph, 1937

John Snyder Sr. Storehouse, log meat house with projecting roof

functions quite differently. An octagonal post is centered inside the building, which is attached to members of the roof structure. This arrangement holds the post upright, but allows it to rotate. Wooden horizontal members were led through the post, and the meat hung from hooks from these tapered pieces. The tree of hams could be turned, and the efficient arrangement of the crossbars accommodated more produce and gave easy access to it. Instead of the typical splayed ventilation slits, this meat house utilized decorative vents. Here, a diamond-shaped form was made in the wall by leaving openings in the brickwork. As will be discussed later in this chapter, some barns of this era also employed this decorative effect.

The square meat house continued to be popular into the 1850s. The only noticeable change in the buildings was that the roof pitches became shallower over time, in keeping with the tastes for shallower pitches on houses. The meat house at AVON BEND is a good example of this later preference. Around 1850 other forms were introduced; meat storage was consolidated with other uses in combination buildings. The multi-use structure at RIGGS-STILES farm has a two-room plan with two side-entry doors on the long side. This arrangement is a complete departure from the plans of the local meat houses that came before.

Riggs-Stiles farm, ca. 1850, combined-use frame building including smokehouse

Lost Drake rectangular stone meat house, built 1799

York Hill rectangular stone meat house

Frederick Rosenberger farm rectangular stone meat house
with offset entry

Mountain View gable-roofed stone meat house with entry on long side

Elmwood rectangular brick meat house

Mount Pleasant rectangular log meat house with offset entry

Southwood rectangular log meat house, south gable

George Eichelberger farm, rectangular log meat house with projecting roof

Spring Hill (Van Deever-Orndorff farm) rectangular log meat house

Traveler's Rest rectangular log meat house with offset entry

Smith-Grantham farm rectangular log meat house with offset entry

Shirley farm rectangular log meat house with offset entry

Gap View farm square log meat house, front elevation

Fertile Plain square log meat house, oblique view

Springwood farm square stone meat house, front elevation

Ripon Lodge square stone meat house, side view

Cold Spring square stone meat house, oblique view

Wild Goose, ca. 1840, square stone meat house

Piedmont square brick meat house with offset entry, oblique view

Richwood Hall square brick meat house, side view

Avon Bend (Logan Osburn farm), ca. 1850, square stone meat house with shallow pitched pyramidal roof

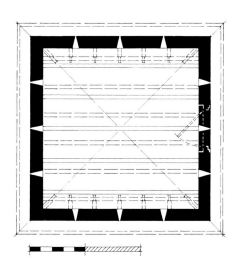

The Bower meat house, plan showing
splayed vent jambs

The Bower meat house, section

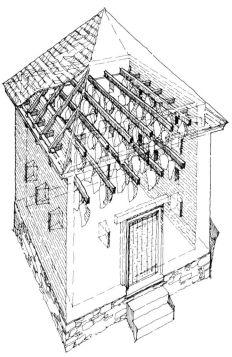

The Bower meat house,
birdseye cutaway perspective

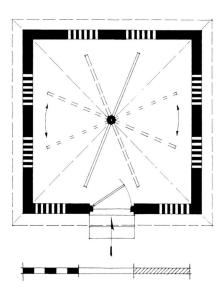

Falling Spring meat house, first-floor plan,
showing rotating meat tree

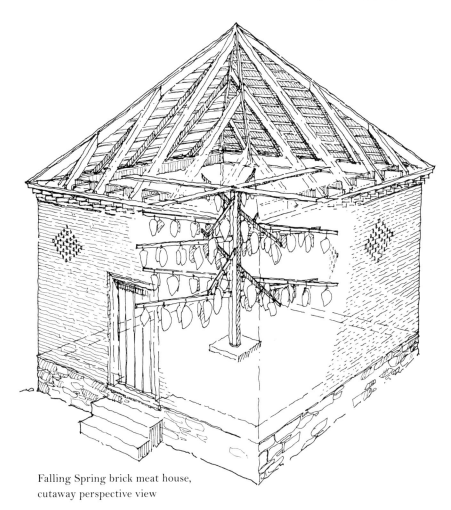

Falling Spring brick meat house,
cutaway perspective view

Slave Quarters

Slave housing was common on the farms of Jefferson County. Roughly half of the county's farm owners held slaves in 1830. By 1850 that percentage had topped 78 percent.[6] In addition to slave labor, local farms utilized paid and indentured laborers, who also required accommodations. Unfortunately, very few quarters have survived. After slavery was abolished, quarters were used for storage, migrant housing, or were simply left to deteriorate. The examples that remain defy neat categorization into plan types. The buildings can be grouped, however, by their fenestration patterns. For this analysis, quarters are categorized by the number of bays on the front elevation.

Two-bay quarters are the most prevalent in the county. Built of log, frame, stone, and brick, these house types are typically humble structures. Unlike the main house of the farm, elevational balance, or symmetry, was not a primary concern. The ELMWOOD quarter is an early survivor of slave housing. This log

building has two doors on the primary elevation and two windows on the rear. Built of diamond-notched logs, this quarter used a two-room plan that may have housed two or more families, or separated the living area and the cooking room. THE BOWER quarter dates to the first decade of the nineteenth century. This log house also has a two-bay front elevation. Again, the two-room plan is used with a single door. The very steep roof pitch allowed for a sleeping loft above the main floor. Another two-bay log example is the SPRINGWOOD quarter. This building has a single-room plan with an inboard chimney. Two-bay quarters also came in more formal arrangements. The brick quarters at BLAKELEY, RION HALL, and NEW HOPEWELL are similar in mass and arrangement. All of these buildings are two stories tall and square in plan. The Blakeley and Rion Hall quarters are gable-entry structures, whereas the door to the New Hopewell quarter opens on the building's long side.

Elmwood quarter, ca. 1795, north gable oblique

The Bower quarter, ca. 1810, restored perspective view

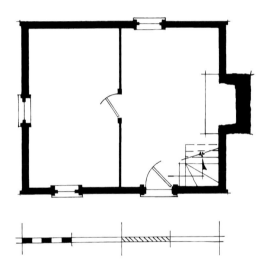

The Bower quarter, first-floor plan

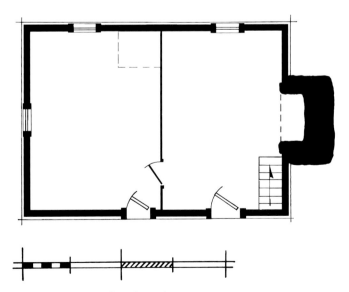

Elmwood quarter, first-floor plan

Springwood quarter, ca. 1820, east elevation

Blakeley quarter, ca. 1825, south elevation

New Hopewell quarter, ca. 1830, south elevation

Claymont Court quarter, ca. 1825, south elevation

Level Green quarter, ca. 1820, front elevation

The Hermitage quarter, ca. 1840, east elevation

Traveler's Rest quarter, ca. 1830, Historic American Buildings Survey photograph, 1937

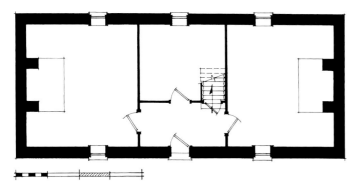

The Hermitage quarter, restored first-floor plan

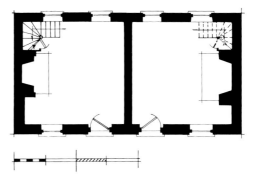

Traveler's Rest quarter, first-floor plan

Three-bay slave quarters can be found in the county, though in smaller quantities. The centered door gave unusual prominence to these buildings, and they tended to be better built, usually of brick or stone. The three-bay front was only used on quarters in situations where the scale of the manor house far exceeded that of the quarter. Farms with large houses, like Claymont Court, Woodbyrne, and Rock Hall, claimed such buildings, where there would be no confusion as to the hierarchy of buildings. The large three-bay quarter at The Hermitage is very similar in scale to the quarter at Rock Hall. This building has an unusual floor plan, with cooking fireplaces at either gable end, which may have supported separate slave families.

Four-bay quarters are rare in the county. Only three were found, and one other was documented by the Historic American Buildings Survey in 1937 before being demolished. The largest of these four-bay structures is the Traveler's Rest quarter. This two-story stone quarter has two front doors. The plan of the house splits the building in half. This arrangement, also used at

Homestead farm near Bakerton, would allow two groups or families, to use the house without sharing living space. Though only one story, the Level Green quarter, now destroyed, had the same duplex plan. In the Historic American Buildings Survey photographs of the building, one of the windows had clearly been a door that was filled in later. This quarter had the same separation plan as the one at Traveler's Rest. The third example of the four-bay form is the Rockland quarter. This log building has none of the formality of the other examples, but shares the four-bay two-door elevation. A sleeping loft sits above the two lower rooms. The plan is not as sternly separated as that at Level Green or Traveler's Rest. Here, the room arrangement resembles a two-room kitchen.

The best built quarters, those of brick and stone, are likely atypical of the period. Small humble log examples were probably the more common slave and servant housing in Jefferson County. The southern end of the county had the greatest concentration of slaves during the nineteenth century, and that is where more slave housing can be found today.

Rockland quarter, ca. 1840, south elevation

Wash Houses

Springwood wash house, ca. 1820, south elevation, oblique view

Springwood wash house fireplace

Fewer wash houses have survived in Jefferson County than have meat houses or kitchens. In many instances, the kitchen doubled as the wash room, so this may account for their local scarcity. The wash house was typically rectangular with a gable-end chimney. This chimney vented a large fireplace used to heat water for cleaning clothes and linens, and for making soap.[7] These buildings are often found nearer the water source than are houses or kitchens. Their more remote siting meant that function usually won out over form, so wash houses appear less symmetrical than kitchens.

The most common type of wash house in the county is the two-bay variety. This building has one door and one window on the front elevation, like those at SPRINGWOOD, SELMA, and HAPPY RETREAT. This two-bay arrangement was used for many different outbuildings, as we will see later in this chapter. A simple one-room plan was used in most wash houses.

The wash house at Selma, near Charles Town, has a more complex layout than other local examples. This two-bay building has the single room with a chimney, but it was designed with a raised brick trough on two sides of the interior, built with a slightly lower floor where the water exits. Water was pumped from a nearby cistern or well into the building using lead piping. It entered a small opening in the stone wall, fell into the plaster-lined trough, and gravity carried the water through the building. If standing water was required, the outlet pipe could be plugged to fill the trough. The use of the water trough would have greatly aided the daily chores. The interior arrangement and its proximity to the house, suggest it may have also served as the dairy.

Certainly the finest wash house in the county was built for R. D. Shepherd around 1845 during the expansion of his farm, WILD GOOSE. The wash house here is made from ashlar cut limestone that has been smoothed and fitted together in exacting fashion. No other building in the county has such precise and sophisticated masonry. It is odd that such a utilitarian building would feature craftsmanship that overshadows that of the property's residence. Still, the building was designed for domestic service and is divided into three work rooms. The largest of these rooms has a stone floor with a perimeter trough against the wall. The smaller rooms have brick ovens used to heat the water for cleaning. The ovens had large copper inserts to hold the water and copper spigots to release the water into waste channels after use. This wash house has little in common with others of the area and speaks to the great wealth of its owner, who was able to commission such a fine outbuilding. Shepherd amassed a great fortune in shipping and retired to his country estate around 1840.

Selma (Bon-Air) wash house, ca. 1830, north elevation

Wild Goose wash house, ca. 1845, east elevation

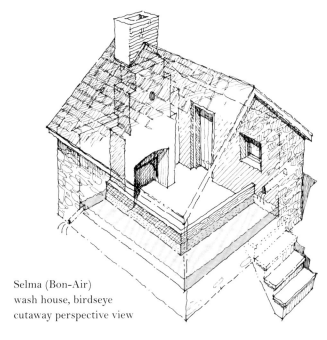

Selma (Bon-Air) wash house, birdseye cutaway perspective view

Wild Goose wash house, view of interior brick wash ovens with copper liners and subterranean water trough

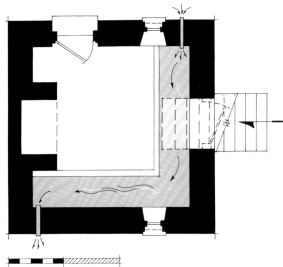

Selma (Bon-Air) wash house, ground-floor plan

Wild Goose wash house, exterior ashlar stonework

139

Springhouses

The availability of water was of primary importance to the settlers of what is now Jefferson County. As discussed in earlier chapters, areas with spring-fed creeks were prime real estate, and locations with dependable springs were the most coveted for house sites. The springhouse was designed to protect such springs from contamination, to store and secure farm produce, and to keep perishable items such as butter and milk cool, often functioning as a dairy. The springhouses surveyed varied little in shape or design, and with one exception were all rectangular, gable roofed, and built of stone. Typically, these buildings were entered on the gable end over or near the water source. Examples of this standard type are found at PIEDMONT, ELMWOOD, LOST DRAKE, ROCK HALL, and COOL SPRING.

As with meat houses, some springhouses had projecting roofs that protected the gable entry from the elements. Springhouses at SHIRLEY farm, WHITE HOUSE farm, ROCKLAND, NEW HOPEWELL, and MORGAN'S SPRING were built with just such overhangs. Wall openings were fitted with pinned frames holding a series of bars. This allowed light and air to enter the building, but not large animals. Also like meat houses, the plank entry doors were secured by interior wooden locks or hasped frame locks. Water flowed from the spring under the wall forming a small stream inside the building. Openings at the foundation of the far end wall allowed the water to travel out to the spring pond, or directly to the creek.

Most springhouses consisted of a single room, known as the spring room, on one floor. Ceilings were not used in the one-

Piedmont spring house, along Evitt's Run

Elmwood springhouse and spring pond along Lucas Run

Lost Drake farm springhouse, south elevation

Shirley farm springhouse, south elevation

Cold Spring springhouse, along Lucas Run, showing water exiting the building

story form, so the roof system was exposed. This arrangement gave added headroom and light to the building. Many springhouses were below grade and accessed by exterior stairs, like the one at Elmwood. Set into the grade, the building took advantage of the earth's insulation to keep the interior temperature cool.

In some cases, excavation was necessary to expose the springhead. This provided an opportunity to bank the springhouse into an elevated grade and gain easy access to a second story. A number of banked springhouses were surveyed. These two-story types had a storage area or usable room on the second floor. The springhouse at THE ROCKS is a good example of this application. SPRINGDALE, COLD SPRING, TAYLOR'S MEADOW, WILLIAM GREEN farm, SHARFF-HOMAR HOUSE, and CLAY HILL also have springhouses of this kind.

The springhouse at TRAVELER'S REST is two stories, yet is not banked. Here, a stair is used to access the upper story. Larger than most other springhouses, it includes several unusual features. The spring pool in the building has a stepped work area. This design may have been developed to allow the building to be used during varying water levels. One of the stepped walls is curved to direct the water toward the end openings.

The design of the springhouse at SPRINGWOOD departed from the typical gable-entry template used throughout the county. This building has a pair of windows flanking the entry, which was placed on the long side. Built in 1819 for Abraham Shepherd, the springhouse functioned as the centerpiece of an interesting grouping of outbuildings removed from the main house. The grade for this building was lowered considerably to allow three separate springs to feed the building. Other than this notable exception, springhouses appear to be rather uniform in design and scale in Jefferson County.

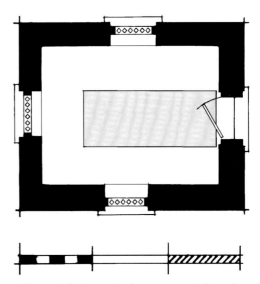

Morgan's Spring springhouse, ground-floor plan

The Rocks banked springhouse, along the Shenandoah River

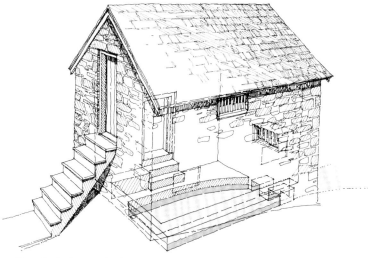

Traveler's Rest springhouse, cutaway perspective view

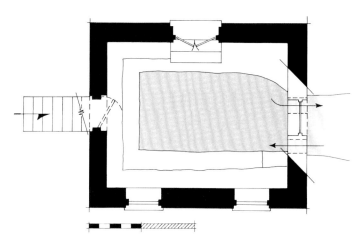

Traveler's Rest springhouse, ground-floor plan

Clay Hill springhouse, oblique view

Traveler's Rest springhouse, interior view showing outlet holes and stepped work area

Springwood outbuildings, a cutaway perspective view of the springhouse, with wash house and quarter behind

Springwood springhouse, 1819, showing exterior spring access in front of the building and water exiting at right

George Eichelberger farm, springhouse, oblique view

Dairies

The local dairy building functioned much like the springhouse, but was not adjacent to running water. The dairies, or milk houses, surveyed in this study are built of stone or brick. The insulative quality of the masonry walls helped to preserve food. Inside the dairy, milk was left to cool, allowing the cream to rise. Later, the cream would be churned into butter.

More modest frame dairies were likely more common but have not survived. In 1762, George Washington commissioned a new dairy to be built at his farm near Summit Point. This modest structure cost just over eleven pounds to construct.[8]

The plans of dairies differed from springhouses in that dairies had raised water troughs running along one or two walls, typically placed along one of the long sides of the building. Troughs were used to store and cool milk and other perishables at a more convenient height. Since cleanliness was a serious concern for dairy foods, these buildings usually had ceilings and walls that were plastered or whitewashed.

Also in contrast to springhouses, local dairies were usually entered on the long side. Beside the door was a single window, while the back side of the building usually featured two windows. These windows allowed light and ventilation, but could be covered with louvered shutters to reduce heat penetration. Dairies at BOIDESTONE'S PLACE and HENKLE farm used exterior stairs, now removed, to reach storage above the ground-floor work area.

Offices

Though relatively rare, offices are found on farms near the residence. These buildings were used by farmers to conduct farm business. Doctors and lawyers who lived out of town also practiced in these small freestanding structures. The offices at WESTERN VIEW, HAWTHORNE, and DUFFIELDS DEPOT are nearly identical in plan, each having two-bay front elevations. The examples built between 1830 and 1850 are similar in scale to the two-bay dairies and wash houses of the same era.

The office at HAREWOOD is older than the previous examples and differs in its configuration. This square structure was built on top of a round, below-grade ice room. The single-room office has a single-bay front and an exterior chimney. The upper room was probably used as a doctor's office in the early nineteenth century. Other single-room offices were found at the SHARFF-HOMAR farm, SPRINGDALE, and BEVERLY. The office at Beverly is a single-bay like the Harewood example and dates to the same era.

In town, offices were generally attached to the house, with entrances on the street, like those at the SPAULDING-BAKER HOUSE, RING HOUSE, M'COUGHTRY LOT IN MIDDLEWAY, and SWEARINGEN-BAKER HOUSE. One of the most interesting offices in the county is the octagonal structure at HAPPY RETREAT. This building may also have been used as a school, though the high quality of the interior trim would suggest an office. There was an early tradition of octagonal school houses in Pennsylvania, but this is the only early eight-sided outbuilding extant in Jefferson County.[9]

Boidestone's Place dairy, ca. 1830, front elevation

Henkle farm dairy, ca. 1830, oblique view

Duffields Depot, 1839, south elevation

Hawthorne office, ca. 1840, front elevation

Office addition to Ring House, ca. 1835, Middleway

Beverly office, ca. 1800, rear gable, Historic American Buildings Survey photograph, 1937

Harewood office, ca. 1810, south gable, Historic American Buildings Survey photograph, 1936

Happy Retreat office, ca. 1800, side view

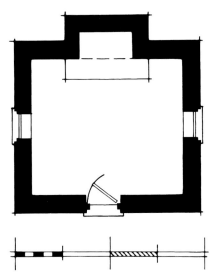

Beverly office, first-floor plan

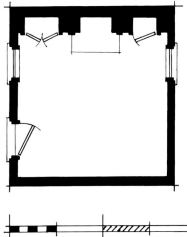
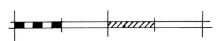

Western View office, first-floor plan

Combined-Use Buildings

Around 1815, farmers began combining various uses into single buildings. This coincided with increased production on valley farms and the proliferation of masonry buildings. Farm production was outpacing domestic consumption. In the preceding decades, storing resources in numerous buildings, most of which were made of wood, distributed the risk of loss. Masonry outbuildings reduced that risk but were also significantly more expensive to build. Cost may have encouraged farmers to be more creative in combining several uses into a single outbuilding.

At CLAREMONT, a two-story stone outbuilding housed the kitchen and smokehouse. The springhouse at NEW HOPEWELL has an upper meat-storage area fitted into the loft. The springhouse at SPRINGDALE has a wash house on the second floor.

By 1835, these multi-use buildings were common on the farms of Jefferson County. One of the most ingenious examples can be seen in the stone structure at ROCK SPRINGS farm. This gable-roofed building functioned as the smokehouse, kitchen, wash house, bakery, and dairy. The two-story building is located at a spring that runs through a low trough cut into the back of the ground floor. The spring water travels through the building and out the other side to a pond. At the entry end, a large cooking fireplace takes up most of the wall. This fireplace has a large wooden lintel and an iron crane to hold kettles and pots. A squirrel-tail oven is attached to the exterior gable wall behind the fireplace. The oven is protected from the elements by the long wall of the building, which projects clear of the gable. A shed roof beds on this projecting wall to keep rainwater from the oven and

New Hopewell springhouse and meat house, ca. 1800, covered gable entry

the entry. Meat could be smoked upstairs with smoke from the first-floor fireplace and oven. That meat was conveniently stored above the kitchen for later use. Diamond-shaped, decorative brick vents allowed air movement in the second-floor meat room. This building represents the trend toward more flexible and efficient use of outbuilding space in the nineteenth century.

Springdale combined-use building, ca. 1830, oblique view

Opposite: Claremont combined-use kitchen and smokehouse building, ca. 1820

Peter Burr farm combined-use building, ca. 1825,
oblique view showing first floor entrance and stair to upper floor,
Historic American Buildings Survey photograph, 1983

William S. Kerney farm springhouse and meat house, ca. 1840,
oblique view showing gable entry to lower floor

Sharff-Homar farm springhouse and office, ca. 1832, north elevation
with diamond-shaped vents in lower room

Cassilis multi-use building with round ice pit below, ca. 1840, north gable

Happy Retreat kitchen, smokehouse, and quarter, ca. 1840, oblique view

Rock Springs combined-use building, ca. 1835, oblique view

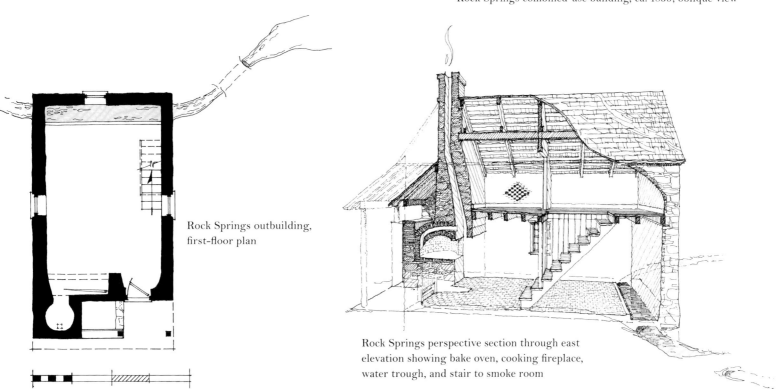

Rock Springs outbuilding,
first-floor plan

Rock Springs perspective section through east
elevation showing bake oven, cooking fireplace,
water trough, and stair to smoke room

149

Blacksmith Shops

The smithy was once a common building on the farms and in the towns of Jefferson County. Individual farms and lots had their own blacksmith shops, or smithies, where iron pieces could be forged. Domestic pieces such as hinges, hinge pintles, hooks, nails, chains, and cookware could all be made on site. Horseshoes, saddle parts, tools, and other agricultural products could also be fabricated or repaired here. Very few of these structures have survived—likely owing to fires—so a typical local building style can not be determined. The blacksmith shops at Springwood, Elmwood, and Walper's Crossroads are three-bay center-entry buildings. The frame smithy at Mount Ellen is gable entry, with a second floor for storage. The formidable stone smithy at the Bell-Fry House on Queen Street in Middleway is gable entry. Though the blacksmith shop at New Hopewell was also designed with gable entry, it had an additional area used for wagon storage. The remaining examples of this utilitarian building show more variety than any other outbuilding type.

Springwood blacksmith shop, front elevation

Engle farm log blacksmith shop, destroyed, photograph courtesy of Robert Orndorff

Mount Ellen blacksmith shop, gable end

New Hopewell blacksmith shop, oblique view showing rear wall and decorative vent cupola

Necessary Houses

Another historic building type that has been almost totally lost in Jefferson County is the privy, or necessary house. Though most households must have had at least one of these structures near the homeplace, only a handful survive. The majority of the county's extant privies date to the early twentieth century. Some earlier privies can still be found in Shepherdstown, Harpers Ferry, and Charles Town. The privy at the WYNKOOP TAVERN is a rare surviving example of this once common building. This brick example, built about 1830, has two separate rooms, each with multiple seats, or holes. A vaulted chamber below the floor captured the waste. The excavation of this privy in 2007 revealed that the building was also the repository of household trash, including broken china, crocks, bottles, and stemware.

Wynkoop Tavern privy, interior view of three hole seats

Wynkoop Tavern privy, ca. 1830, attached to bakehouse, Shepherdstown

Family Burial Grounds

During the eighteenth and nineteenth centuries, many of Jefferson County's residents were laid to rest on the family farm. With few exceptions, funerary markers in the county during the period of survey were very modest in design. Family cemeteries remain at ELMWOOD, SNOW HILL, RETIREMENT, VAN SANT farm, CHAPLINE farm, WILDWOOD, LINDEN SPRING, BUCKLES farm, HAREWOOD, WALPER'S CROSSROADS, JOHNSON farm, YORK HILL, and many other county farms. Slave cemeteries are also common throughout the county, though not well documented.

Only two architecturally significant markers were found outside the church graveyards of the towns—one at the Briscoe family cemetery behind PIEDMONT and the other at Abraham Snyder's farm, PLEASANT VALLEY. Beyond these unusual examples, people of Jefferson County chose understated markers, or even simple pointed stones, to mark their graves. Like other local material culture, grave marker designs and profiles changed over time. The earliest extant markers are carved sandstone blocks with rounded tops, probably quarried along Ridge Road between Bardane and Duffields. Early-nineteenth-century markers were made of limestone and had more intricate profiles. By the mid-nineteenth century the standard marker top was a shallow arch flanked by projecting ears. Though graveyards can be found on numerous county farms, many have been lost or forgotten.

Piedmont, Briscoe family grave marker

Pleasant Valley farm, Snyder family cemetery

Stone Walls and Stone Fences

A number of stone walls and fences remain scattered through-out Jefferson County. They are both functional and decorative. The stone for most fences was cleared from the farm fields. The irregularly shaped stones were generally laid into the wall without mortar. This technique is called "drystacking." Field stones were usually used for fences rather than houses since they had already been weathered and would be more likely to crack under the load of a structural wall. Drystacked fences remain at WHITE HOUSE farm, SHIRLEY farm, MARTIN MILLER farm, BELLEVUE, ALTONA, VINTON, LITTLE ELMINGTON, ALLEMONG farm, and SPRINGDALE, among others. The length of Shepherd Grade near Shepherdstown also has remnants of the stone walls built at the direction of R. D. Shepherd in the 1840s. Dry-stacked fences were also used to enclose barnyards. Examples of this use are found at the SHARFF-HOMAR farm, WILLOWDALE, and SPRINGDALE.

More formal cut stone walls required masons, and thus were less common. Fine, cut stone walls like those at WILD GOOSE are rare in the county. Functional retaining walls are fairly common, though usually small in scale.

Wild Goose, cut stone walls

Shirley farm, drystacked fieldstone walls

York Hill bank barn, built 1812 for John Snyder, south gable

Glenburnie bank barn, ca. 1815, oblique view

Prato Rio bank barn, built 1828 for John and Jacob Sharff, Historic American Buildings Survey photograph, 1937

Little Elmington bank barn, ca. 1830, asymmetrical gable

Pleasant Valley stone bank barn, 1849, asymmetrical gable with brick gable top

Rees-Daniels farm bank barn, ca. 1850, symmetrical gable

Barns

An entire book could be devoted to the various barns found in Jefferson County. Only a brief discussion will be included here to familiarize the reader with the different types of barns found on the county's farms before 1850.

The most recognizable and iconic structure on the Jefferson County farm is the bank barn. These large two-story structures can still be found in significant numbers throughout the county. As the name implies, these barns are "banked" into the land. The second floor is accessed on one side from the higher ground, the entrance to the first floor is on the opposite side at the lower elevation. This barn type is known as the "Sweitzer" or Pennsylvania barn. Along with its functional siting, the cantilevered forebay is the defining feature of the barn. This overhang protects the lower area from the weather while allowing additional storage above. Generally, the forebay was oriented to the east for those barns built before about 1840. Later nineteenth- and twentieth-century bank barns typically faced the forebay to the south.

The lower level of the barn, built of stone, housed animals in stalls. The upper floor was usually divided into three sections—a flat threshing floor centered between two haymows—and could be built of stone, brick, log, or frame. Most of the extant bank barns date from after the Civil War. A few, though, have survived from the early nineteenth century, with stone bank barns faring the best. These earlier barns can be identified by their asymmetrical gable ends. Later bank barns usually have symmetrical gable ends.

Surviving stone bank barns include those at York Hill, Glenburnie, Needwood Farm, Pleasant Valley, Rees-Daniels farm, Adam Link farm, Alexander Link farm, and Little Elmington. Most of these barns have asymmetrical gables and lie in the area between Ridge Road and Duffields.

Two brick bank barns remain in the county. The oldest of these, built in 1832, stands at the Jacob Homar farm near Leetown. The other brick example is the enormous bank barn at Altona, built in 1855. Though brick was a common material for houses it was rarely used for outbuildings in Jefferson County. The stone bank barn at Pleasant Valley was built in 1849 for Abraham Snyder. Its unusual brick gable tops have decorative diamond-shaped, or diapered, vents.

One log bank barn is known to survive in Jefferson County. The big barn at Boidestone's Place was built with reused pieces of an eighteenth-century log house. Here two log cribs flank the threshing floor.

The most numerous bank barns are those of frame construction. Frame examples are found at Elmwood, Grubb farm, Henkle farm, Snow Hill, Linden Spring, Billmyer Mill farm, and many other places in the county.

The bank barn is believed to have been brought to the Shenandoah Valley by German descendants who used the form

Jacob Homar bank barn, 1832, Leetown vicinity

widely in Pennsylvania. This distinctive barn type can be found all over the parts of Pennsylvania and Maryland that were settled by Germans in the eighteenth century. Origins of this interesting building type appear in central Europe. Precursors to the Sweitzer barn, dating to the sixteenth and seventeenth centuries, stand today in Switzerland and eastern Austria.[10] These European forerunners are log structures with low stone foundations. Bank barns, without forebays, that have stonework similar to local barns are found in the Lake District of England. These Cumbrian barns are contemporaries of the local bank barns dating from the eighteenth century into the twentieth.[11]

Another type of early barn common in the county was the ground barn, a single-level structure. The ground barn, like the bank barn, was used for hay and grain storage and animal housing. Many of the farms surveyed by Jonathan Clark in 1786 had ground barns, however few of these early structures survive.[12] Most of the ground barns surveyed were built after 1850, yet a few earlier examples exist. One of these is the log ground barn at Springdale. The barn has been altered but retains its original log walls and ground-floor arrangement.

A handful of early stables, those built of stone, can be found in the county. The earliest is at White House farm, which has recently been restored. Other examples are the stable at Leeland and the ruin at Retirement farm. The stable is another building type that has all but vanished from the county's farmsteads. Those few that survive were all built of stone.

In contrast, corncribs can be found on most farms in Jefferson County. Many of these date to the late nineteenth or early twentieth centuries. Traveler's Rest has the earliest extant corncrib surveyed. This structure is built of logs rather than of frame like the multitude of later examples. Harewood has an early nineteenth-century corncrib and Altona has two.

Boidestone's Place bank barn, ca. 1810, asymmetrical gable

Aspen Pool bank barn, ca. 1830, symmetrical gable, frame construction

Ripon Lodge bank barn, ca. 1833, symmetrical gable

Western View bank barn, ca. 1835, with asymmetrical gable

Cassilis bank barn, ca. 1840, asymmetrical gable

Woodbyrne bank barn, ca. 1850, symmetrical gable

Altona brick bank barn, 1855, asymmetrical gable

Mountain View bank barn, ca. 1880, symmetrical gable

Hendricks farm bank barn, built ca. 1880, symmetrical gable

Traveler's Rest bank barn, ca. 1900, symmetrical gable

Taylor's Meadow bank barn, ca. 1880, symmetrical gable

Springwood bank barn, ca. 1880, symmetrical gable

Prato Rio bank barn, interior view, Historic American Buildings Survey photograph, 1937

Glenburnie barn door showing early nineteenth-century hardware

Springdale ground barn, interior view showing log partition and side walls

Boidestone's Place bank barn, interior view of log crib and threshing floor

Adam Link farm bank barn, interior view of framing, built in 1844 by W. Grubb

These later buildings conform to the standard corncrib template for the area: a rectangular structure with a wide open-air central passage flanked by vertical storage cribs. Wagons were pulled into the opening to be unloaded. Hinged doors high on the interior crib walls open for access to the structure. Lower doors allow for unloading of the building's storage. Corncribs were covered with vertical siding that was spaced enough to allow air to dry the supply of corn but tight enough to prevent animals from entering.[13]

Two granaries were found during the survey. The stone granary at NEW HOPEWELL was built in 1833 for James Hite. This structure has a rough-cast plaster interior, a wide paired-door entry on the long side, and an open floorplan. An exterior stair on the gable end permits access to the second floor and is covered by a projecting roof. Though the building looks vaguely residential, it has no chimneys, ceilings, interior finishes, or other necessary elements of domestic life. The McPherson family built the frame granary at BARLEYWOOD in the 1850s. This structure is one of the only pre–Civil War buildings in Jefferson County built on a brick foundation, rather than stone. Most granaries were incorporated into a bank barn's forebay interior, or added as an offshot shed. These were conveniently located to the barn's threshing floor and animals.

The farmsteads of Jefferson County had numerous outbuildings with specific uses, each contributing to the production of the farm. The rich variety in siting, scale, materials, fabrication, and function of these structures traces the development of local agricultural and architectural trends. These functional buildings also show the ingenuity of local farm families who adapted to the land by using the natural environment to their benefit. Surviving outbuildings stand as an important element of the county's agricultural heritage and architectural history.

White House farm stable, eighteenth century

Altona corncrib, ca. 1850

Altona corn crib, interior view of framing and spaced vertical siding

New Hopewell granary, interior view of rough-coat plaster and wide entry doors

New Hopewell granary, 1833, west elevation

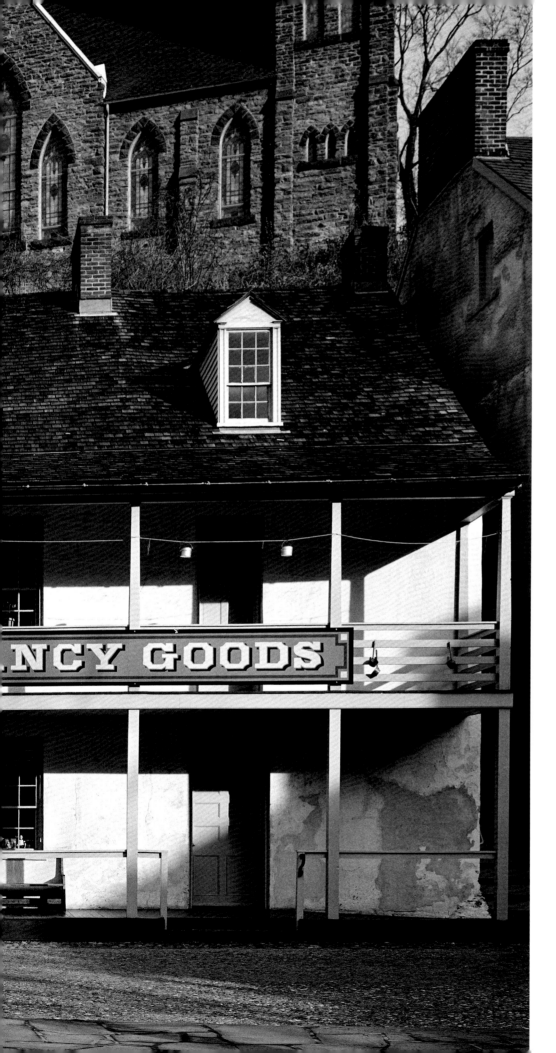

Chapter Five

Town Houses

1780–1835

John G. Wilson House (Stagecoach Inn),
1826, Shenandoah Street, Harpers Ferry

Jefferson County's Early Town Houses

At the close of the eighteenth century, three chartered towns stood in present-day Jefferson County: Mecklenburg, Charlestown, and Smithfield. The earliest of these villages was Mecklenburg, incorporated by the Virginia House of Burgesses and Council of Virginia in 1762. The town was renamed Shepherd's Town in 1798 in honor of its founder, Thomas Shepherd. With fifty acres laid out in a grid, Shepherdstown originally contained lots measuring 103 feet wide by 206 feet deep.[1] These were half-acre lots with the short dimension facing the street. After incorporation, many of these rectangular lots were subdivided into long narrow parcels, further limiting street frontage. Most lots in Shepherdstown were divided into thirds, each with roughly thirty-four feet along the street. In many cases, these frontage dimensions drove the decision for one house type over another. To maximize the value and utility of lots with limited frontage, houses were often built to cover the entire lot width at the street. Service wings were typically added to the backs of buildings. Because the lots were usually quite deep, ample reserve was available in the rear for outbuildings and gardens. Fire was a serious concern in early towns, and it certainly factored into decisions about building. Butting a house to a neighboring one was the most economical use of space, but it increased the risk of a fire spreading from that adjacent structure. In many cases small alleys were left between houses to allow access to the rear of the lot and to suppress the spread of fire.

Charlestown (now Charles Town) was laid out in half-acre lots in 1787. The long sides of these lots faced the street, and this wider frontage gave owners more choice in house plan and placement. Charles Town developed more slowly than Shepherdstown, however. Shepherdstown owner and sole trustee Thomas Shepherd

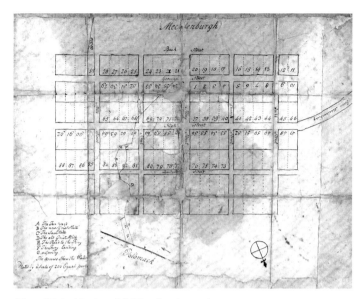

Plat of "Mecklenburgh" (Shepherdstown), ca. 1790, courtesy of Historic Shepherdstown and Museum

Map of Charlestown, Jefferson Co., W.Va. (Charles Town), ca. 1880

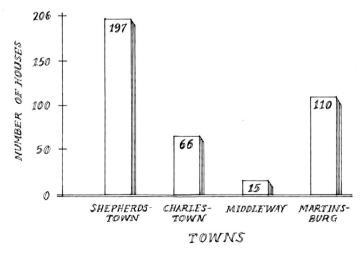

Number of town houses from the 1798 U.S. Direct House Tax for Berkeley County

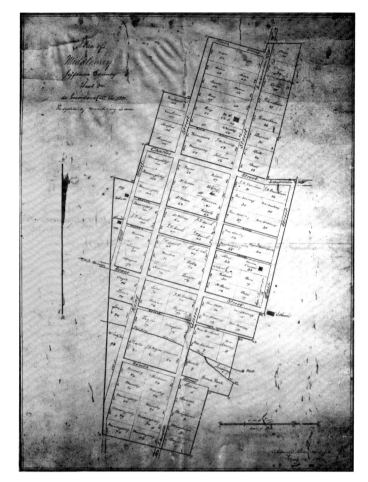

Plan of Middleway by S. Howell Brown, 1883

Samuel Offutt House, North Lawrence Street, Charles Town, Historic American Buildings Survey photograph, 1937

Opposite: Row of early houses on West German Street, Shepherdstown

Robert Harper House, ca. 1780, Harpers Ferry, rear view

(and, later his youngest son, Abraham) required that a house of at least sixteen-by-twenty feet be built on his town's open lots, but building covenants were not included in sales of Charles Town's unimproved lots, so property speculation prevailed there. In many cases, the earliest property owner held entire blocks. Since there was no incentive to improve each lot, Charles Town grew at a slower rate. It wasn't until 1801, with the formation of Jefferson County, that Charles Town began to flourish as the new county seat. By that time, Shepherdstown was one of the largest population centers in the Shenandoah Valley, with its street fronts densely packed with houses and shops. The differences in layout and density of these two towns can still be seen today.

The town of Middleway, originally Smithfield, was the third official town, sited about seven miles west of Charles Town near Opequon Creek. Incorporated in 1798, the lots of the town were typically 90-by-180 feet. This village retains a number of early houses of differing plan type, but side-hall is the town's dominant form. In Middleway, which never achieved the popularity of Charles Town, Harpers Ferry, or Shepherdstown, the lots were not subdivided as often. Thus, the houses of Middleway have generous spaces between them along the street fronts. The loose groupings of buildings along the town grid allow Middleway to retain its rural character.

The town of Bolivar, adjacent to Harpers Ferry, was incorporated in 1825 and by 1840 had over five hundred residents.[2] The majority of the historic houses in Bolivar date to its boom period from 1835 to 1850. Many of the new inhabitants were employed at various local industrial enterprises, such as the National Armory. Housing for these workers was largely constructed of compressed brick. This building material was not

Opposite: View of Shenandoah Street, Harpers Ferry, showing large urban buildings

used extensively in other parts of the county but can be seen frequently along Bolivar's Washington and Union streets.

Though not officially incorporated until 1851, Harpers Ferry was settled in the eighteenth century.[3] A handful of early buildings are sprinkled among the lower town, known then as "Shenandoah Falls at Mr. Harper's Ferry."[4] The oldest of these is the Robert Harper House, which dates to about 1780. Armory worker housing accounts for the majority of the earliest buildings in this part of town.

Like Bolivar, Harpers Ferry has a large number of houses dating to the arrival of the Baltimore and Ohio Railroad and the Chesapeake and Ohio Canal in the mid-1830s. These later buildings reflect changes occurring in the American urban landscape of that time, where new ideas and aesthetics were taking hold across the country. At both Harpers Ferry and Bolivar, new machine-made bricks were laid with tight joints like those in the town house construction of Baltimore and Philadelphia. These pressed bricks have a more consistent shape and color than older local

bricks. The faces of the later bricks were also smoother, a look that appealed to building patrons of the mid-nineteenth century.[5]

The scale of American urban buildings also changed in the railroad era. The three-story brick buildings along Shenandoah Street in Harpers Ferry speak to the increasing urban land values of the time, as well as the departure from traditional two-story house templates. American cities were becoming larger and residents more comfortable with new urban architecture. New commercial building forms such as the Wager Building in Harpers Ferry signaled changes coming for the interior of the county. Because the introduction of the railroad and canal brought such significant changes in architecture of the county, this chapter will focus on houses built before their arrival.

Restricted by lot sizes, town houses underwent modifications that were unnecessary in the country. As with their rural contemporaries, though, early town houses in Jefferson County can be categorized in three distinct types: side-hall, center-hall, and hall-and-parlor.

Daniel Bedinger House, ca. 1790, East German Street, Shepherdstown

William Chapline House (Chapline-Shenton House), 1795, North Princess Street, Shepherdstown

Joseph McMurran House, 1798, East German Street, Shepherdstown

Michael Fouke Sr. House, 1786, West German Street, Shepherdstown

Side-Hall Town Houses

The most popular town house plan of Jefferson County's early period was the side-hall. In most cases, the side-hall town house was two rooms deep, or double-pile. This arrangement allowed maximum use of the narrow street frontage. By 1800, few lots on Shepherdstown's German Street were wide enough for proper center-hall houses. Forty feet was a typical length of a small-scale center-hall farmhouse, but few lots remained on the main streets with this much frontage. Without the room to build a center-hall house, many early builders and their patrons were left with the option of the side-hall plan or hall-and-parlor plan. The side-hall plan appears to have worked better in towns, since it allowed for a rear wing to be added more easily. The door placement of the hall-and-parlor house resulted in a more awkward rear-wing arrangement, which may account for its decline in popularity among town dwellers. The side-hall plan was used in large numbers in all three of the county's earliest towns.

The DANIEL BEDINGER HOUSE in Shepherdstown is a classic example of the double-pile, side-hall town house. Built about 1790, this brick house measures thirty feet across the front and thirty-four feet deep. Though the partition wall was removed between the two first-floor rooms in the 1830s, the house originally had a pair of sixteen-by-eighteen-foot rooms accessed by a side stair hall. This simple, effective arrangement made excellent use of the deep lots in town.

The WILLIAM CHAPLINE HOUSE on Princess Street in Shepherdstown exemplifies the useful nature of the side-hall plan in a town setting. This fine brick town house, now known as the Chapline-Shenton House, expanded the standard local three-bay form. At thirty-two feet across the front, the house width was not practical for a center-hall plan. Chapline added a fourth bay to the standard side-hall template to provide more light, giving an extra window to the front parlor and front bedchamber. The residence possesses all of the telltale attributes of Shepherdstown's late-eighteenth-century houses, such as the molded watertable, carved wooden lintels, and modillioned cornice.

The same four-bay arrangement is found at the JOSEPH McMURRAN HOUSE on East German Street, which was completed in 1798. This side-hall house also features excellent exterior detailing and may have been built by the same craftsmen as the Chapline House.

Now known as The Manse, the JOHN KEARSLEY HOUSE on the northwest corner of Church and German streets was built in 1816. This formal side-hall house has a rear service wing along the street that forms a private interior courtyard. Jefferson County has many side-hall houses built with perpendicular service wings.

John Kearsley House (The Manse), 1816, West German Street, Shepherdstown

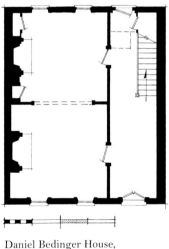

Daniel Bedinger House, first-floor plan

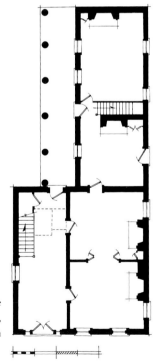

John Kearsley House (The Manse), first-floor plan

Solomon Entler House, 1825, New Street, Shepherdstown, original service wing behind and later front addition to right of the entry

Dr. Thomas Hammond House, 1844, West German Street, Shepherdstown

As mentioned in earlier chapters, additions to the side-hall plan are efficient and could be made aesthetically pleasing by balancing the front elevation. Occassionaly there was room for such additions in town settings, and the side-hall HENRY BOTELER HOUSE on West German Street was given just such front extension. In this case, however, the alley between it and the adjacent house was incorporated into the improvement, allowing access through the building on the ground level. The MICHAEL COOKUS HOUSE, on East High Street, was constructed as a three-bay side-hall house in 1798. A later addition transformed this frame building into a center-hall plan. The same extension occurred at the SOLOMON ENTLER HOUSE on New Street. This side-hall house, constructed for Entler in 1825, received a two-bay addition in the late nineteenth century, balancing the facade.

Other examples of early side-hall houses in Shepherdstown include: REICHSTINE-McELROY HOUSE, BENJAMIN TOWNER HOUSE, BELTZHOOVER HOUSE, JACOB ISHLAR HOUSE, and HISER-SHUGART HOUSE.

Only one early side-hall house constructed of stone exists in Shepherdstown. The STALEY HEIRS HOUSE on West German Street in Shepherdstown was built in 1835. Though the owners chose a typical plan, the material selection diverged from their town neighbors. Stone houses are common in the farmland surrounding the towns, but not within town limits. One reason for this lack of stone buildings may be the wall thickness required to construct in local stone. Most stone houses have walls at least eighteen inches thick, while similar load-bearing exterior walls of brick would only need to be twelve inches thick. A house could easily gain a foot of interior space in both width and length by using brick—a distinct advantage in a town's restricted space. It is not surprising then that stone was much more popular on the farm, where lot sizes were not an issue. Frame construction enabled owners to gain even more space; however, the fire protection afforded by masonry made it a practical choice in urban settings where fire spread easily.

Reichstine-McElroy House, ca. 1815, West German Street, Shepherdstown

Benjamin Towner House, 1832, East German Street, Shepherdstown

Staley Heirs House, 1835, West German Street, Shepherdstown

Warner Briscoe House, 1832, West German Street, Shepherdstown

The early residents of Middleway favored the efficient side-hall arrangement. More than half of the town's houses built before 1835 are side-hall plan.

The GRANTHAM-STONE HOUSE stands at the corner of Middleway's main intersection. This frame structure had been a side-hall house before being enlarged in 1828 and renovated into a hotel in 1850. The house has a standard rear service wing housing its kitchen and dining room.

On the adjacent corner, SCOLLAY HALL (Eckhart-Scollay House) is composed of two adjoining side-hall houses, the central log section dating to 1800 and the brick side-hall addition built in 1843—an unusual arrangement. The plan's single-room depth is typical in Middleway but not common in more densely built towns of the county where the double-pile plan was favored. Other examples of the side-hall plan in Middleway include the ELIZABETH STRIDER HOUSE, JOHN MOYER HOUSE, and DANIEL FRY HOUSE. Both the Moyer and Fry Houses were originally side-hall plan houses that later became a center-hall by the addition.

The side-hall plan was not popular in Harpers Ferry or Bolivar, however, where commercial and residential uses were often mixed in the nineteenth century. These mixed-use buildings were typically built with center entries.

Like those in Middleway and Shepherdstown, Charles Town's early builders frequently employed the side-hall plan. Many of these can still be seen on the side streets on the north side of town. Builders and their clients used the plan to maximum advantage on each particular lot.

The THOMAS GRIGGS SR. HOUSE on North Lawrence Street is an early log example of this plan type. Now stuccoed, this house has a two-bay mid-nineteenth-century addition. Here, the hall was placed on the corner, giving a measure of privacy to the living spaces.

The RANKIN-HAMMOND-LEE HOUSE on West Liberty Street utilized the side-hall plan, until a later expansion to the hall side and rear transformed the house into a center-hall plan. The additions were made for Robert C. Lee about 1820; though a modest-sized town house, this log building has refined interior detailing.

Constructed in 1828, the SAMUEL HOWELL HOUSE along Evitt's Run in Charles Town is a solid nineteenth-century side-hall house. As an added detail, the front elevation is topped with a molded brick cornice. Like the John Kearsley House, Thomas Griggs Sr. House, Solomon Entler House, and Jacob Haines House, the service wing cloisters the rear yard from the public street.

The side-hall town house remained popular during the entire survey period. The plan's economical use of lot space and adaptability to additions and wings made it a logical choice for town settings.

Scollay Hall (Eckhart-Scollay House), ca. 1800 and 1843, Queen Street, Middleway

Elizabeth Strider House, ca. 1805, Queen Street, Middleway

John Moyer (Myer) House, ca. 1818, Queen Street, Middleway

Daniel Fry House, ca. 1805, Queen Street, Middleway

Thomas Griggs Sr. House, 1797, North Lawrence Street, Charles Town

Three side-hall houses, Liberty and West streets, Charles Town

Rankin-Hammond-Lee House, ca. 1795, West Liberty Street, Charles Town

Samuel Howell House, 1828, West Washington Street, Charles Town

Fanny Sweeny House, 1834, South West Street, Charles Town

Hall-and-Parlor Town Houses

Owing to their commercial setting, town houses are far more likely to have been remodeled than farmhouses. For this reason, and on account of the hall-and-parlor plan's decline in popularity in the early nineteenth century, these town houses are exceedingly rare today in Jefferson County. However, hall-and-parlor houses can still be found on side streets where commercial activity was limited.

The JOHN LOCKE HOUSE (Star Lodge) in Charles Town is one such remnant. The house was built about 1796 on South Lawrence Street. Although this stone double-parlor house has

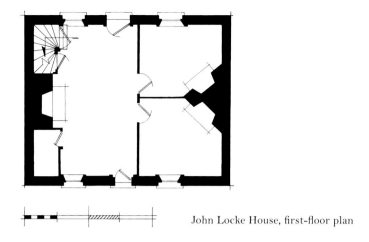

John Locke House, first-floor plan

John Locke House (Star Lodge), ca. 1796, South Lawrence Street, Charles Town

been modified over time, the original plan is unmistakable. The arrangement and scale of the house is similar to several contemporary local farmhouses.

The CATO MOORE HOUSE on Washington Street in Shepherdstown employs the single-parlor plan. Built in 1786, the house is one of a handful of frame town house survivors. The side wing is also very early and is built of wooden slabs.

The DR. EDWARD TIFFIN HOUSE on Charles Town's Liberty Street began with the hall-and-parlor plan. Dr. Tiffin's home was built of logs in 1788, though they were covered with a brick veneer about 1850. Subsequent renovations have altered its plan and appearance, but this notable Charles Town residence remains.

Another early Charles Town hall-and-parlor structure is the WILLIAM CHERRY HOUSE. Located at the corner of Liberty and West streets, this early house typifies the massing of the local three-bay hall-and-parlor type. Like the John Locke House, the Cherry House was built using the double-parlor plan. Along with the Dr. Edward Tiffin House and REVEREND HILL HOUSE, William Cherry's residence is one of Charles Town's oldest extant dwellings.

Bedinger House, ca. 1785, North Princess Street, Shepherdstown

Cato Moore House (Crooked House), 1786, Washington Street, Shepherdstown

Dr. Edward Tiffin House, ca. 1790, West Liberty Street, Charles Town

William Cherry House, 1788, West Liberty Street, Charles Town

Henry Fizer House, ca. 1795, West German Street, Shepherdstown

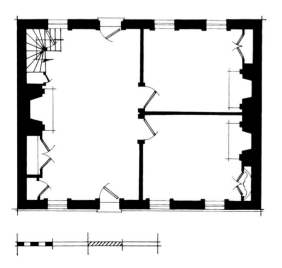
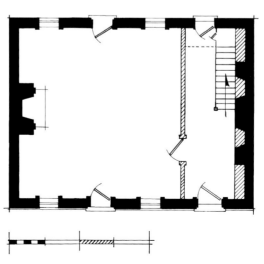

Henry Fizer House (Fizer-Morrow Store), restored first-floor plan, ca. 1795, original hall-and-parlor plan (left) and remodeled first-floor plan, ca. 1825 (right)

The four-bay hall-and-parlor house, common in other parts of the region, is found rarely in Jefferson County. Only one farmhouse example, Melvin Hill, exists in the entire county. Town houses with this fenestration are found in relative abundance in Shepherdstown, where ten early examples of four-bay hall-and-parlor exist. The HENRY FIZER HOUSE on West German Street, Shepherdstown, built in about 1795, was converted into a store with an open plan early in the nineteenth century. The original hall-and-parlor arrangement can be seen in the restored plan. This brick house has carved wooden lintels, watertable, and fine modillioned cornice typical for Shepherdstown's earliest brick buildings. Other Shepherdstown four-bay examples include the CATY HILL HOUSE and DAVID KEPLINGER HOUSE.

The DR. NICHOLAS SCHELL HOUSE, located on High Street in Shepherdstown, was built of logs in 1787. A modified hall-and-parlor, the plan of this house utilized a rear chamber for the stair, as opposed to an enclosed or boxed corner stair, which is more typical in the country. Since German-born Schell moved to Shepherdstown from eastern Pennsylvania, where this plan type is common, this house is a good example of a first-generation resident of the area introducing a building plan more typical of another region.[6]

The FOUKE-SHINDLER HOUSE was built about 1795 by Michael Fouke. The house originally had a hall-and-parlor plan. Around 1815 Conrad Shindler Jr. added a rear wing and changed the plan to center-hall with an in-board hall stair. During this major renovation, the front elevation was changed from four bays to three.

Dr. Nicholas Schell House, 1787, High Street, Shepherdstown, restored perspective view

Fouke-Shindler House, first-floor plan, ca. 1815, showing Shindler renovation and rear addition

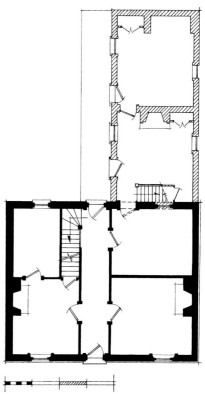

Fouke-Shindler House, ca. 1790, West German Street, Shepherdstown

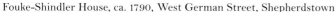

Weltzheimer Tavern, ca. 1810, North Princess Street, Shepherdstown

John Mark Building, ca, 1809, and John Line Building, ca. 1810, New Street, Shepherdstown

Another four-bay hall-and-parlor town house is the WELTZHEIMER TAVERN on Shepherdstown's Princess Street. Built about 1810, the exterior detailing reveals that this house likely shared the same builder as other early brick houses in Shepherdstown, namely the Henry Fizer House, Daniel Bedinger House, Jacob Staley House, William Chapline House, Fouke-Shindler House, Joseph McMurran House, and Wynkoop Tavern. Two town houses in the region, Martinsburg's O'Hara House and the 41 S. Loudoun Street House in Winchester, Virginia, share exterior features such as molded watertables, belt courses, and carved wooden lintels. The Weltzheimer Tavern, Henry Fizer House, and Fouke-Shindler House, however, are the only hall-and-parlor examples in this interesting group.

In the early nineteenth century two similar four-bay story-and-a-half houses were built on New Street. Both the JOHN LINE BUILDING and JOHN MARK BUILDING were built as rental units. These sturdy brick houses have half-exterior chimneys, which were common in the Virginia Piedmont but very rare in Jefferson County. Exterior detailing was kept to a minimum on this pair of side-street houses, in contrast to the more ornate brick houses along German Street.

The CATHERINE WELTZHEIMER HOUSE on High Street stands as a rare log four-bay hall-and-parlor type. Though very small, this residence has the standard corner stair and other plan features of the hall-and-parlor type. Built about 1817 for tavern keeper Catherine Weltzheimer, this house is the last survivor of many log buildings that once lined this stretch of High Street.

The town of Middleway also has a number of hall-and-parlor houses, including the SHAULL-SMITH HOUSE, MERCHANT-JANNEY HOUSE, JOSEPH MINGHINI HOUSE, and BELL-FRY HOUSE on Queen Street, and the SEBASTIAN EATY HOUSE and HARMON McKNIGHT HOUSE on King Street.

Catherine Weltzheimer House, ca. 1817, High Street, Shepherdstown

Merchant-Janney House, ca. 1798, originally a central entry hall-and-parlor house, Queen Street, Middleway

Bell-Fry House, ca. 1810, Queen Street, Middleway

Thomas Chew House, 1826, South Charles Street, Charles Town

Dr. Nicholas Marmion House, 1829, Washington Street, Harpers Ferry

Caty Hill House, ca. 1797, South Princess Street, Shepherdstown

Philip Shutt House, 1792, New Street, Shepherdstown

David Keplinger House, ca. 1820 and ca. 1840,
West German Street, Shepherdstown

177

Wynkoop Tavern (Selby-Hamtramck House), ca. 1790,
East German Street, Shepherdstown

John Ware House, 1804, East Washington Street, Charles Town

George Tate House (Tate-Fairfax-Muse House), 1800,
East Washington Street, Charles Town

Center-Hall Town Houses

Only the largest town lots could accommodate the long center-hall houses that proved so popular in the countryside. After the original lots had been subdivided, it often was difficult to fit a center-hall house in town. Some lots did, however, remain large enough for these house types, and some builders found unconventional ways to pocket them into tighter spaces. Center-hall town houses were less numerous than side-hall examples, though they represent the best detailed of the county's town residences.

The largest and most refined of Jefferson County's early center-hall town houses is the WYNKOOP TAVERN, also known as the Selby-Hamtramck House. Built of brick in about 1790, this double-pile house is an imposing presence on lower German Street. An unusually generous lot enabled this house to clear nearly fifty feet in width. Paired chimneys like those found on either gable of the Wynkoop Tavern are only used locally on mansions such as The Bower and The Hill.

Standing on the northwest corner of German and King streets, the PHILIP SHEETZ HOUSE occupies Shepherdstown's lot number one. This early brick structure was finished in 1790. Before a nineteenth-century remodel, the center-hall house had radiused or segmental jack arches over its openings. These treatments, along with a molded ogee watertable, speak to the building's age. Though the remodeling has eliminated many of these early features, two radius arches can still be seen over the basement entrance front and gable window.

The JOHN WARE HOUSE in Charles Town is also an early five-bay center-hall house. Like the Philip Sheetz House and Fouke-Shindler House, the building underwent an extensive remodel, but here the fine early detailing was retained. Though built in 1804, the house has features of the previous century, such as its heavy cornice and its narrow gable-end windows—which are reminiscent of those at HAREWOOD, BEVERLY, and the WILLIAM TATE HOUSE, all of which are located in the Charles Town area.

The CHRISTIAN CLISE HOUSE on New Street in Shepherdstown came to be a center-hall house by addition. Originally a single-room log house, the structure gained a three-bay addition early on, which resulted in a balanced five-bay facade typical for center-hall houses. The original section dates to 1786 and was expanded by James McCauley, who added the fine central stair in 1819.

The GEORGE TATE HOUSE, now known as the Tate-Fairfax-Muse House, occupies the southeastern corner of Washington and Samuel streets in Charles Town. Again, the entry and windows were altered in the mid-nineteenth century, but its scale and handsome detailing make the house a Charles Town landmark. The west gable features blackened header bricks, which add visual interest to the wall at the corner.

Philip Sheetz House, 1790, West German Street, Shepherdstown

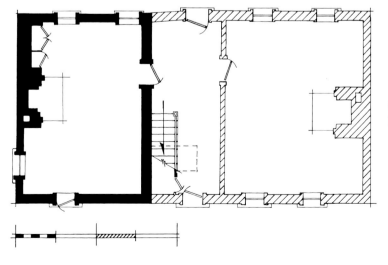

Clise-McCauley House, 1786 and 1819,
New Street, Shepherdstown

179

As Charles Town's business district developed in the nineteenth century, many of the earliest houses were replaced by commercial buildings. The WILLIAM TATE HOUSE in Charles Town, built in 1808, is a notable center-hall house that survived this modernization. The house served as the local branch of the Bank of Virginia from 1818 until the end of the Civil War. This fine brick home has a decorative cornice as well as narrow gable-end windows.

Located on the very edge of Shepherdstown, WINGERD COTTAGE qualifies as a town house, although it looks more like a neighboring farmhouse. Built about 1810 by John Wingerd, this five-bay brick house stands one-and-a-half stories. The double-pile plan includes a wide hallway and an early end wing.

A special varietal of the center-hall plan was used for several Shepherdstown houses during the last decade of the eighteenth

Spaulding-Baker House, 1793, West German Street, Shepherdstown

century. This new plan appears to have been developed in order to fit center-hall houses onto smaller lots. The SPAULDING-BAKER HOUSE, built by William Spaulding in 1793, is an excellent example of this unusual form. It appears from outside to be a typical center-hall type. With the main block of the house only thirty-five feet in width, the hall needed to be very narrow in order to allow usable rooms to either side. But with a hall width of less than five feet, there was not enough room for a standard stair. The solution to this dilemma was to move the stair out of the narrow hall and into a rear room, creating a boxed winder stair inside the wall. This adaptation allowed for unrestricted access through the narrow center-hall passage. This arrangement is also used in the Michael Cookus House, Jacob Staley House, Fouke-Shindler House, and other early Shepherdstown buildings. Evidently, William Spaulding spent more on his elegant home than he could afford. In 1793 Magdalene Bedinger of Shepherdstown warned her son in Kentucky not to incur debt in building a house as it was "the principle [*sic*] cause of Mr. Spaulding's ruin."[7]

The JACOB STALEY HOUSE, on East German Street, was built in 1791. This house boasts the county's most refined brickwork of the period, with molded watertable, beltcoursing, and projecting keyed brick lintels. The original plan of the house was very similar to both the Fouke-Shindler and Spaulding-Baker houses. The front elevation width of thirty-seven feet allowed more room than many other town examples of five-bay houses, but not as much as local farmhouses. Existing local center-hall farmhouses average over forty-three feet in length. Like at the Spaulding-Baker House, an off-hall winder stair is used to open the narrow central passage.

The JAMES STRODE HOUSE is another grand center-hall house on German Street. As in the previous two examples, the stair was located in the rear corner of the center-hall in order to reduce the hall width. The entry and windows were enlarged about 1830 by the Lane Family, but the house was built in 1795.

William Tate House, 1808, West Washington Street, Charles Town

Jacob Staley House (Parran House), 1791, East German Street, Shepherdstown

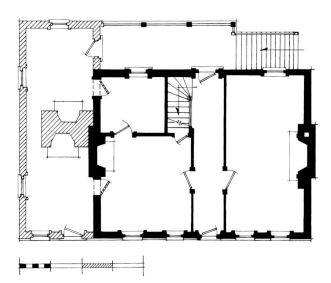

Spaulding-Baker House, first-floor plan showing office addition

James Strode House (Lane House), 1795, West German Street, Shepherdstown

181

Swearingen-Baker House, 1815, New Street, Shepherdstown

From 1800 to 1820, several center-hall houses were built in the towns of Jefferson County. Some examples dating to that period are the GEORGE WEIS HOUSE, JOHN MOTTER HOUSE, and the SWEARINGEN-BAKER HOUSE in Shepherdstown, the WILLIAM McSHERRY HOUSE and WILLIAM STEPHENSON HOUSE in Middleway, and the JOHN GRAHAM TAVERN in Bolivar.

Built about 1808, the JACOB HAINES HOUSE on the Southwest corner of German and Princess streets shows how lot size and location informed the design and plan of a town house. The nearly square plan emphasizes both street-side facades at this prominent intersection. The German Street five-bay front was the most formal, though the four-bay Princess Street elevation was also highly developed. Here, the molded cornice continues across the entire gable of the building. The use of interior chimneys, which have since been removed, optimized the fenestration at this important corner. This arrangement of interior chimneys is Jefferson County's sole example of a formal Georgian plan, found commonly in the northern states.

George Weis House, 1819, West German Street, Shepherdstown

John Motter House, ca. 1810, East German Street, Shepherdstown, restored
perspective view with the side-hall Henry Boteler House to the left before later additions

Jacob Haines House, ca. 1808, and Joseph McMurran House, 1795, restored perspective view

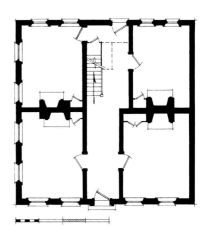

Jacob Haines House,
restored first-floor plan

Each of the county's early towns retain an example of a six-bay center-hall house. These houses make the most of the lot width and accommodate a larger common room on one side of the hall. The Conrad Kounslar House in Middleway and Snively Tavern in Shepherdstown were built with this extra bay. In addition to serving as residences, six-bay houses were typically used for commercial purposes. These two examples served as a store and inn, respectively. Other county examples of the six-bay center-hall design are the John G. Wilson Building in Harpers Ferry, the Willoughby W. Lane House in Charles Town, and the Edward Kelly House on Union Street in Bolivar, each designed to combine residential and commercial uses. With this exception, town houses followed the same plan templates as contemporary farmhouses throughout the county. The exterior detailing was generally more ornate in town house examples, though the interior work was comparable to rural examples.

The abundant early town houses in Bolivar, Harpers Ferry, Charles Town, and Shepherdstown showcase the unique range of the county's vernacular. Later nineteenth-century towns, such as Kabletown, Summit Point, Halltown, and Leetown, have interesting houses as well, though these fall outside the date range of this study. The three principal house types found in the early towns have variations that express the character and nuance of the place. The detailing, materials, siting, and scale of each town house serve to enrich its neighbor, and each town weaves its own distinctive fabric from these historic threads. Therefore, preserving early structures must be a priority for towns that want to retain their heritage and individuality.

Conrad Kounslar House, 1830, Queen Street, Middleway

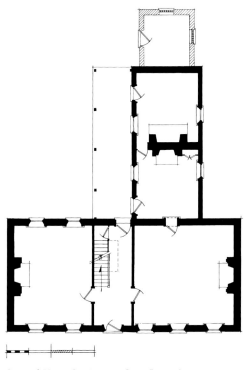

Conrad Kounslar House, first-floor plan

Dr. Lee Griggs House, 1829, Congress Street, Charles Town, demolished,
photo courtesy of Robert Orndorff

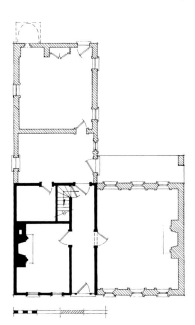

Snively Tavern (Hestant-Snively House), first-
floor plan with 1832 additions to side and rear

Opposite: John G. Wilson House (Stagecoach Inn), 1826, Shenandoah Street, Harpers Ferry

185

Chapter Six

Siting and Construction

Shortt Warehouse, ca. 1840, Princess Street, Shepherdstown

Siting and Orientation

Most of the existing eighteenth- and early-nineteenth-century country houses in Jefferson County were built adjacent to springs or creeks. The importance of having a nearby source of fresh water at a time when household water had to be carried in is obvious. Certainly, the largest farmhouses were situated within easy access of good springs, and several of the earliest residences, like the MICHAEL BURKETT HOUSE, were built directly over springs. However, by the 1820s most of the land adjacent to the county's plentiful springs had been taken. From this time on, dug wells and cisterns were the source of domestic water for newly constructed houses. As slave ownership on county farms increased throughout the nineteenth century, proximity of the house to water would have been less of a concern to homeowners since enslaved laborers likely bore the brunt of water collection and delivery.[1]

The siting of homes away from water coincides with a period of departure from their traditional orientations. Most of the eighteenth-century and early-nineteenth-century houses surveyed were built facing the east or south. By contrast, west-facing houses were nearly absent from the record until after 1825, with only three early houses, THE BOWER, CALEDONIA, and LANSDALE, built with that orientation.

The south-facing house benefits from maximum light in the winter months. Many houses oriented to the south also have fewer bays on the north wall to reduce heat loss during cold periods. Extreme weather from the west can be minimized in this scenario by presenting a blank gable to that direction. East-facing houses utilize the light well in the winter months, and without a fenestrated south gable, reduce sun-generated heat in the summer. The rear or west wall of the east-facing house, however, is exposed to the worst of the weather so fewer bays were usually built on that side. The negative impact of the elements was

Builders felling trees and measuring lumber, *The London Country Builder's Vade Mecum*, William Salmon, 1748

Illustration of typical house siting

minimized further by siting a house on a rise with higher ground to the west or north. East-facing houses such as the George Reynolds House and the Adam Link House are steeply banked into hills with higher ground behind. This type of siting was common in Jefferson County's undulating landscape.

The Casper Walper House, built in 1805, is a notable exception to the east- and south-facing homes of this period. This residence served as an inn, or ordinary, as well as the home of the proprietor. Walper oriented his house to the southwest at right angles to the adjacent roadway. Here the siting followed the commercial purpose of the structure and not climate concerns. This road-facing house orientation became much more common later in the nineteenth century.

By the 1830s, there appears to have been a reaction against the traditional understanding of the benefits associated with the east-facing or south-facing house. At this time many of the largest houses, such as Woodbury, Cassilis, Springland, and Western View were built facing the west. The trend can also be seen with the orientation of smaller farmhouses like Boidestone's Place, Mantipike, and The Hermitage. There may be more symbolic or emotional reasons for this change. From the frontier period of the Shenandoah Valley to the time before the railroad's arrival, settlements were culturally and economically oriented to the port cities of the east and places from which the inhabitants migrated. As the frontier moved west in the nineteenth century, there may have been a feeling that the future of the country lay in that direction.[2] Also, the burgeoning sentimentality of the early Victorian styles were emerging in America. This changing emotional climate may have led to the popularity in Jefferson County of the west-facing house with its view of the setting sun.

House siting should also be viewed within the context of neighboring houses. Historian Warren Hofstra identifies loose groupings of farms in particular parts of the lower Shenandoah Valley as "open country neighborhoods."[3] An example of one such community in Jefferson County can be found along Ridge Road. Here, a string of early houses follows the road, not in proximity, but certainly within sight of one another. Other examples of open country neighborhoods include the Upper Bullskin and the Lucas Run groupings, each of which are organized along a creek. In such neighborhoods, some unusual orientations are employed where an advantageous view or perspective can be achieved. North-facing Rock Springs, for example, has a sight line of contemporary houses and a long view of the road to both the north and south.

Upper Bullskin Run open country neighborhood

Lucas Run open country neighborhood

Massing

A simple rectangle was the standard form of Jefferson County's early houses. These houses, whether one room deep or two, developed some consistent sizes. The common single-pile house was built between eighteen and twenty feet wide. This width is roughly equivalent to the ancient English measurement of the rod—also called a perch or a pole—equalling sixteen feet six inches.[4] This distance could be safely spanned by floor joists without the use of a summer beam or structural bearing wall underneath. In longer spans, one of these two supporting systems is necessary. The summer beam is a large structural member that supports floor joists either by running under them or by having the joists mortised into this perpendicular support. In Britain, builders and surveyors had been using the measurement of the statute pole for at least five centuries, and it was certainly a common dimension on the new continent.[5] The other typical measurement for joists was the woodland pole, which is eighteen feet long. So the joist length—between sixteen-and-a-half and eighteen feet—and the exterior wall thickness account for the end wall width of the single-pile house. Builders may have found through generations of experience that joist distances over eighteen feet, without the aid of a summer beam, caused floor deflection, or worse, structural failure.

While the gable side measurements developed nearly uniformly, the lengths of these buildings vary more. Center-hall single-pile farmhouses generally measure between thirty-eight and sixty-five feet in length. Center-hall houses in town can be as small as thirty-one feet, like the William Stephenson House in Middleway. The county's hall-and-parlor houses tend to be smaller, averaging thirty feet in length, but with the depth of double-pile plans. Smaller still are the early single-pile side-hall farmhouses. The double-pile house utilizes a summer beam or structural bearing wall to increase the width of the building and therefore the necessary span of the floor joists. These houses tend to be twenty-five to thirty feet deep, and the lengths are similar to their single-pile cousins.

Local building heights appear to be driven simply by interior ceiling heights rather than any aesthetic preference or mechanical threshold. In addition to creating more imposing spaces, higher ceilings made for cooler summer interior temperatures and correspondingly colder winter interior temperatures. In Jefferson County, the masonry buildings appear to have been built with a bias toward summer comfort. For the first floor, ceiling heights averaged ten feet for houses built before 1835. Most of the larger houses have ceilings of ten feet six inches to eleven feet six inches on the first floor, with slightly lower heights on the second floor. Larger houses such as Harewood, Elmwood, and The Bower boast eleven- to twelve-foot room heights. Snow Hill, on the other hand, had a contrary arrangement. With ceilings at just nine feet, this south-facing house may have been intended to maintain comfort in the winter months. Town houses generally had lower ceiling heights than contemporary farmhouses.

Measurements from *The London Country Builder's Vade Mecum* by William Salmon, 1748

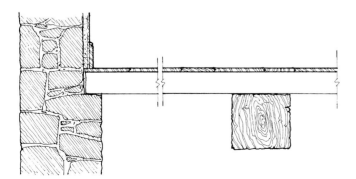

Floor system showing standard summer beam

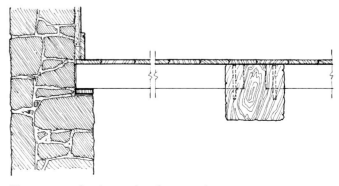

Floor system showing pocketed summer beam

Foundations and Floor Systems

Although some buildings were erected on crawl spaces, most houses in the survey had full basements. After the manual excavation of the basement area, local masons built limestone foundation walls between eighteen and thirty inches thick. These walls stepped in at the basement ceiling height to create a ledge on which to rest the first floor joists. A handful of houses had floor joists pocketed into the wall instead of sitting on an open shelf. With either of these joist systems, a summer beam would run under the floor joists of double-pile houses built before 1800, pocketing into the masonry gable walls. After the turn of the nineteenth century, Jefferson County builders typically mortised the floor joists into the summer beam, which could then sit flush against the flooring. This technique, already used on the upper floors, took more time to construct but allowed for shorter joist lengths and more head height in the basement area. Houses that did not have summer beams were single-pile in plan. In some houses a thin leveler board was placed on the foundation shelf below the joist ends. The joist would sit on the board, which provided a flat surface for the timber. As an added benefit this leveler could be replaced easily if rot was found, before the damage had spread to the joist ends.

Floor joist sitting on masonry shelf with wooden leveler board, Sallie Melvin House

Floor joists mortised into central beam, Belvedere

Hewn floor joists laid into wall pockets, Prato Rio

191

Houses with inboard chimneys had corresponding foundations in the basements against the gable wall. Most of these foundations were laid as stone piers with a bridging segmental arched opening. This opening has the appearance of a fireplace, but is simply a support for the masonry mass above. Other chimney foundation types commonly found are a pair of piers with a bridging wooden lintel, as at the WILLIAM HENDRICKS HOUSE and BELLEVUE, or solid masonry construction. In houses with a cooking fireplace in the basement, the top of the firebox opening was commonly supported by a large wooden lintel, as at COLD SPRING and the CLISE-MCCAULEY HOUSE. The underside of this wooden piece would be chamfered. Other cooking fireplaces were formed with masonry arches, like those at ELMWOOD and the GEORGE REYNOLDS HOUSE.

Builders used many different methods to support the triangular mass of corner chimneys. The most common was a corbeling support that tapered sharply outward from the two perpendicular walls at the gable, as at the NATHAN HAINES HOUSE, RICHARD MORGAN HOUSE, and ADAM LINK HOUSE. In a few cases, the three-sided support began at the basement floor.

Load-bearing masonry walls were laid across the width of the basement when masonry partition walls were used on floors above. This construction allowed for shorter summer beams and divided the basement into distinct rooms, as at BELVEDERE and WOODBYRNE. As another benefit, the flooring of the hall could be turned perpendicular to the other rooms. Without bearing walls the flooring could only be changed with the introduction of pocketed joists. Visually, this flooring arrangement made a house appear to be deeper upon entry. Hall flooring running from front door to back door was also easier to sweep.

In the basement, many houses had locked rooms for storing valuable foodstuffs, such as hams. These storage rooms were usually constructed from bearing walls and plank dividing walls. Most bearing walls were built of stone, and if the room was used for food storage the stone was roughcast with plaster, or at least whitewashed. Sometimes brick was used for interior basement walls. In houses such as FERTILE PLAIN and GLEN-BURNIE, large relieving arches provided generous openings between below-grade rooms.

Brick chimney foundation, William Hendricks House

Brick and stone chimney foundation, George Tate House

Stone chimney foundation, Bellevue

Stone chimney foundation, Reverend Black House

Stone chimney foundation, McPherson Mill House

Stone chimney foundation, Van Deever-Orndorff House

Basement cooking fireplace with masonry arch and engaged summer beam, Elmwood

Basement cooking fireplace with masonry arch
and engaged summer beam, George Reynolds House

Basement cooking fireplace with wooden lintel
and engaged summer beam, Cold Spring

Opposite: Brick relieving arch in central basement wall, Fertile Plain

Corbeled chimney support, John Rion House

Corbeled chimney support for corner fireplace, Adam Link House

Typically, basements had a series of horizontal vent windows laid across the long walls. These windows allowed air to flow through the basement and were covered with barred frames to prevent unwanted access. The survey revealed two favored forms of basement access: a stair below the main staircase allowing entry from the interior of the house, or an at-grade door giving access from outside. The exterior basement door was usually placed on the gable end of the building, though this door is located on the front elevation on some houses. Depending on the lay of the land, the house would be banked either laterally or longitudinally into a rise to allow access from two different planes at grade level. Usually large and constructed of reinforced vertical planks, the basement door could be locked and then bar-secured inside. The basement was often better defended than the rest of the house. Only a few examples of paneled basement doors were found during the survey; perhaps these decorative features were not worth the extra expense. The wide basement door was typically hung on iron pintles driven into the thick wooden door frame. Strap hinges, which reinforced the heavy door and carried the weight to the frame, attached to the pintles.

Basement vent window with horizontal bars, Harewood

Vent window with vertical bars, Shenstone

Basement vent window, New Hopewell

196

Paneled basement entry door, William Hendricks House

Plank basement entry door, Adam Link House

Strap hinge attached to pintle driven into door frame,
Michael Cookus House

Longitudinal banking

Lateral banking

Wall Materials

The material chosen to construct the body of each house depended on many factors. In the county's earliest houses, cultural familiarity may have dictated the wall material—since newly arrived settlers likely preferred materials that they knew how to work with. Economically, brick was typically the most expensive building material, followed by stone, then frame. Log was the least expensive of the available building materials, and log houses could be constructed quickly. Still, there are many examples in Jefferson County of grand houses being built of stone rather than brick, or log rather than frame. Certainly cultural preferences and economics were at work in these decisions, but there were other variables as well. Material availability, especially early on, was obviously a consideration. Brick was rarely used in early houses because it was not locally manufactured until the 1790s. Likewise, dimensional lumber was probably difficult to obtain until local sawmills were developed. Performance also played a role in the selection of one material over another. For example, stone would weather better in a damper environment than wood or brick. This chapter weighs the benefits and detractions of each of the four common building materials used for early residential construction in Jefferson County.

Limestone outcroppings in farm field, Harewood

Shutt's Brew House (Stone Row), New Street, Shepherdstown

199

Stone

Limestone was a resource that every Jefferson County farmer had on site, most likely in the form of outcroppings in his fields. This native material was durable and free. Nevertheless, most owners would need to buy lime mortar and hire masons to erect the walls of the house—both significant expenses.[6] Stone quarrying also took more time and effort than felling and preparing trees for lumber. Limestone had to be hauled to town sites, and the thicker wall masses required took up too much of the restricted space in town. For these reasons and because of the increased availability of brick, very few stone houses were constructed in downtown Shepherdstown, Charles Town, or Middleway. Of the county's towns, Harpers Ferry had more stone buildings. The material for this town's buildings was shale instead of limestone, which was quarried out of the cliffs in the lower town. This quarrying, usually into the rear of the lot, had the added benefit of creating more usable lot space. So, in this particular location, owners had an incentive to use stone.

In residential stone construction, wall thicknesses generally ranged from sixteen inches to twenty-two inches on the first floor and stepped in again at the second-floor level.

Rock outcroppings, so ubiquitous throughout the county, were generally the source for wall stone. Most wall stone was quarried from buried strata. Quarried stone could be shaped more easily than loose fieldstone, whereas weathered surface rock was brittle and thus much harder to work. Few buildings with ashlar stonework are found in the county for this reason. By contrast, the early stone houses of central Kentucky were commonly built with quarried stone that was cut into rectangular ashlar pieces, like brickwork.[7] This difference in masonry styles may have a cultural explanation, or may be due to the particular qualities of the limestone in each area.

The application of lime mortar between stones varied little during the study period. Local houses were usually pointed into a hipped joint. This type of projecting dressing is known as the "V joint" because of its shape. Original pointing can still be found under porches and otherwise protected areas of exterior walls. The plasticity of the high-lime mortar used in these walls allowed the pointing to adjust to weather conditions without cracking or spalling. Most mortars used today do not have this critical flexibility and when used in restoration they damage historic structures.

In towns stone was more commonly used for industrial buildings, such as mills. The heavy mill works and the vibrations they created necessitated heavy stone bearing walls. The damp environs of water-powered mills also made stone the perfect material choice. Stone walls offered the insulative quality, weight, and durability required in other industrial uses, as well. Examples of early stone industrial buildings in Jefferson County include Arc Mill, Hopewell Mill, Shutt's Brew House, Shortt Warehouse, and the Duffields Depot.

In the countryside, stone was a popular house material until the 1840s, when harder, machine-made brick became a cost-effective replacement. Many of Jefferson County's finest houses, like FALLING SPRING, WHEATLAND, WILLIAM WILLIS HOUSE, and WOODBURY, were made of stone long after brick was readily available. These examples were commissioned by families with Tidewater lineage, who would have been expected to favor brick. But as we have seen, the choice of building material was a multifaceted issue.

Early stonework with original V-joint pointing, Millbrook

Small stone quoins and wall pieces, Prato Rio

Stone quoins, Cold Spring

Log

Log buildings were very popular in Jefferson County's early development. These structures could be erected quickly with largely free materials, but their durability was severely limited. Log houses made up about 20 percent of the residences surveyed, but they were undoubtedly the most common domestic material in the study period, as documented in "the Jonathan Clark Notebook" from 1786 and the 1798 house tax.[8] Though log structures were numerous during this time, relatively few have survived the ravages of nature, neglect, and the Civil War. Still, there are enough examples remaining to make assessments of the construction techniques used in these buildings.

Log houses were built with interlocking timbers. The space between the logs was filled with stone or wooden chinking laid diagonally. The chinking was then daubed with a mud mixture of clay, sand, water, and lime. In some cases, the building never received siding. However, most surviving log buildings did have lapped or batten siding, which certainly helped to preserve them. If siding was intended, the foundation was sometimes laid out past the plane of the log crib in order to be flush with the clapboard sheathing.

The interlocking corners, known as notches, were prepared in several different fashions depending on the era and the builder. The most common notching technique found in the county is the V-notch. This locking form seems to have been popular from the end of the eighteenth century until the middle of the nineteenth century. As a general rule, the pitch of the notch flattens through time in the nineteenth century. However, this dating technique cannot always be trusted. Log buildings dating from 1840 to 1900 tend to utilize the flat, or square notch, which is pinned through the top of the corner with a dowel or spike to keep it from moving. The diamond notch is another corner form found in Jefferson County. This corner was more difficult to fabricate and is generally found on the oldest log structures. Examples of diamond-notched buildings in the county include the kitchen at Aspen Hill, the smokehouse at Gap View, and the Josiah Swearingen House. Dovetailed or half-dovetailed examples were not found in the survey, though some log buildings with this type of notching have been moved out of the county.[9] Several early log buildings in this survey, such as the Clise-McCauley House and Nicholas Schell House are still covered with siding, preventing the identification of the notching type. Despite the type of notching, log structures were favored throughout the county as economical and expedient housing. Prefabricated log buildings were even available in the area to those who needed immediate shelter, as was advertised in the local *Potomac Guardian* newspaper in August 1799.[10] Here, a log crib was prepared for use on any site "ready hewed, with rafters, joints, etc."

V-notched logs, Level Green kitchen,
Historic American Buildings Survey photograph, 1936

Advertisement, *Baltimore Patriot &
Evening Advertiser*, May 6, 1814

V-notch joint, Wayside kitchen

Shallow V-notch, Hawthorne kitchen

Diamond notch, Gap View smokehouse

Square notch, Green Hill (George B. Beall House)

Opposite: V-notched logs, Harmon McKnight House, 1798, Middleway

Samuel Offutt House, 211 North Lawrence Street, Charles Town, diamond-notched crib with later brick chimney and V-notched side addition, photograph courtesy of Robert Orndorff

Frame

Frame buildings were erected early on, but the use of frame construction dwindled locally from the 1790s until the development of balloon framing in the mid-nineteenth century. Given the popularity of frame fabrication in other parts of Virginia and the early availability of frame lumber in Jefferson County, this fact is quite surprising. Few frame-constructed buildings were found in this survey. Just nineteen houses, or less than 10 percent of the study group, are frame built. Jonathan Clark noted many frame houses on his tour of the area in 1786, but few if any of the structures he cataloged have survived. Probably the finest examples of this construction in Jefferson County are THE HILL, MOUNT EARY, and NEW HOPEWELL. Covered with lapped siding, these houses have spacious rooms and fine detailing. Again, it is rare to be able to document specific framing techniques because most house frames remain covered on the inside and outside until serious deterioration occurs. The house joiners who built these structures are just as elusive. Local house joiners such as William M'Coughtry are known only through their newspaper advertisements.[11] These same newspapers frequently contain notices of carpenters tools available at farm sales, which leads one to conclude that at least some of the local buildings were erected by farmers rather than professional joiners.

Jefferson County's sole mid-eighteenth-century survivor of frame construction is the PETER BURR HOUSE. Important as a rare example of early timber-framed construction in the valley, the Burr House retains its original end-lapped siding and is one of only three stacked two-room plans in the area. The framing consists of vertical members tenoned and nailed to the larger horizontal beams, which were exposed on the interior. Diagonal mortise–and–tennon bracing gave extra rigidity to the large gable walls. The areas between the vertical members were infilled with soft bricks and mud.

By the 1820s "soft brick" was commonly being used for insulation in frame structures. Stacked between the framing members, the brick also acted as a fire-stop. This practice of nogging, as it is known, became quite common for frame buildings in the later part of the period of study. After the arrival of the canal and railroads to the county, frame building began to steadily increase. By the Civil War, standard balloon framing was by far the most common building technique locally.

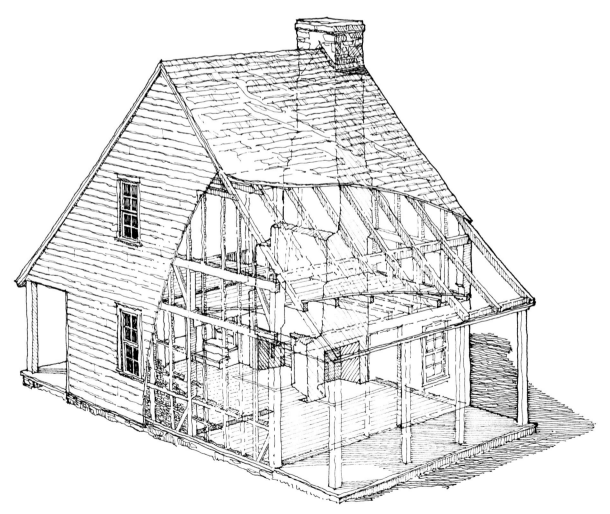

Peter Burr House, cutaway perspective view showing framing with brick and mud nogging piled between vertical members

Brick

In Jefferson County's first century of settlement, brick houses stood as much as symbols of refinement as dwellings. Taxed at the highest rates and built of a manufactured material, the brick house was the most costly.[12] Yet the brick building functioned largely as a stone one, so not much was gained in the bargain. In brick construction, walls could be laid thinner than stone, thereby allowing a bit more floor space. Thinner walls, however, lose more thermal warmth in the winter and cool air in the summer. In towns, where houses commonly joined one another on the gable walls, there was less thermal loss than in the country.

Brick was recognized as the premier building material of Jefferson County's early houses. Brickyards, such as the one owned by the Welsh family, were operating in Shepherdstown by the 1790s.[13] Some of the county's brick farmhouses were built with bricks made on site, while others were erected with material purchased from brickyards near towns, or after 1840, brought in from Baltimore.

Every brick house in this survey was built upon a stone foundation. Bricks rested on a bed of mortar whose ingredients differed by location. Generally, sand, water, and lime were mixed together with smaller amounts of clay or loam to form the mortar. This flexible composition allowed absorbed water to leave the wall through evaporation. Its plasticity also gave the bricks room to expand and contract.

Brickwork detail, Piedmont

Typical Flemish bond brickwork

Framed Openings

The construction techniques of framed openings—doors and windows—changed over the course of the study period. The earliest door and window frames were thick mortise-and-tenon pieces joined in the corners with wooden pins, or treenails, as they were known at the time.[14] Some frames were mitered using double-pinned corners, like those at Harewood. Most frames, however, were simply butt joined with a single pin for each corner. These frames generally utilized heavy wooden sills, though some of the finer examples predating 1815 had sills with molded profiles. These decorative pieces were especially prevalent in Shepherdstown. In masonry buildings, frames were laid in the openings as the walls were built. Moldings were applied directly to the frame after the masonry work was completed. In later construction, lighter mitered frames supplanted the heavy mortise-and-tenon frames. The smaller reveal of the later frames was made possible by recessing the bulk of the framing in the wall, leaving only the edge of the frame visible.

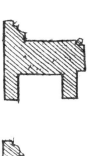

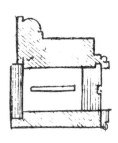

Window sill and stool profiles, *The Carpenter's Company of the City and County of Philadelphia 1786 Rule Book*, plate X

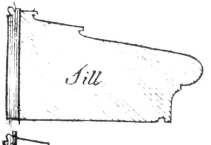

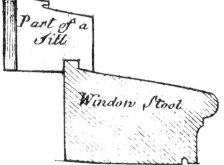

Pinned butt-joined door frame, Yates-Beall meat house

Roof Systems

The roofs of the earliest houses in the county carried only thin wooden shingles made of local oak or white pine. Even when wet, this covering applied very little load to the roof structure. Snow could add significant weight, but early roofs were steeply pitched and designed to shed the burden. Despite this reality, the earliest houses in the survey had the most substantial roof structures. Most of these houses utilized either principal-rafter roof systems or common rafters with collar ties. Principal-rafter systems used heavier members at intervals and common rafters between. This configuration was more complicated to build since it involved joining the principal members to tie beams and interlocking them with purlins, the horizontal beams. The purlins would then support the common rafters between the principal members. Heavy roof framing like this can be seen at several early houses, including Elmwood, Glenburnie, Prato Rio, and Straithmore. At Elmwood vertical struts were used to further brace the principal rafters. Thick diagonal bracing helped to interlock the rafters at Glenburnie.

Common-rafter roofs, consisting of smaller, uniform rafters, were the most widely used in the area. This roof type was less demanding to construct. Light roof loads made common rafter systems adequate for most houses, though the earliest were usually braced with collar ties. Collar ties were attached to the rafters with a half-dovetailed joint and pinned in place, like those at McPherson Mill House, Daniel Bedinger House, and Adam Link House. These horizontal braces, known at the time as collar beams, gave extra support to the roof framing and kept the roof from spreading.[15] In both common- and principal-rafter roofs, the rafters were half-lapped and pinned together at the peak. Paired rafters were commonly incised with Roman numerals to ensure that the matching rafters, made on the ground, were installed together.

Roof framing of a different sort is found at White House Tavern near Summit Point. The earliest section of this house employs a false plate that is rotated to match the roof angle. The false plate is laid into a cut in projecting beams—almost like notching—holding the rafters in place. Though uncommon in Jefferson County, this technique can be found in numerous early- and mid-eighteenth-century buildings of Tidewater Maryland and Virginia.[16]

Houses with hipped roofs were among the best built in the county. The design of local hipped-roof systems usually consisted of a heavy principal-rafter system. The hipped rafters were cut to allow the sloping intersection of the roof planes. The sturdy roof framing reflected the care and cost of the rest of the building. Houses such as Harewood, Mount Eary, Belvedere, Cedar Lawn, Cassilis, Springland, Altona, and Vinton utilized hipped roofs. All of these examples are found near Charles Town.

Rafter with incised Roman numerals and shingle roof, Reichstine-McElroy House

Collar tie-beam pinned into rafter with half-dovetail joint, McPherson Mill House

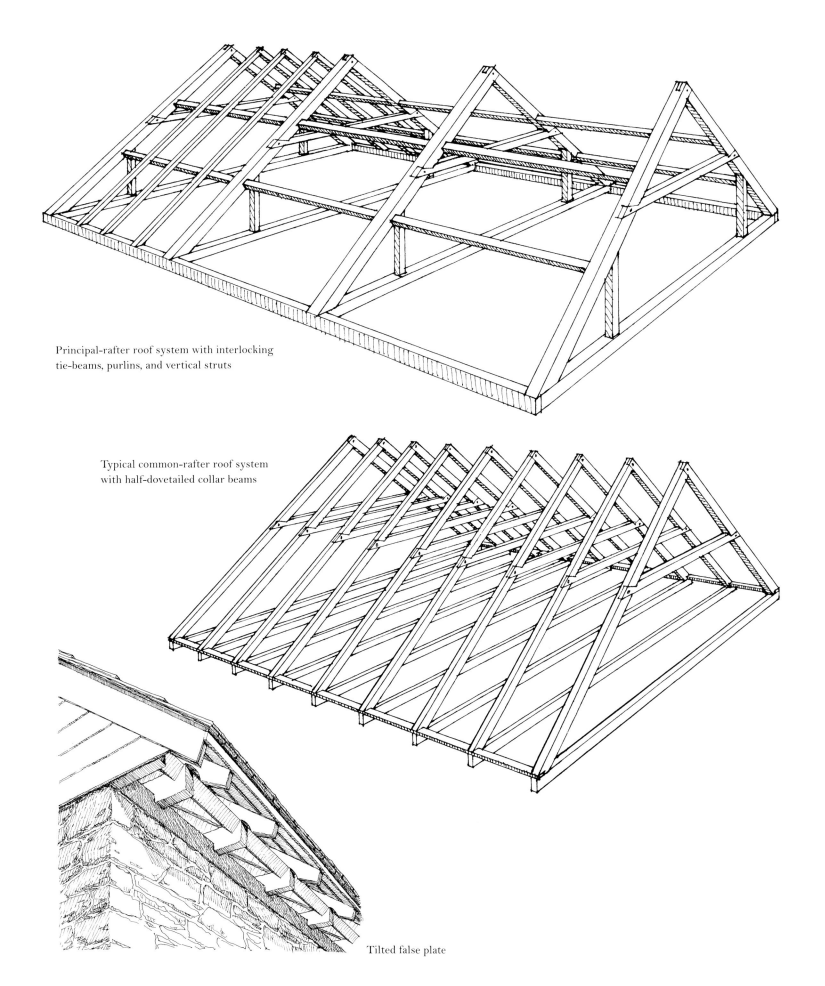

Principal-rafter roof system with interlocking
tie-beams, purlins, and vertical struts

Typical common-rafter roof system
with half-dovetailed collar beams

Tilted false plate

208

As the nineteenth century progressed, only houses that were built to hold slate roofs used anything more substantial than a common-rafter design. Later houses such as the Jacob Moler House and Western View had large hewn members braced and pinned to deal with the weight of slate. Wooden shingles were the standard roofing material until after the Civil War when metal became widely available. Roofing shingles were prone to fire and some interesting strategies were employed to reduce that risk. Recipes for fire-proofing paints and chemical mixtures were advertised in local newspapers.[17] Metal roofs brought some relief to the constant fear of roof fires. This new watertight material also allowed for flatter roof pitches, as shingles require steeper slopes to shed water. Many stylish houses in the Charles Town area had roofs that were shallow or nearly flat. These novel arrangements were made possible by the availability of metal roofing material imported from the coastal cities.

The building techniques that developed over the first one hundred years of European settlement in what is now Jefferson County reflect the interplay between economic and cultural forces. House design, composition, and scale were directly related to these changing determinants. Available raw materials and the local land forms also played a pivotal role in shaping the local architecture, inspiring differing rationales for building throughout the county. Together these factors created an assemblage of residential buildings with notable diversity that share many physical traits.

John Dangerfield House, 1859, Harpers Ferry, shallow-pitched roof with stepped parapet end walls

Chapter Seven

Exterior Features

Eave chimneys on rear elevation,
Peter and Jacob Williamson House

Exterior Details as Historic Clues

A building's exterior detailing reveals information not only about that structure and its age, but also about the people who were involved in its design and construction. Certain facets of Jefferson County's early house designs are repeated through time, while other components evolve into new features. Such details assist the historian to date buildings and even to identify the work of particular craftsmen. This chapter will trace the exterior features of the county's houses and how the development, alteration, and disappearance of this detailing helps to determine a building's period and style.

Small quoins, or cornerstones, and field pieces, Harewood

Stone Detailing

Stone buildings abound in Jefferson County. The style of local stonework differs according to the structure's age and function. In residential construction, the earliest houses have the smallest stonework. The size of cornerstones, or quoins, are the most telling detail in the area. Structures built before 1790 generally display corners less than ten inches in height. The corner size increased in the years up to 1820 when corners averaged sixteen inches. In the houses near the end of the survey period, 1820 to 1835, quoins commonly reached over twenty inches tall. This transformation in corner size can be seen in three local houses built between the late eighteenth

Large quoins and field pieces, Staley Heirs House, Shepherdstown

Small ashlar stonework, Traveler's Rest

century and 1835. The typical corner of the Peter and Jacob Williamson House (1782) measured just eight inches tall compared to the quoins of Rockland (1812) that averaged thirteen inches. The Isaac Clymer House (1835) has corners over twenty-four inches tall. These large quoins correspond to the scale of pieces used in local bank barn foundations of the same period. Also by the 1830s, the neighboring work of the Chesapeake and Ohio Canal masons could be examined by local builders and their clients. In this canal work, enormous stones were dressed smoothly and fitted tightly together to better contain the canal water. Domestic stonework of the 1830s and early 1840s reflects this preference for larger, ashlar corner material throughout the county. This increased aesthetic preference for larger stones is also evident in the development of arch treatments, as we will see later in this chapter.

The stonework of earlier houses typically emphasizes the horizontal aspect. The body of the wall is composed of longer and thinner rocks laid parallel to the ground. Local eighteenth-century stonework also has more surface irregularity, or texture, than does later work. The wall surface becomes smoother and the wall and corner pieces larger in subsequent eras.

Large stonework of a lock on the Chesapeake and Ohio Canal near Shepherdsown

Stone Arches

Some of the most distinctive elements of local masonry houses are arches. Though decorative, the arch functions to carry the weight of the wall over windows and door openings. Various building techniques can be seen locally that address fenestration. Most of these techniques are referred to as arches, even though some are actually flat. Typically, the arches used locally are known as jack arches, which refer to the splayed arrangement of the arch pieces. Radiused jack arches are utilized on some of the earliest stone houses in the county. Vertical stones, splayed at the ends, are laid in a relieving arch over the first-floor openings. The window frames of the second floor carry much less weight and therefore received flat jack arches. Radiused jack arches are rare, since few masonry buildings exist from their period of use. Only four of the county's extant stone houses have radiused jack arches: PRATO RIO, HAREWOOD, VAN DEEVER-ORNDORFF HOUSE, and RICHARD MORGAN HOUSE.

By the late eighteenth century, flat jack arches had become the dominant detail type over all openings. Evidently, builders responded to the changing tastes of county patrons by laying the stones into flat, splayed arrangements. Though structurally superior, the radiused jack arch was gradually phased out. With the considerable heft of the typical window or door frame and the average scale of the buildings, the flat jack arch made an adequate support. By 1785, local stone houses typically used flat jack arches. As time passed, these stone arch pieces became more square, or ashlar. By 1815, stone arch pieces were precisely cut and arranged with flanking shoulder stones. Some sandstone examples with keystones, such as those at ROCKLAND (1812) and LANSDALE (ca. 1810), can be seen in the area near Ridge Road. The sandstone quarried in the vicinity of the ridge could be shaped much more easily than the more common limestone and was, therefore, an ideal material for decorative arches. The large, rusticated pieces at Lansdale may have been inspired by one of the many colonial-era plan books showing Palladian rusticated details, such as *The London Art of Building* by William Salmon or William Pain's *The Builder's Companion*.[1]

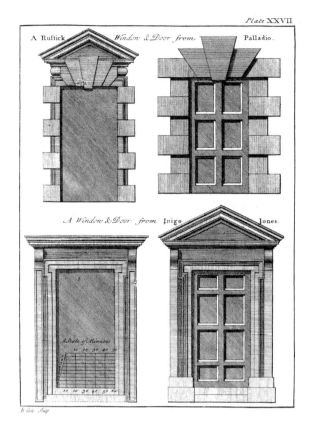

Rusticated door, William Salmon, *The London Art of Building*, 1748

Radiused jack arch over first-floor windows, Harewood

Flat jack arch with key, Cold Spring

Flat jack arch with squared shoulder stones, Conrad Kounslar House

Decorative sandstone flat jack arch with key
and shoulder stones, Rockland

Single-piece stone header, York Hill

215

Brick Detailing

As discussed in earlier chapters, brick was used rarely in Jefferson County until after the Revolution. By the 1790s, brick had become a common building material in the towns of the county, and was gaining acceptance on farms. There were several reasons for this growing popularity. As the local economy rebounded from wartime woes, patrons could afford the expense of this building material. Brick was also increasingly available. At least one brickyard had opened in the county by the last decade of the eighteenth century.[2] Brick also reduced the risk of fire. In town, buildings were susceptible, so masonry buildings were preferred by those who could afford them. In 1796, Shepherdstown resident Henry Bedinger described the anxiety of property owners in town as they "run everyday of their lives the Risk of their property which in a few hours may be in ashes."[3] In addition to fire protection, brick allowed for reduced wall thickness. This saved space was especially important in town, where lot sizes dictated building plan and scale. Finally, brick houses were viewed as fashionable and functioned as status symbols to local families. This social benefit had to be weighed against tax assessments that were higher for brick houses than stone dwellings.

Brick bond patterns in Jefferson County were fairly uniform throughout the study period. The repeating organization of the bond pattern reflects the style and period. The front elevations of most pre-1835 brick houses surveyed were laid in Flemish bond. This formal pattern alternates stretchers and headers, the long sides and the ends of the bricks respectively. On some of the most formal houses, Flemish bond would also be used on the sides or rear wall. In most examples, however, the secondary elevations were laid in common bonds, ranging from three courses of stretchers for every course of headers to five stretcher courses per header course. Three-to-one bond was used locally until 1815, after which, secondary elevations were laid in five-to-one bond.

Glazed or vitrified headers were occasionally used as a decorative device in Flemish bond exterior walls. Though they were never used on the front elevation, this elaborate work enhanced the sides and rear of houses such as the GEORGE TATE HOUSE, GLENBURNIE, ELMWOOD, BEVERLY, and SNOW HILL. The use of darkened headers after the Revolution was rare in other parts of Virginia but remained in use during the rest of the eighteenth century in the Shenandoah Valley.[4] In Jefferson County, this form of Flemish bond died out by 1815.

The standard Flemish bond, without glazed headers, lasted several decades longer, finally petering out in the 1840s. In areas of the coastal mid-Atlantic, the old Flemish bond pattern had been discarded earlier as an antiquated detail. It appears that local builders and owners preferred this traditional pattern for the front elevations. By the second half of the nineteenth century, Flemish bond had disappeared from residential buildings, though it was still used on public buildings and churches. Stylish later houses, such as JOHN STEPHENS HOUSE (1841) in Shepherdstown, and Charles Town's GEORGE SAPPINGTON HOUSE (1843) and ANDREW HUNTER HOUSE (1845), and the farmhouse WOODLAWN (1850), were laid entirely in common bond. Many of the brick buildings in Bolivar and Harpers Ferry of the 1840s and 1850s also had common-bond facades.

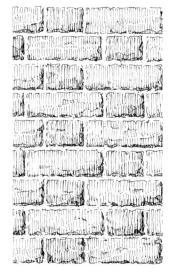

Flemish bond—
rows of alternating headers
and stretchers

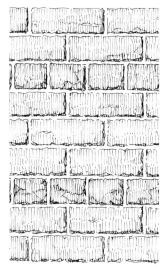

Common bond—
three rows of stretchers for
every row of headers

Three-to-one common bond with glazed headers, Glenburnie

Brick Arches

As with stone houses, only three of Jefferson County's brick houses—JOHN RION HOUSE, PHILIP SHEETZ HOUSE, and TAYLOR'S MEADOW—utilize radiused jack arches. Not coincidentally, these are among the oldest brick buildings extant in the county. As with radiused jack arches of stone, few brick buildings survive from the period when this detail was common. Brick houses post-dating the Revolution, which were also laid in a splayed fashion, used flat jack arches over openings. Typically, these arches were constructed of wedge-shaped bricks, or voussoirs, one-and-a-half bricks tall on the first floor and a single brick high over the second floor windows. Rubbed bricks with their smoother texture were sometimes used to visually accentuate the arch. These softer bricks, called samels, were easier to form into the voussoir shape. Only the most refined houses in the county, such as Elmwood, utilized rubbed brick detailing.

A handful of late-eighteenth-century brick houses used decorative wooden flat arches over the windows. This carved piece is applied over a functional brick flat arch. These wooden details are made to simulate finely cut stone flat arches found in urban areas of the late eighteenth century. All known county examples of this unusual detailing are in Shepherdstown and date to the 1790s.

Carved wooden arch,
William Chapline House

Flat jack arch in brick,
Snow Hill

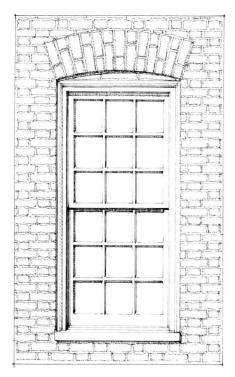

Radiused jack arch, brick-and-a-half course
used locally before 1790

Flat jack arch, brick-and-a-half course used
locally from about 1790 to about 1840

Flat jack arch, single brick course used
locally after 1835

Belt Courses

The belt course became a decorative element among the post-Revolutionary brick houses of Jefferson County. A projecting band of bricks, usually three courses, extends across the building horizontally in these examples. The belt course, or string course, is located between the first- and second-floor windows, typically on the front elevation only. This stylistic feature can be seen on several houses along German Street in Shepherdstown, such as the JACOB STALEY HOUSE. PIEDMONT is the only known farmhouse in the county to feature a belt course. This detail was short-lived locally, so that by 1800 the belt course ceased to be used in either town or country.

Water Tables

The earliest masonry buildings in the county, whether brick or stone, share some distinctive features. One of these is the water table, where the plane of the exterior wall steps inward above the building's foundation. By the late eighteenth century, the water table had become a stylized plinth course, whose antecedents in Europe had been used to divert water from the foundation. On local brick houses, the water table is topped by molded bricks. Though the PHILIP SHEETZ HOUSE and the DANIEL BEDINGER HOUSE in Shepherdstown utilize ogee shaped (S-shaped) water tables, all of the other examples feature ovolo, or quarter-round profiles. The location of the water table varies, though one to two feet above the foundation is most common. This placement is different from that in many other parts of the mid-Atlantic,

Belt course and water table, Jacob Staley House

Brick ovolo water table, Elmwood

where the water table usually defines the bottom of the first floor. Water tables may ornament the front elevation only, or continue around all sides of the building, as at Elmwood. With stone houses, the water table is simply a flat shelf directly below the first-floor level. The earliest stone houses surveyed, such as Harewood, Richard Morgan House, Mount Hammond, Robert Harper House, Traveler's Rest, and Avon Hill, utilize this feature. However, water tables ceased to be used locally on stone houses by 1790. This feature is much more common on their brick counterparts, where water tables continued to be used until the turn of the nineteenth century. There are no known brick houses with water tables built after 1800 in Jefferson County.

Penciling

In the early nineteenth century, it became common to apply red iron-oxide paint to brick buildings.[5] The paint gave a uniform color to the body of the house and improved its weather seal. To complete the look, the mortar joints were painted, or "penciled" with white or black paint. The remnants of this treatment can still be seen under eaves and porches, where the brick has been protected from the elements.

Brick ovolo water table, Wynkoop Tavern

Brick ogee watertable, Philip Sheetz House

Date Stones and Inscriptions

Unfortunately, the inscription of dates and names on buildings was not as common in Jefferson County as it was in some areas, like Lancaster County, Pennsylvania.[6] However rare, there are local examples of date stones. The most formal of these may have been cut by masons adept at making funerary markers; many of the shapes can be found in the burial yards of the county. Other dates are crudely cut into brick or stone. More formal stone examples, cut into sandstone, are found at ROCKLAND and YORK HILL, both in the area of Ridge Road. These stones were laid near the peak of the gable, unlike most of the other date stones, which are at or near the edge of the front elevation.

Date stone, Rockland, "1812"

Date stone, Peter and Jacob Williamson House, "1782"

Date and initials, Casper Walper House, "FC 1805." The initials may indicate work of a craftsman with the masonic rank of "Fellow Craft"

Date stone, Nicholas Shaull House, "year 1816"

Date stone, Springwood springhouse, "A.E.S. 1819"

220

John Motter headstone, 1833, Lutheran Graveyard, Shepherdstown

Jacob Entler headstone, 1800, Lutheran Graveyard, Shepherdstown

Decorative head and foot stones, Lutheran Graveyard, Shepherdstown

Sheathing Details of Log and Frame Buildings

The detailing of log and frame buildings differs substantially from their masonry contemporaries. No relieving arches are necessary in either of these construction types, so these opportunities for decoration and structural expression are absent. Most local log and frame buildings were sheathed in horizontal lapped siding. The PETER BURR HOUSE retains the county's earliest siding sample. The wooden siding on this frame house is attached by hand-forged nails and side lapped (bevel joined at the ends) and top lapped. Other siding types were simply top lapped. Siding would be cut with or without a bead on the bottom edge and randomly spaced up the wall. Some log houses, like HAWTHORNE and the original part of the SNIVELY TAVERN,

were covered with stucco. This stucco was applied to diagonally fastened lath nailed directly to the outside of the log crib. While drying, the stucco could be scored to give the appearance of ashlar stonework. Few log houses that were left uncovered exist today, though the documentary evidence suggests that such houses had been numerous.[7] The siding protected the logs and gave a degree of aesthetic finish to the building. The most typical siding detail or decorative element was a simple bead. Only one house in the survey had more elaborate ornament to its horizontal clapboards—the MICHAEL FOUKE SR. HOUSE on West German Street of Shepherdstown. The wide, rusticated siding of this house was later augmented with Victorian details.

Typical lapped siding, Grantham-Stone House, Middleway

Lapped siding, Peter Burr House

Molded siding, Scollay Hall

Beaded siding, Riverside

Scored stucco over log, Hawthorne

Wooden Details: *Millwork*

A wide range of applied detail, or millwork, can be found on the exteriors of the houses surveyed. As styles and building techniques evolved, millwork changed to meet new needs and tastes. Subtle transformations occurred in some detailing, while other elements were drastically altered, expanded, or eliminated.

The entry door and surround is a good place to begin the discussion of these evolving forms. Most of Jefferson County's earliest houses, those built before 1815, share a simple entry form: a six-panel door topped by a four-light transom. The heavy frame that secured this door and transom typically had a simple casing with a quarter-round or ovolo backband. The stout frame would be pinned in the upper and lower corners.

The entry jamb could be paneled or flush with the exterior wall. In some of the more formal houses, paired doors were used at the front entry. Houses such as Avon Hill, Prato Rio, Mount Eary, Harewood, and John Rion House are early examples of the paired-door entry. Because this entry was wider, an extra pane would be added to the typical four-light transom. The weak point of the paired doors was at the center where they joined; therefore, forced access was a concern. For security, many of these entries were braced from the inside with removable wooden or iron bars. After the turn of the nineteenth century, paired doors were utilized in only the largest and most formal houses, such as Cedar Lawn, Belvedere, Mountain View, and Glenburnie.

Wide entry, originally a paired door, with five-light transom, Elmwood, 1797

Framed entry with four-light transom, Adam Link House, ca. 1800

Opposite: Pedimented frontispiece of central pavilion entry, Piedmont, ca. 1790

A more decorative alternative to the standard entry utilized half-round transoms. Three local houses—PIEDMONT, CASPER WALPER HOUSE, and RICHWOOD HALL—have these unusually developed entries. The half-round light in each of these houses is placed over the door with flanking reeded or fluted pilasters. These ornate entry types are found more commonly in towns, such as Alexandria or Philadelphia, than in rural Jefferson County. Piedmont boasts the county's only formal, pedimented frontispiece, which surrounds an eight-panel door with matching jamb panels.

As discussed earlier, the center-hall house became the dominant plan type by the start of the nineteenth century. When BELVEDERE, a three-bay center-hall house, was built before 1820, an entry with sidelights and extended transom were part of the design. This is the earliest known use of sidelights in the county.

Accomplishing their twofold purpose of adding focus and importance to the center bay while allowing much-needed light into the hall, sidelights gained increasing popularity throughout the county. There are three types of side-lit entries that appear in the county around 1820: half-round transom, elliptical transom, and rectangular transom.

The early form of the half-round transom discussed previously in this chapter was enlarged at CLAYMONT COURT, TUDOR HALL, and SHENSTONE, all built in 1820. These formidable brick houses expanded the scale of the earlier half-round light and added sidelights below. These, along with the pediment attic light at HAZELFIELD, are the only examples of the tall half-round light in the county. This scarcity may be due in part to the massive ceiling height required to fit one of these overscaled windows.

Half-round transom with decorative tracery, Casper Walper House, 1805

Paneled entry with four-light transom, George Reynolds House, 1812

Opposite: Large half-round first-floor entry with sidelights and second-floor elliptical fanlight with sidelights, Claymont Court, 1820 and 1838

Detail of half-round transom and triglyph frieze,
Richwood Hall, ca. 1815

Half-round fanlight with webb tracery and sidelights, Shenstone, 1820

The entry of the Solomon Entler House in Shepherdstown, built in 1825, is the oldest documented use of the elliptical, or half-oval, fanlight in the county. Later examples of this ornamental detail can be seen at Cedar Lawn (1829), James Strode House (ca. 1830), Martin Billmyer House (1831), Snively Tavern (1832), Woodbury (1833), Altona (1834), and Boidestone's Place (1835). Only three fanlights were found that post-date 1835, those at Rion Hall (1836), Shannon Hill (1840), and Scollay Hall (1843). Some fanlights utilized lead muntins formed into profiles, which were accompanied by decorative rosettes at junctures, to secure panes of glass. The fanlight has become an iconic symbol of the county's antebellum homes; however, it had a rather short period of use. Many early houses were retrofitted with elliptical fanlight windows during the colonial revival in the early twentieth century, so dating a house solely by entry type is not advised.

By the early 1840s, the fanlight had fallen out of favor and had been replaced by boxy rectangular entry forms, as seen at Walnut Hill, Ripon Lodge, and both Moler Houses near Bakerton. This entry usually had a six- or seven-light rectangular transom over the door with sidelights flanking. An eight-panel door typically accompanied these rectangular, side-lit entries. This new panel configuration allowed the door's upper panels to correspond with the division of the vertical sidelights. Houses such as the Southwood (1833), Jacob Moler House (1834), Falling Spring (1834), Clay Hill (1835), Springland (1835), Rose Lawn (1840), Eastwood (1841), Fruit Hill (1842), Windward (1842), Glenwood (1844), La Grange (1845), Walnut Hill (ca. 1845), Vinton (1848), and Beallair (1850) used the wide, rectangular transom arrangement. Similar entries were added to earlier houses such as Rockland, Gap View, George Tate House, Beverly, and New Hopewell in the mid-nineteenth century.

Transom tracery also became popular locally during the late 1830s and 1840s. Various geometric motifs were used to decorate the transom space. At Boidestone's Place, Jacob Moler House, and Windward, both the transom and sidelights were fitted with ornate leaded pieces. As the nineteenth century progressed, sidelight entries became standard decorative elements for larger houses of the county.

Opposite: Elliptical fanlight, 1825,
Solomon Entler House, Shepherdstown

Elliptical fanlight added ca. 1830 to the earlier James Strode House, Shepherdstown

Elliptical fanlight with decorative sidelight tracery and eight-panel door, Woodbury, 1833

Decorative tracery of transom and sidelights with eight-panel door, Jacob Moler House, 1834

Detail of decorative sidelight tracery, Jacob Moler House, 1834

Transom and sidelight entry with eight-panel door, Falling Spring, 1834

Detail of decorative carved band over entry, Falling Spring, 1834

Elliptical fanlight with standard sidelight division and six-panel door, Boidestone's Place, 1835

Transom and sidelight entry with eight-panel door, Uriah Kerney House, 1840

Decorative tracery of transom and sidelights with eight-panel door, Eastwood (John Humphreys House), 1841

Transom and sidelight entry with paired doors, Fruit Hill, 1842

Sidelight entry with decorative tracery and single-panel paired doors, Windward, 1842

Elliptical fanlight with decorative sidelight tracery and eight-panel paired door, Scollay Hall, 1843

Paneled entry with narrow sidelights and eight-panel door,
La Grange, 1845

Later entry form added, ca. 1845, to earlier house, Ripon Lodge

Sidelight entry with decorative diamond tracery and two-panel paired
doors, Beallair, 1850

Later entry form, William Norris House, 1851

233

Windows

The appeal of well-lit rooms in the eighteenth and early nineteenth centuries was widespread. Historian Richard Bushman notes that "more light gave gentry rooms an entirely different feel from the rooms of ordinary houses," which in contrast were experienced as "shadowy, rough, and crowded."[8] However, ample interior light was a luxury that not all house patrons could afford. The number of windows and the amount of glazing reflected wealth and status, in Jefferson County as in other parts of the country. Thus, the largest houses tend to have more numerous and larger windows.

In construction, the windows were similar no matter their size. Nearly all windows were double-hung sash type, having two sliding sashes. A few casement windows were found in secondary spaces such as kitchens, basements, and attics dating to the 1830s and 1840s. These windows consist of a pair of hinged sashes that typically open into the room. The substantive variation in the windows of the surveyed houses can be categorized by period. Generally, the earlier houses had smaller windows with larger frames. The overall window sizes and individual light pane sizes grew through time, as availability of larger glass increased.[9] Windows of the earliest houses have wide frames pinned at the corners, with a number of different window divisions. These earlier windows have wider muntin bars than nineteenth-century examples. Pre-1815 houses utilized sash divisions of nine-over-nine, nine-over-six, six-over-nine, and six-over-six. Larger houses of this period also used twelve-over-twelve and twelve-over-eight sash arrangements. Occasionally, larger windows with more divisions were used on the front elevation with smaller windows used on the rear. Elmwood is an example of this arrangement, where twelve-light sashes carry the front of the house while nine-piece sashes light the rear. This house also demonstrates the use of the dropped landing window, the placement of which creates an asymmetrical rear elevation. The landing window was placed at a convenient height to give light to the stair, which made it lower than the other second-story windows. A few houses, like Glenburnie and Piedmont, balanced the rear elevation as well. In center-hall houses where a symmetrical rear elevation was intended, the stair landing is forced to bisect the central second-floor window. If the stair did not continue to the attic and a symmetrical rear elevation was desired, that central window would be out of reach on the interior. Clearly a choice had to be made between practicality and formality. At elegant houses such as Prospect Hall, Harewood, Snow Hill, and Beverly, form was chosen over function.

Early windows typically had moldings applied directly to their frames. In a few eighteenth-century houses, the molding profile was cut directly into the frame itself. Windows in houses dating after 1825 are typically set in frames with rounded, or bullnosed profiles. These frames were prevalent through the 1840s, when thin window frames with only a simple bead for ornament became fashionable.

As discussed in the previous chapter, small horizontal cellar windows were standard in houses of all sizes and plans, providing ventilation and light to the below-grade spaces. Typically, the frames of these windows included wooden bars on the outside face to deter animals and intruders. The bars are square in profile and set diagonally into the frame. This window type can also be seen on most local bank barn foundations.

Balanced rear elevation with dropped landing window, Piedmont

Applied casing, Piedmont

Bullnosed frame profile, Boidestone's Place

Basement vent window, John Kearsley House

Opposite: Balanced rear elevation with dropped landing window, Glenburnie

Shutters

Shutters functioned as an integral part of the temperature control system of early local houses. During the warmest seasons, shutters were closed to reduce sunlight, and thus the interior temperature. Closed shutters allowed air to flow through the louvers even during inclement weather. To mount the shutters, drive pintles, or mounting pins, had to be led directly into the wide window frame. Strap hinges seated on the pintles, known at the time as hooks, which allowed shutter movement.[10] In early houses the shutter itself was typically paneled on the first floor and fitted with fixed louvers on the second.

A few early houses, like ELMWOOD and PROSPECT HALL, retain their original shutters. Once protective porches became common, shutters fared much better, and many original examples can still be seen, such as those at CALEDONIA and numerous 1830s examples.

Around 1815, louvered shutters began to be made for the first-floor openings in Jefferson County. As window frame reveals decreased in size, cast-iron hinges were used to hang shutters. Cast hinges were mounted to the sides of the window frame instead of through the frame. The cast hinges were easier to mount than drive pintles, but they were not nearly as strong.

Shutters were held open against the house with hooks known now as shutter dogs. Many different designs of these restraints were used throughout the county. Like other hardware, the earliest shutter dogs were hand forged. Some had decorative elements such as scrolled ends or rat-tails, while others were purely functional without any embellishment. By the 1830s, cast-iron shutter dogs were being imported into the county from urban foundries. Examples of these highly decorative pieces were emblazoned with flowers, shells, or eagles.

Original paneled shutters, Elmwood,
Historic American Buildings Survey photograph, 1937

Louvered shutters, Prospect Hall

Iron boot scrapers were another standard appointment to local houses, usually found near the entry door, either fastened to a stone block that could be moved, or into the stone stair tread. These functional pieces were sometimes fashioned into decorative forms. Scrolled ends were the most common, but finer designs, such as the unusually intricate boot scraper at Richwood Hall, were utilized in the county.

Mounting blocks were another convenient and useful feature that were positioned near the house. The blocks allowed a rider an easier dismount from horseback. They were typically made of several large limestone blocks that were stacked to form a short stair. Several examples still stand in front of houses on German Street in Shepherdstown and surrounding farms such as Rockland and Fruit Hill.

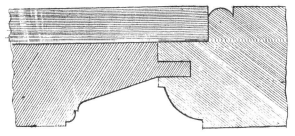

Paneled shutter detail, *The Carpenter's Company of the City and County of Philadelphia 1786 Rule Book*, plate XI

Upper and lower bifurcated shutters for window with jib-door, Woodbury

Utilitarian plank shutters for outbuilding hung on strap hinges, New Hopewell

Shutter dog, Wynkoop Tavern

Shutter dog and interior latch mechanism, Caledonia

Sill-applied shutter dog, Hawthorne office

Shutter dog, Grantham-Hall House

Shutter dog, Scollay Hall

Decorative cast-iron shutter dog, Claymont Court

Decorative spiral-end boot scraper in limestone stair tread, Scollay Hall

Facet-topped boot scraper in sandstone base block, Richwood Hall

Mounting blocks, Claymont Court

Mounting blocks, Rockland

239

Cornices and Friezes

The cornice in residential construction is partly decorative and partly functional. It covers the juncture of the roof rafters with the wall plate at the eave. The cornice also creates a projecting surface for the roofing material to rest on, thereby aiding it in shedding water away from the building. Most local cornices are simply long hollow boxes applied perpendicularly to the rafter ends. These are known as box cornices, which are typically ornamented by a simple molding, called a bed molding, at the juncture of the soffit and fascia—the vertical and horizontal elements of the cornice. More refined cornices are found throughout the county on larger and more elaborate houses. The degree of cornice development and detailing in Jefferson County depended upon the relative formality of a house, but also on the era in which the building was constructed.

The earliest houses in the county have some of the most developed cornice detailing. Many buildings dating to the eighteenth century have modillioned cornices, where brackets project from the underside of the soffit, perpendicular to the fascia. The carved wooden modillions are lined in series along the entire length of the cornice. The classical cornice of Harewood is the county's earliest existing use of this cornice type. In some examples, a dentil band or Wall-of-Troy band rides below the modillions, further accenting the composition. Such ornate cornice detailing can be found at large brick houses like ELMWOOD, CASPER WALPER HOUSE, and PIEDMONT. On the DANIEL BEDINGER HOUSE and FOUKE-SHINDLER HOUSE in Shepherdstown, the spaces between modillions are decorated with unusual geometric and shell motifs.

After 1815, milled cornice details became more understated throughout the county. Heavy modillions were replaced by light features like roped bed molds and interlocking track bands. Shepherdstown's HENRY BOTELER HOUSE and SNIVELY TAVERN are good examples of these designs. The more ornate versions of these were generally reserved for town, but some farmhouse examples exist. There are a handful of early-nineteenth-century transitional examples, such as the JACOB HAINES HOUSE and THE HILL, that retained highly decorative cornices. In general, however, the nineteenth-century wooden cornice consisted of a simple bed mold applied to the frieze below the soffit.

Brick proved to be a good material for cornices—since they were exposed to weather—and it became a popular replacement for the rot-prone wooden soffit and fascia. Simple stepped brick cornices were built in the county beginning in the mid-1820s. Finer brick cornices also began to appear in that decade. Houses like SHENSTONE (1820), the JOHN GRAHAM TAVERN (1821), WILLIAM GROVE HOUSE (1826), STRODE-LANE HOUSE (ca. 1830 remodel), and the MARTIN BILLMYER HOUSE (1831) utilized molded bricks to compose their decorative projecting cornices. These projecting cornices with compound moldings are rare in other parts of Virginia, but relatively common in the Shenandoah Valley.[11]

Modillioned cornice, Harewood, Historic American Buildings Survey photograph, 1937

By the 1830s, stone houses began using brick for both the cornice and chimney. Many houses in and around Harpers Ferry utilized a sawtooth arrangement, where bricks projected diagonally from the wall below. Examples of sawtooth brick cornices on stone farmhouses include Richwood Farm, the Michael Foley House, the stone addition to Hawthorne, and the Isaac Clymer House.

As use of brick cornices expanded in the 1830s, brick parapet walls began to appear. These stepped gable-end walls cleanly resolved the otherwise awkward brick cornice return, giving the projecting cornice a termination plane. The parapet roof detail was used earlier in towns as a device for separating adjacent roofs, thereby reducing the threat of fires. Though more common in town, pre-1835 farmhouse examples of this developed roofing detail were found at Jacob Moler House, Woodbury, and Falling Spring.

Another brick cornice detail was the projecting brick dentil band, as at Rose Hill, Rock Springs, and Dr. Thomas Hammond House in Shepherdstown. Each of these dates between 1840 and 1850.

More formal houses such as Cassilis (1834), Springland (1835), Ranson House (ca. 1845), and Vinton (1848), had intricate cornices composed of molded bricks with different reveals. These highly developed compositions required oversize square bricks to be made for the corner pieces.

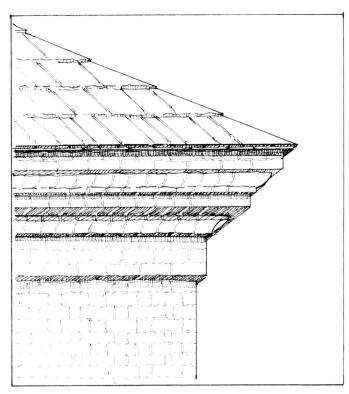

Highly developed projecting molded brick cornice

Modillioned cornice with rope mold and Greek-key band, Casper Walper House

Simple wooden cornice bed mold, Henry Strider House

Corbeled brick soffit with sawtooth band, Rezin Cross House

Molded brick cornice, Martin Billmyer House (Rock Springs)

Brick dentiled cornice, Rose Hill

Chimneys

The earliest chimneys in the county were probably built of wood and mud. "The Jonathan Clark Notebook" lists a number of houses as having "cat and clay" chimneys, such as Thomas Boydston's "old round log dwelling house . . . with outside cat & clay chm."[12] These stacks were wood frames parged on the interior with clay to reduce the possibility of burning. No examples of this primitive chimney type have survived in Jefferson County. Chimneys of the houses surveyed are constructed of either stone or brick. Generally, these chimneys are located at the gable ends of houses, either inside the gable wall (inboard) or outside the gable wall (outboard). Inboard chimneys are the most numerous, accounting for roughly 70 percent of surveyed houses. Outboard chimneys are more common on log buildings. Interestingly, the exterior end chimneys can be found in larger numbers in the Opequon Creek watershed, on the western edge of the county.

The third chimney type, the half-outboard chimney, projects into the room and out of the end wall. This arrangement was

Inboard chimneys, Ambrose Timberlake House

Outboard stone chimney, The Hermitage

Opposite: Half-outboard chimney, Jones Mill House

rarely used in Jefferson County. Half-outboard chimney examples include the SPAULDING-BAKER HOUSE and the JOHN MARK BUILDING in Shepherdstown, the ROCK HALL quarter, Charles Town's DR. EDWARD TIFFIN HOUSE, and JONES MILL HOUSE on the Berkeley County line. This chimney arrangement is quite common on the eastern slope of the Blue Ridge and Virginia's Tidewater. Why local builders did not utilize half-outboard chimneys in larger numbers is unknown.

A fourth chimney type, the eave chimney, was used on some of the oldest houses in the county. This chimney pierces the roof, not at the peak, but near the eave. Early houses such as the MICHAEL BURKETT HOUSE, TRAVELER'S REST, PRATO RIO, and PETER AND JACOB WILLIAMSON HOUSE have this unusual chimney placement. In all but one case, eave chimneys were located on the rear elevation, obscuring the stack from the front of the building. These chimneys share a banded drip-edge detail that most of the earliest chimneys had toward their tops. Large stone-topped chimneys became less frequent as brick became more widely used outside of towns. More farmhouse chimneys were built of brick since it created thinner profiles. Even stone houses commonly utilized brick chimneys after 1815: RIPON LODGE, MOUNT PLEASANT, HAZELFIELD, GEORGE REYNOLDS HOUSE, SIMEON SHUNK HOUSE, LANSDALE, OLIVER CROMWELL HOUSE, ISAAC CLYMER HOUSE, GAP VIEW, FALLING SPRING, and the MICHAEL FOLEY HOUSE.

Not until the 1820s did brick chimneys become more numerous than stone chimneys. In many stone house, built between the 1810s and the 1840s stone chimneys are topped with brick. This mixing of materials is hidden in the case of inboard chimney stacks. However, many examples of exterior stone and brick chimneys were found, typically on less formal houses and kitchens.

Stone and brick chimney, Vinemont

Stone and brick chimney, Pleasant Valley

Rake Details

The surveyed houses showed two typical treatments of the rake, or sloping gable edge, of the roof. The broken rake beds against the chimney, which interrupts the roof's rise toward the peak. This rake treatment was most common before 1820 on gable-roofed buildings. Some of the more stylized houses employed the unbroken, or continuous rake. In this configuration, a molded rake board projects past the plane of the end wall and meets the other rake at the roof's peak. The continuous rake required more finish material, and thus, would have been more costly to construct.

Roof Coverings

Wooden shingles were the dominant roof covering in the area until slate and tin roofing materials were imported in the mid-nineteenth century. Early houses are described in the documentary record as being "covered with wood."[13] In addition to shingles, some early houses used long wooden poles to weigh down the covering. Despite being a fire risk, shingle roofs were by far the most common surface material. In the 1830s, with the arrival of the railroad and canal, slate began to be imported for roofing in Jefferson County. This costly and heavy material required more substantial roof framing.

The exterior detailing of each house in this survey depended on factors such as period of construction, material, and cost. The composition of exterior design elements represented choices made by builders and owners. These details are expressions of their cultures, ambitions, and experiences. Though there is wide variation in exterior detailing, repetition of elements serves to link those houses of similar eras, showing the local preferences of that time.

Broken rake

Continuous rake

Chapter Eight

Interior Detailing

Daniel Bedinger House, Shepherdstown, ca. 1790,
mantels and fanlight added ca. 1835

Integrated Design

As with exterior elements, the interior detailing in Jefferson County's early houses features integrated designs. Certain door types, for example, accompany specific casings and those combinations are used with complementary mantels to form detail packages. The detailing of a local building, then, can be viewed as a stylistic vocabulary from a specific time and place, and the detail palette of a particular historic structure will usually be similar to other buildings of that time in the immediate area. Detailing can be a useful component in determining the date of construction or subsequent renovation. Telltale clues can be observed where the original detail integration has been altered.

As in most parts of the mid-Atlantic region, a hierarchy of detailing developed in Jefferson County's early houses. The most formal design components were reserved for those rooms most frequented by guests. Entry halls and parlors, therefore, were the most elaborately detailed spaces in the house. Dining rooms tended to have slightly less intricate features. The next lower level in detail sophistication was used in private rooms and passages, like bedchambers. These rooms, however, had better detailing than that of workrooms or storage spaces, such as kitchens, closets, and basements.

Front entry with flanking windows, Piedmont, ca. 1790

Entries

The formality of the front entry of the surveyed houses varies through time and with pretense of the structure. As discussed in the previous chapter, three types occur with frequency: transom entry, fanlight entry, and sidelight entry. Nearly every house had some type of glazing over the door, even where hall windows were present. Obviously, light was essential for the use of the hall, but matters of security, scale, and symmetry occasioned varying entry arrangements.

The earliest entry form, the transom entry, places a simple four-light transom over the door, like the one in the Adam Link House. In more formal houses, especially in the eighteenth century, a paired door was used. Only two houses, Harewood and Western View, made use of a double transom. This four-over-four-pane arrangement greatly increased light in a central hall that had no other first-floor light source. The inherent problem of limited light in the center-hall plan spurred some inventive adaptations of the simple transom. Formal houses such as Piedmont, Richwood Hall, Mountain View, and The Hill used narrow windows flanking the front door to add light to their large entry halls. Most hallways, however, were not wide enough to employ this device.

Starting in the mid-1820s, elliptical fanlights became fashionable in Jefferson County. These half-oval windows rested above the combined width of the door and its flanking sidelights. This new arrangement gave much more light to the hall than the simple transom. By the late 1830s, however, the fanlight had faded in popularity. The expanding acceptance of Greek Revival detailing inspired an enlarged transom and sidelight arrangement. The entryways of many older houses were modified with this newer arrangement in order to add light to stair halls and update the front elevation. For all of the light allowed by this large glazing around the door, security was certainly compromised. Many houses built well into the nineteenth century, such as the Isaac Clymer House and George W. Moler House, still used the old transom, probably in response to security concerns. Many of these houses employed heavy iron or wooden security bars to brace the entrance.

Four-light transom, Adam Link House, ca. 1795

Double transom over paired door front entry, Harewood, 1770

Paired-door entry with flanking windows, Mountain View, ca. 1813

Paired-door fanlight entry,
Cedar Lawn, 1829

Eight-panel door and fanlight entry,
Woodbury, 1833

Decorative transom entry,
Springland, 1835

Decorative transom entry, Caledonia, 1816

Fanlight-topped entry, Boidestone's Place, 1835

Hook for security bar,
George W. Moler House, 1834

Sidelight entry, William B. Willis House, 1841

Casings (Architraves)

The molded surrounds of openings, known as casings, come in an assortment of designs in Jefferson County. The casing, also called the architrave, is made of planed pieces of wood that are applied to door and window frames. Seen through time, the dizzying array of casing details in Jefferson County can be categorized easily into two basic types: stepped and symmetrical.

Stepped casings are much like picture frames. The outside molding is built up from the plane of the wall, and the inner levels step down successively closer to the opening. These casing types were used in the earliest houses and continued to be popular throughout the entire survey period. Symmetrical casings, trim that has level profiles that do not step down toward the opening, came into vogue locally in the 1820s and continued to be used through the Victorian era.

Stepped Casings

The stepped casing is composed of three primary features: backband, field, and bead. The outermost part of the casing is formed by an applied piece known as the backband. This molded feature projects farthest from the wall plane. The middle part of the composition, called the field, is a flat section that terminates in a bead or a small molded edge depending on whether the casing is single field or double field. The single-field casing utilizes only one flat plane after the backband, terminating with a bead. The double-field casing has two planes that step down to the bead. Generally, the larger double-field casing is reserved for prominent places on the first floor of a house. It would, therefore, be the major casing of a residence, and in its earliest forms would have been mitered, or cut diagonally, in the corners. The single-field casing, or minor casing, would be used on the second floor or in secondary spaces such as bedchambers. Having only two pieces, the single-field type was usually butt joined at the corner.

The backband was molded into a variety of profiles. In local houses built before 1790, the backband was either ovolo (convex) or ogee (S-shaped) in profile. By the early nineteenth century,

Mitred double-field stepped casing, Harewood, 1770

ovolo was more common. The stepped casing reached its most developed form locally in the 1790s. The use of crossettes, or eared corners, expanded the local style. Crossettes, only seen in the area's most formally detailed houses, died out after 1815, when symmetrical casings first appeared. The unusually developed hall architraves of the WYNKOOP TAVERN included molded key blocks in the center of the crossette casings. Other houses with crossettes include SOJOURNER'S INN, PIEDMONT, GLENBURNIE, and THE HILL. Interior pedimented casings were attempted at only one of the surveyed houses. The joiner of the SPAULDING-BAKER HOUSE in Shepherdstown executed a vernacular version of the pedimented architrave in the tight entry hall. Between 1800 and 1820 another backband profile for stepped casings—a modified ogee, or composite profile—became favored along the western edge of the county, from Shepherdstown to Middleway. This form seems to have been used by a particular joiner since all of the houses using this casing have similar detailing: MICHAEL SHAULL HOUSE, NICHOLAS SHAULL HOUSE, FREDERICK ROSENBERGER HOUSE, JOHN MOYER HOUSE, SHARFF-HOMAR HOUSE, CASPER WALPER HOUSE, JOHN MOTTER HOUSE, and GEORGE WEIS HOUSE. The plane for this profile was commonly used on furniture skirts of chests and desks, so perhaps the joiner of these houses was also a cabinetmaker, like Andrew Woods of Charles Town. Several advertisements in the newspapers of this time mention joiners, such as Robert Gregory in Martinsburg, that were employed making buildings and cabinetry.[1]

By the mid-1820s, new backband profiles were applied locally, including those that featured steep Grecian ogee forms with raised beads, or astragals. Widespread use of Grecian motifs characterized the millwork of the 1830s.

The inside edges of all stepped casings have a bead, the type of which depends upon the era of construction. Early structures feature the smallest beads; more developed forms appeared in the first half of the nineteenth century. The termination of the casing at the floor was also a matter of hierarchy. The most formal spaces of the house, such as the entry hall, would typically feature plinth blocks at the casing base. In private rooms, or in less formal houses, the casing would run to the floor.

Crossette stepped casing with projecting key block, Wynkoop Tavern, ca. 1790

Crossette stepped casing, Sojourner's Inn, ca. 1790

Butt-joined double-field stepped casing, Beverly, ca. 1800

Mitered double-field stepped casing with ogee backband,
White House Tavern, ca. 1800

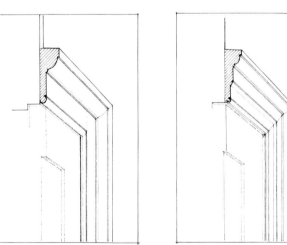

Single-field casing
with ovolo backband

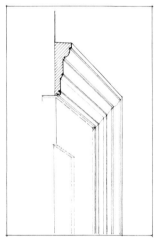

Double-field casing
with ovolo backband

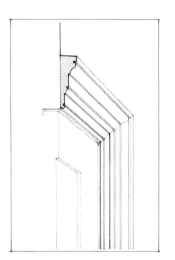

Double-field casing
with ogee backband

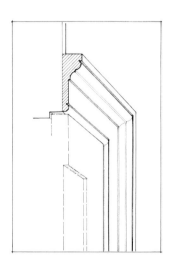

Single-field casing with
composite profile backband

Opposite: Gouge-decorated casing, Richwood Hall, ca. 1815

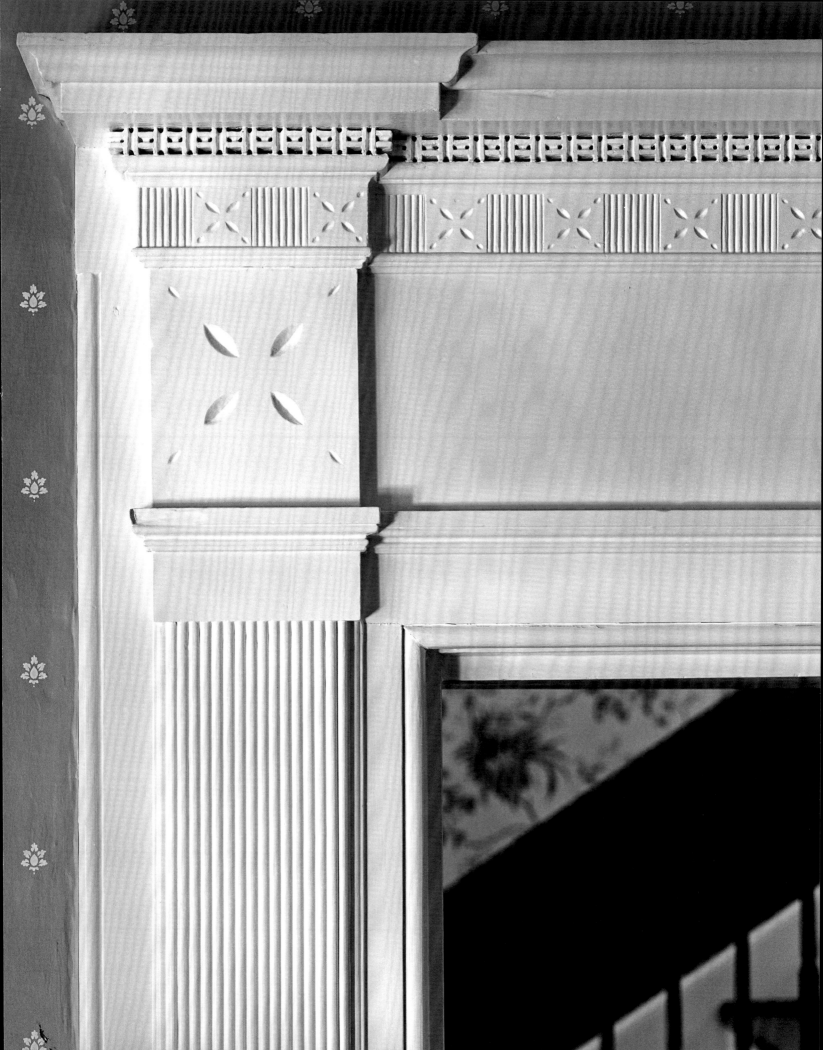

Symmetrical Casings

The first houses in the county to use symmetrical casings date to the period between 1815 and 1820. This trim has uniform inside and outside edges, so that if the two halves of the profile were bisected longitudinally they would mirror one another. Because of this symmetry, no backband is utilized. The horizontal and vertical planes of this casing terminate with a corner block, known locally as a bull's-eye, as it is deeply incised with circular patterns. The earliest symmetrical profiles were the most ornate. The major casings at RICHWOOD HALL surpassed all other local types in their intricacy: the casings are reeded, the corner blocks medallioned or incised, and the architrave top features a double Wall-of-Troy band. Other ornate symmetrical casings were found at the SWEARINGEN-BAKER HOUSE, BELVEDERE, and LINDEN SPRING, all built between 1815 and 1820. In these formally detailed houses, vertical projecting fins decorate the symmetrical trim. As time went on, however, the profiles became more hard edged and regularized until they were simply grooved. The forms of the late 1830s were more rudimentary, losing delicate features such as the small molded panel edges known as stickings. By the 1840s, with houses like BARLEYWOOD, ROSE HILL, BEALLAIR, and VINTON, the local symmetrical casings were wide, unadorned boards with flat corner blocks. These austere casings had little or no worked faces—quite a contrast to the busy designs just a few decades earlier. The evolution from complex late-Federal forms into the harsh simplicity of Jefferson County's Greek Revival can be traced clearly in these casings.

Symmetrical casing, Belvedere, ca. 1818

Symmetrical casing, Western View, 1831

Symmetrical casing, Ripon Lodge, ca. 1835

Symmetrical casing, William B. Willis House, 1841

Symmetrical casing, Rose Hill, 1850

Greek Revival pediment casings, Vinton, 1848

Pediment crossette casing likely imported to Jefferson County, Beallair, 1850

Stairs

With the growing popularity of center-hall and side-hall plans after the Revolution, the staircase became the most prominent piece of millwork in the houses of Jefferson County. Before this time, the county's hall-and-parlor houses encased the tight winding stair in a corner of the hall. These houses celebrated the paneled chimney walls, not the utilitarian stair. However, once the stair was put on display in the hall, rich detailing was devised to showcase this significant element.

Most of the stairs surveyed are open-well types, those with an open shaft between the runs of stairs. Secondary stairs were commonly winders with wedge-shaped stair treads. The ingenuity, creativity, and skill of local joiners is apparent in each design. This section identifies the various features that make the stair, and traces the development of each form.

Stairway and landing,
Belvedere, ca. 1818

Square fluted newel, Harewood, 1770

Stair Rail

The stair rail is a composite of three milled elements: newel (the large posts at the ends of stairs), baluster (the vertical supports between the newels), and handrail (the diagonal railing). Newels are the primary features of the stair's composition. Most of the newel posts built in the eighteenth century in what is now Jefferson County were turned, tapering pieces of walnut with blockish square tops. Examples of this design can be found at the DANIEL BEDINGER HOUSE, WYNKOOP TAVERN, GEORGE TATE HOUSE, WILLIAM CHAPLINE HOUSE, and TRAVELER'S REST. Early unturned newels such as the square fluted newel at HAREWOOD were rare in the county. Balusters dating to the eighteenth century were all turned, with varying degrees of sophistication. The recurrence of certain baluster profiles can provide clues to identify the work of particular craftsmen. The early handrail was typically large and molded, and in most cases, goosenecked in a graceful sweep up to the landing newel.

Square-topped newel, Traveler's Rest, ca. 1781

Square-topped newel, Daniel Bedinger House, ca. 1790

By 1810, a newel with a raised grip-top became popular in the northern and eastern parts of the county. This utilitarian feature aided the climbing of stairs, and examples can be found in LANSDALE, SIMEON SHUNK HOUSE, CASPER WALPER HOUSE, SOJOURNER'S INN, CLAREMONT, ALLSTADT HOUSE, COLD SPRING, FERTILE PLAIN, and GLENBURNIE in the country; and the HENRY BOTELER HOUSE, JOHN KEARSLEY HOUSE, CLISE-MCCAULEY HOUSE, and JACOB HAINES HOUSE in town. Their similarity, proximity, and dates of construction, make it likely that the same craftsmen built these stairs.

Also at this time, unturned rectangular balusters became the dominant forms of handrail supports. These simple pieces stood in stark contrast to the earlier sculptural balusters. Finer houses, however, continued to use turned balusters until 1815. Squared balusters were usually set parallel to the stair edge, though occasionally they were angled, or "set on the diamond," as at GLENBURNIE and ROCK SPRING.

In the central and southern parts of the county during the early nineteenth century, craftsmen continued to use turned newel posts, for the most part with rounded integral tops, as evidenced by the stair designs at SNOW HILL, HOPEWELL, RICHWOOD HALL, HAZELFIELD, PROSPECT HALL, and CALEDONIA. Again, many of these stairs were likely built by the same joiners and turners. Several newels, like those at ROCK SPRING, HOPEWELL, and VINEMONT, are identical in profile and construction and could be the work of a single craftsman.

A handful of square newels were used in the southern end of the county during the first quarter of the nineteenth century. The SHARFF-HOMAR HOUSE, DANIEL HAINES HOUSE, TULIP HILL, DANIEL HEFFLEBOWER HOUSE, BEVERLY, and MICHAEL SHAULL HOUSE each utilized unadorned or reeded square newel posts. Interestingly, most of the owners of these southern Jefferson County houses originated in Pennsylvania, not the Tidewater; it appears that these owners preferred simpler detailing than their neighbors with Virginian ancestry.

By the 1820s, the fashion for round or oval handrails brought about a change in newel design. Unlike previous newel types, these turned pieces joined the rail from below allowing the rail to pass over the newel top. Examples were found at CLAY HILL, CEDAR LAWN, WESTERN VIEW, ASPEN POOL, WILLIAM S. KERNEY HOUSE, URIAH KERNEY HOUSE, FALLING SPRING, and SOUTHWOOD. The newels of the 1830s typically utilized this overshot design with a turned cuff near the top of the newel. In the 1840s the overshot became even more expressive and curvilinear, culminating in the acorn-top newels seen in and around

Square-topped newel, Elmwood, 1797

Shepherdstown at houses such as ROCKLAND, SPRINGDALE, ROSE HILL, JOHN STEPHENS HOUSE, and the STALEY HEIRS HOUSE.

Full-blown Greek Revival houses of this period commonly had massive barrel newels, which sometimes rested on octagonal bases. All examples of the barrel type, including those at ASPEN HILL, HAPPY RETREAT, BARLEYWOOD, CLAYMONT COURT, WILLIAM B. WILLIS HOUSE, GEORGE EICHELBERGER SR. HOUSE, WILLIAM NORRIS HOUSE, VINTON, WOODLAWN, and EASTWOOD, are located in the central and southern parts of the county, where there appears to be a distinct preference for heavy Greek Revival elements. In contrast, residents in the northern end of Jefferson County preferred details derivative of the more delicate Federal style in this era.

Another newel type that was used, though sparingly, was the twist newel. Only three examples predating 1835 exist in the county: THE HILL, BELVEDERE, and WOODBURY. Both Belvedere and Woodbury combined this newel with a graceful elliptical stair. Two other county houses, WILD GOOSE (1842) and ROSE BRAKE (1855), utilized this newel type in later years.

Opposite: Square-topped newel, Wynkoop Tavern, ca. 1790

Turned newel, Piedmont, ca. 1790

Grip-top newel, Jacob Haines House, ca. 1808

Grip-top newel, John Kearsley House, 1816

Grip-top newel, Clise-McCauley House, added 1819

Turned newel, Hopewell, ca. 1810

Turned newel, Vinemont, ca. 1815

Overshot newel with cuffed turning, Falling Spring, 1834

Overshot newel with cuffed turning, William S. Kerney House, 1837

Acorn newel, Rockland, added ca. 1840

Acorn newel, Rose Hill, 1850

Twist newel, The Hill, ca. 1815

Twist newel, Wild Goose, 1842

Barrel newel, William B. Willis House, 1841

Barrel newel, New Hopewell, added ca. 1845

Barrel newel, George Eichelberger House, 1849

Barrel newel, Woodlawn, 1850

267

Newel Drops

The newel ends that hang from landings and upper floors were sometimes turned into decorative forms called newel drops. Many different types of turnings were used locally to ornament and resolve this hanging member. Simple turnip-shaped forms were the most common, like those at the WILLIAM CHAPLINE HOUSE. Some intricately turned drops were found at the JACOB MOLER HOUSE and WESTERN VIEW. By the 1830s, however, most newels were cut flush with the ceilings and left unadorned. This simplification is consistent with other changes happening in the local detailing of the Greek Revival period.

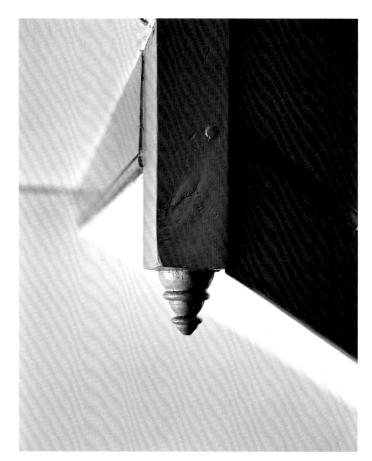

Newel drop, Daniel Bedinger House, ca. 1790

Turnip newel drop, William Chapline House, 1795

Turned newel drop, Jacob Moler House, 1834

Stair Rail Resolutions

Most of the houses surveyed in Jefferson County are two-story structures with stairs that lead to the attic. In houses with this arrangement, different designs were employed to link the stair rail termination at the end of the second flight of stairs and the start of the third flight. Some designs eliminated the space behind the rail by cutting straight across the landing to the adjacent risers. Though this is an economical use of space, the resulting intersection appears as an awkward collision of parts. The landings at the HENRY BOTELER HOUSE, WYNKOOP TAVERN, and the CASPER WALPER HOUSE all use this design, though more elegant solutions were devised in other county houses. Notable ingenious arrangements include the reverse curve of PIEDMONT, and the arcing rails of FERTILE PLAIN, WILLIAM S. KERNEY HOUSE, MARTIN MILLER HOUSE, WILLIAM GROVE HOUSE, and MOUNT ELLEN. The most successful and beautiful, however, is the sinuous resolution of the rail at GLENBURNIE. Here, the heavy handrail curves back gracefully to the recessed newel.

S-curved stair rail connection, Glenburnie, ca. 1815

Stair rail termination, Wynkoop Tavern, ca. 1790

Stair rail termination, Henry Boteler House, 1817

Angled stair rail connection viewed from above, Elmwood, 1797

Radiused stair rail connection, Fertile Plain, ca. 1818

Stair rail termination, Casper Walper House, 1805

Stair Wall Features

Elements of stair wall detailing include wainscot, engaged newels, and shadow rails. The last two ornamental features mirror the action of the stair's real newels and rails along the wall. The use of wainscot, the paneled or flat boarding under the shadow baluster, declined as the eighteenth century came to a close. Houses with paneled wainscoting, like HAREWOOD and BEVERLY, were among the most formal in the county. The finely detailed RICHWOOD HALL is the only nineteenth-century house with paneled wainscoting. Later houses with wainscoting employed diagonal planking instead of underpaneling; examples of this plain wainscot are found at PROSPECT HALL, HAZELFIELD, and MOUNT ELLEN. All of these houses utilized shadow rails and engaged newels. As time progressed, however, these elements became less common. Most of the houses of the 1840s and 1850s had no stair wall features, or earlier appointments such as chair rail.

Decorative profiled landing return, Richwood Hall, ca. 1815

Shadow baluster and engaged newel, Lansdale, ca. 1810

Shadow baluster and engaged newel, Caledonia, 1816

Shadow baluster and engaged newels with paneled wainscot,
Richwood Hall, ca. 1815

Square newel, paneled wainscot, and shadow baluster, Beverly, ca. 1800

273

Incised scroll bracket, Piedmont, ca. 1790

Incised scroll bracket, William Chapline House, 1795

Incised stair brackets, Prospect Hall, ca. 1810

Incised stair brackets, Woodbyrne, ca. 1810

Stair Brackets

The returning edge of the stair riser, or stair bracket, is the location of some of the most interesting and original detailing in all of the houses surveyed. Stair brackets in Jefferson County's earliest houses have a profiled edge. Some of the bracket profiles like those at COLD SPRING and CLAREMONT were quite simple, while brackets at TAYLOR'S MEADOW, HAREWOOD, and the GEORGE TATE HOUSE were more refined and singularly original. The brackets of early-nineteenth-century local houses became more complex, yet showed more similarity. A group of early-nineteenth-century profiled stair brackets in the Shepherdstown area are nearly identical and may all be the work of the same craftsman. These brackets, used at LANSDALE, GLENBURNIE, JOHN MOTTER HOUSE, GEORGE WEIS HOUSE, DAVID KEPLINGER HOUSE, CASPER WALPER HOUSE, DR. THOMAS HAMMOND HOUSE, and

SWEARINGEN-SHEPHERD HOUSE, have Chippendale-inspired cutaways and spurs that resemble furniture skirt expressions.

Another local stair bracket form is the incised bracket. Few eighteenth-century houses used incised stair brackets, but the WILLIAM SHENTON HOUSE has these ornate features. By the turn of the nineteenth century, however, the incised stair bracket became more commonplace throughout the county. The scroll-incised brackets at the SAMUEL MENDENHALL HOUSE, WOODBYRNE, and PROSPECT HALL are quite similar and date to the first decade of the nineteenth century. Similar designs can be seen in numerous houses in the Winchester, Virginia area. Another grouping of similar brackets are those in and around Shepherdstown at LINDEN SPRING, FERTILE PLAIN, CLISE-MCCAULEY HOUSE, JOHN KEARSLEY HOUSE, and SWEARINGEN-BAKER HOUSE, built between

Profiled stair brackets, Cold Spring, ca. 1800

Profiled stair bracket, William McSherry House, ca. 1810

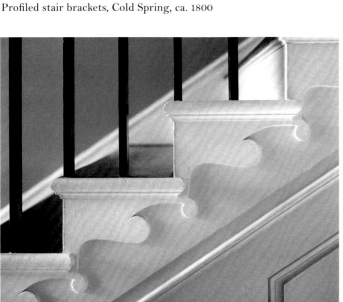

Profiled stair brackets, Woodlawn, 1850

Wave brackets, La Grange, 1845

1815 and 1819. Similar incised stair brackets can be found in the southern end of the county at CALEDONIA, SNOW HILL, and the DANIEL HAINES HOUSE. The incised brackets at the MICHAEL SHAULL HOUSE, HAZELFIELD, SHENSTONE, RIVERSIDE, and RICHWOOD HALL are nearly identical, as are those of PIEDMONT and THE HILL. In addition to handsome brackets, RICHWOOD HALL has the only example of decorative basket-mold profile on the landing returns in the county.

Later incised brackets include the highly developed ones at WESTERN VIEW, FALLING SPRING, and JACOB MOLER HOUSE, the design of which was taken from a plate in Owen Biddle's *The Young Carpenter's Assistant*.[2] The unusual spurred spiral profile of the brackets at ROSEMONT can also be found in the Winchester area, but they are not common in Jefferson County.[3]

In the 1830s, a new bracket design, the wave form, became popular throughout the county. This profile proved to be very adaptable to the more irregular stairs of the period. Wave brackets can be seen at CEDAR LAWN, CASSILIS, RICHARD MORGAN HOUSE, ASPEN HILL, CLAY HILL, ROCKLAND, WOODBURY, LA GRANGE, STRAITHMORE, and WOODLAWN, and in many other local houses. Craftsmen developed endless variations on this theme, at times carrying the waves horizontally across the landing face. The incised wave brackets at BEALLAIR show the variety and novelty employed by local craftsmen. A few houses, such as LITTLE ELMINGTON, MANTIPIKE, HOPEWELL, SOUTHWOOD, ROCK SPRINGS, MARTIN MILLER HOUSE, and VINEMONT, have plain, undecorated stair ends, but such lack of ornament is not common in the county.

Incised stair brackets, Swearingen-Baker House, 1815

Incised stair brackets, Linden Spring, ca. 1818

Incised stair brackets, John Kearsley House, 1816

Incised stair brackets, Mount Ellen, ca. 1818

Incised stair brackets, Clise-McCauley House, added 1819

Incised stair brackets, William B. Willis House, 1841

Decorative stair brackets, Rosemont, 1830

Decorative stair bracket, Falling Spring, 1834

Profiled stair brackets,
Harewood, 1770

Profiled stair brackets,
Wynkoop Tavern, ca. 1790

Profiled stair bracket,
George Tate House, 1800

Profiled stair brackets,
Casper Walper House, 1805

Profiled stair brackets,
Lansdale, ca. 1810

Profiled stair brackets,
John Motter House, ca. 1810

Profiled stair bracket,
Claremont, ca. 1818

Profiled stair brackets,
George Weis House, 1819

Incised and profiled stair bracket,
Beallair, 1850

Decorative stair brackets, Joseph
McMurran House, added ca. 1825

Decorative stair brackets,
Dr. John R. Hayden House, 1826

Decorative stair brackets,
Jacob Moler House, 1834

Decorative stair brackets,
Western View, 1831

Decorative stair bracket,
Jacob Moler House, 1834

Wave stair brackets,
Woodbury, 1833

Wave stair brackets,
Clay Hill, 1835

Wave stair brackets,
Staley Heirs House, 1835

Wave stair brackets,
Rockland, added ca. 1840

Walls and Ceilings

Five interior wall materials were used in the early houses surveyed: log, frame, plank, lapped plank, and masonry. Log walls were seen both plastered and exposed. The space between the logs was filled with diagonally laid stone or wood, called chinking, which was then daubed over with a mixture of clay, sand, and lime. In larger, more formal log houses, the log walls were plastered to achieve a more refined effect. In these cases the logs were lathed and plastered much the same way as frame walls.

Plank walls were employed to a great extent in the eighteenth century, but their use tapered out by 1815. Tongue-and-groove beaded planks of random width were set vertically to form a partition wall. They were placed into a groove cut in the flooring which was then covered by a molded strip. The partition was also nailed into a molded top piece that held the wall boards in place. Because the planks were only one inch thick, a receiving casing was used to bed and secure partition doors. With space at a premium in early houses, the plank wall had no

equal in economizing floor area. Plank walls were found in the Adam Link House, McPherson Mill House, Clise-McCauley House, Hopewell, Nathan Haines House, Samuel Mendenhall House, Snow Hill, and Michael Dorsey Mill House, among others.

Many houses also had lapped-plank partition walls, formed by overlapping boards that then had lath and plaster applied to them. The resulting wall would measure three to four inches in thickness. Exposed rough-hewn walls were generally reserved for basements, since their rugged appearance was not refined enough for living areas.

Masonry interior walls were commonly found in larger houses, even used for interior partition walls. These walls, certainly the most structurally substantial, were used to effect maximum stability. Joist spans could be reduced and floor deflection decreased by utilizing this relatively costly arrangement. Plaster was applied directly to the interior side of these masonry walls.

Exposed log walls and plank partition wall, Elmwood quarter

Plaster-covered frame wall above a lapped-plank basement wall, Cold Spring

In most cases, the walls and ceilings of the houses surveyed were finished with plaster. A few log houses and summer kitchens remained unfinished, but these were uncommon. The baseboard, or washboard as it was called, neatly resolved the junction of the floor and wall planes. The trim, including the washboards, chair rail, and casings, were affixed before the plaster was applied.

Decorative plaster was found in fewer than ten houses in Jefferson County. Some simple ceiling medallions were installed in local houses in the 1830s and 1840s. These finned, circular motifs were confined to the entry halls, usually surrounding a lantern hook. Houses such as the HENRY STRIDER HOUSE, JACOB MOLER HOUSE, WOODBYRNE, ROCKLAND, BARLEYWOOD, and the URIAH KERNEY HOUSE had these types of entry hall medallions. The fine medallions in the double parlor of HAPPY RETREAT are the only such pair in the county, and display unusual sophistication for the area.

Ceiling medallion, Happy Retreat

Plank wall and enclosed stair, Snow Hill

Chair rail and door casing, Piedmont

Paneled end wall, ca. 1780, Taylor's Meadow

Paneled end wall, Adam Link House, ca. 1795

Cornice detail showing gauge decoration, drawing room, Woodbyrne, ca. 1810

Unbalanced paneled wall, ca. 1765, Richard Morgan House

End wall paneling detail, ca. 1810, Woodbyrne

The most refined houses of the eighteenth century often had paneled walls. These wall types were the most elaborate and expensive. Hall-and-parlor houses typically employed paneled walls on the gable end of the hall in order to present the projecting corner stair as cohesively as possible. These paneled walls utilize a cornice, or crown molding, to resolve the juncture of the wall and ceiling. Crown molding was only found in houses with paneled walls.

Several examples of hall-and-parlor end walls include the Adam Link House, Nathan Haines House, Taylor's Meadow, and Melvin Hill. The fine paneled walls at Woodbyrne, built about 1810, are atypical of nineteenth-century construction, and the reason for this can be found in the will of Battaile Muse—which mandated this antiquated style for the house of his heir.[4]

By far the most ornate, refined, and architectural of the paneled walls in Jefferson County were built in the eighteenth century. The paneling at Harewood, Mount Eary, New Hopewell, the Nathan Haines House, and Traveler's Rest are the county's best examples. The detailing of these four houses is unusually formal compared to their neighbors and may have been designed by Jefferson County's resident architect, John Ariss, who lived near Summit Point from 1769 until his death in 1799. Only Traveler's Rest is known to have been planned by Ariss, but the other three houses have remarkable sophistication for their period in the Virginia backcountry. The construction dates of these houses coincide with Ariss's time in the county. In each case, the chimney wall of each house is sheathed by rigidly symmetrical panels. The formality of the paneling stands in stark contrast to the typical unbalanced treatments at houses such as Richard Morgan House and Taylor's Meadow, which predate Ariss's arrival to the area. By the last decade of the eighteenth century, paneled walls were uncommon in the county, as tastes shifted away from heavy Georgian elements. Large houses built after 1790, such as Elmwood and the George Tate House, would utilize plastered walls instead of paneled wall surfaces.

Paneled end wall of dining room, Harewood, 1770

Northwest corner of drawing room, Harewood

Cornice detailing, drawing room, Harewood

Plinth detail of truncated column, drawing room, Harewood

North wall, drawing room, Harewood, 1770

West wall, drawing room,
Harewood

Paneled chimney breast, Traveler's Rest addition design by John Ariss, 1781

End wall paneling, east parlor, Traveler's Rest, 1773

Parlor paneling, Nathan Haines House, ca. 1770

Opposite: Paneled end wall with later applied mantel, New Hopewell, 1774

Cornice detail, drawing room, New Hopewell, 1774

Paneled wainscot with later enlarged window and casing, New Hopewell, 1774

Doors

Like the other stylistic elements in the houses studied, doors speak of a time and place. Door detailing and construction also give valuable information about a house, such as its age and how particular rooms were used. This discussion of doors will be grouped by panel types.

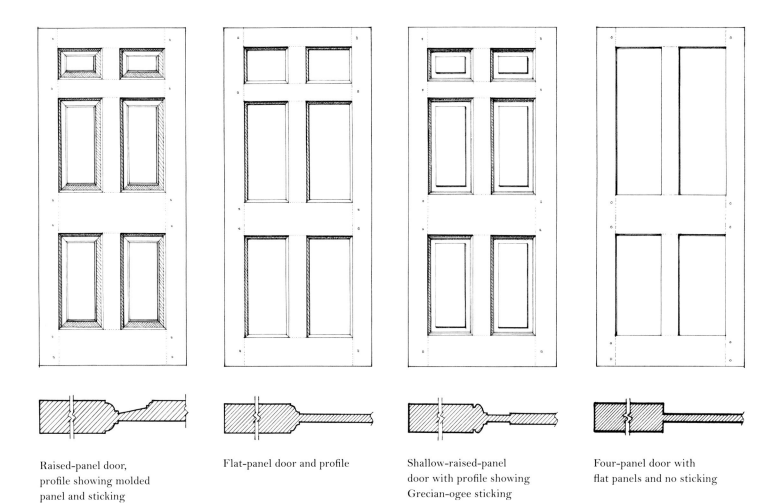

Raised-panel door, profile showing molded panel and sticking

Flat-panel door and profile

Shallow-raised-panel door with profile showing Grecian-ogee sticking

Four-panel door with flat panels and no sticking

Raised-Panel Doors

Doors with raised panels are the earliest surviving door types in Jefferson County. These will be defined as true raised-panel doors in order to differentiate them from later doors with shallow raised panels.

All extant local eighteenth-century houses were equipped with true raised-panel doors. Six panels is the most common arrangement for older doors, however, some of the earliest houses in the county, like the NATHAN HAINES HOUSE and AVON HILL, employed four-panel doors in secondary locations. At the CLISE-MCCAULEY HOUSE in Shepherdstown, a rare five-panel door was found. Though true raised-panel doors were used until about 1815, they are seen more commonly in eighteenth-century houses. The formal, hall side of these doors often had molded panels. A simple ovolo profile was planed across the edges of the

raised panel, to give a more refined appearance. Later raised-panel types are similar in construction to their antecedents, but for the molded sticking at the panel edge.

The sticking, a small molding on the edge of the panel opening, changed through time just as the other elements of detail packages evolved. Door thickness also changed by era. The earliest interior doors were usually made ⅞ inch thick. Over time, door thickness expanded likely due to the depletion of the local high-quality pine. Evidently, the younger woods used later on would warp at less than an inch. By the 1840s, the thickness of local interior doors had swelled to over an inch-and-a-half, requiring heavier hinges to bear the increased weight. The beefy doors at the MICHAEL FOLEY HOUSE, BARLEYWOOD, and BEALLAIR exemplify how much door thickness had changed in the nineteenth century.

Raised five-panel door, Christian Clise House, 1786

True raised panel door, Mountain View, ca. 1813

Reinforced Doors

Some exterior doors were reinforced on the back with vertical, horizontal, or diagonal boards. The reinforcing pieces were applied to the otherwise typical raised-panel door with many short rose-head nails. Known locally as Indian doors, these heavy entries hang on drive pintles and swing on long strap hinges that give rigidity to the whole. The common name is a fallacy, as the existing examples were built well after any conflicts with native peoples. In contrast to the other millwork of the stair halls where they are seen, these doors have an unrefined character. In the case of reinforced doors, security concerns appear to have trumped aesthetics. Examples of these doors are found at the Adam Link House, William Chapline House, Elmwood, Prospect Hall, Piedmont, and Woodbyrne. By 1815, reinforced entry doors were rarely used, except for basement entries and meat houses.

Vertically reinforced door, Elmwood, 1797

Diagonally reinforced door, Woodbyrne, ca. 1810

Flat-Panel Doors

Flat-panel doors have no raised element. They are simply adorned by a small molded sticking along the panel edge. These understated doors appear locally in the last decade of the eighteenth century and may have started as a reaction against the heavy look of the raised panel. PIEDMONT appears to be the first house in the county to incorporate doors with flat panels. In the stair hall the paneled door jambs have flat panels and the doors are hung with the flat side to the hall. Though the room side of the door had raised panels, the hierarchy favored the newer, flat panel. After this precedent, other houses, like ELMWOOD in 1797, CASPER WALPER HOUSE in 1805, and CALEDONIA in 1816, utilized the flat-panel door until the true raised panel was abandoned completely.

Flush-Panel Doors

The weather side of exterior doors began to be made with flush panels locally in the late eighteenth century. The panel had a bead that marked its outline against the stiles and rails, the vertical and horizontal members of the door. This design kept water from collecting on projecting or recessed pieces. For a brief time, between 1805 and 1815, flush-panel doors were used inside as well, as at THE BOWER and GLENBURNIE. At WOODBYRNE, flush-panel doors were employed throughout the first floor, but the older raised-panel types were used upstairs. Since the flush-panel was more stylish, the hierarchy of detailing can be seen in the door placement.

Flat-panel door, drawing room, ca. 1790, Piedmont

Flush-panel door and jamb, Piedmont

Shallow-Raised-Panel Doors

The most common panel configuration encountered during the survey was the shallow-raised panel. This panel has a rectangular panel expression that only slightly projects from the panel floor creating a small shadow line, but without the heavy projection of the true-raised panel. A small Grecian-ogee sticking ornaments the panel frame. These doors were popular from 1820 through 1840 and can be seen all over Jefferson County. Faux-graining was very common locally during this period. Examples of these doors with their original grain painted finishes intact can be found at WESTERN VIEW, JACOB MOLER HOUSE, GEORGE EICHELBERGER HOUSE, and ISAAC CLYMER HOUSE among others.

After 1840, the sticking was rarely applied, giving doors harder edges and a utilitarian look. The two-panel and four-panel doors of the 1840s and 1850s used this unadorned treatment with flat panels. As was discussed earlier in this chapter, the casings and mantels of this period were also stripped of most details. Some front doors of this later period were made with hipped panels. Again, this same panel type can be found on the mantels of the mid-nineteenth century.

Shallow-raised-panel door, Springland, 1835

Pair of eight-panel pocket doors, Woodbury, 1833

Pair of hinged eight-panel doors, Springland

Vertical two-panel door, Ripon Lodge, added ca. 1840

Faux-grain-painted six-panel door, George Eichelberger House, 1849

Vertical hipped two-panel door, Woodlawn, 1850

Four-panel door without stickings, Rose Hill, 1850

Hardware

Original hardware that was found still extant in the surveyed houses includes hinges, locks, escutcheons, firetool hooks, lantern hooks, shutter dogs, boot scrapers, and security bars. Both imported and locally made pieces can often be seen in the same house. Bar iron was being produced in Jefferson County by the mid-eighteenth century, so some of the earliest hardware was made with local materials.[5] However, with the arrival of the railroad and canal in the 1830s, hardware items were typically imported from urban areas of America and Europe.

Hinges

Three basic hinge types were used in Jefferson County in the eighteenth century. Locally made strap hinges were used on many larger doors, such as entry and basement doors. A flat bar of iron, like a strap, was nailed to the top and bottom of door, while the loop ends of the straps extended out from the edge of the door. These hinge ends rested on iron pintles driven into the door frame. Individual blacksmiths used slight variations on the basic strap hinge template. In general, the earlier varieties were thinner in profile than those being forged by the 1830s. This difference was likely due to the relative scarcity of the iron in earlier decades and the heavier doors used in later houses. Domestic strap hinges dating after 1815 often have decorative ends forming spades, hearts, or tails, in addition to being wider.

Another early hinge type, the H-and-L, was used in more formal areas, in place of the more utilitarian strap hinge. These two-piece hinges were screwed to the face of door with the door side forming an L shape and the combined vertical shafts of the two pieces forming an H. Larger forms of this hinge type were found on the most important doors. Fine early houses such as Elmwood, Adam Link House, Glenburnie, New Hopewell, Harewood, Snow Hill, and Taylor's Meadow utilized H-and-L hinges. Smaller versions were used on secondary spaces, though never in basements or attics. Many of these were made locally, though some were imported.

Knuckle hinges, similar to modern hinge designs, were used in the last decade of the eighteenth century and became the nearly universal domestic hinge by the early nineteenth century. Early knuckle hinges were smaller than the cast versions that would be common by 1830.

A few examples of lifting hinges were found, such as those in the John Rion House and at Sojourner's Inn. This hinge lifted the door slightly as it opened, allowing the door to swing over an obstruction, such as a carpet. The rounded hinge profile was routed to align with the casing bead, giving this arrangement a finely resolved appearance. By the end of the survey period, heavy cast hinges produced in cities, by Baldwin, E&T Company, Thos. Clark, and others, were being imported into Jefferson County.

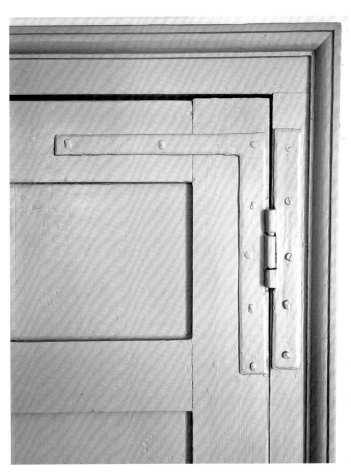

H-and-L hinge, Clise-McCauley House

H-and-L hinges, Taylor's Meadow

Opposite: Entry door hung with strap hinges, Prospect Hall

Locks

Iron rim locks and Dutch elbow locks were used throughout Jefferson County, from the earliest houses to the end of the survey period. The cases of these locks were typically fabricated of sheet iron and screwed to the face of doors. Period locks in the English tradition use knobs to operate the latchbolt. In this system, the latch bolt moves horizontally in and out of the keeper, which is mounted on the door frame. Only two houses used brass-plated rim locks: HAREWOOD and RICHWOOD HALL. These formal locks were certainly not a typical embellishment in the county. German or Pennsylvania-type locks, known as Dutch elbow locks, were far more common in the surveyed houses. These locks utilize a vertically moving latch bolt that closes on to a piece called a striker. The striker was either screwed into the door casing or driven into the frame. Though Dutch elbow locks were also made of sheet iron, their operating mechanisms are very different. The impetus for the level action of this lock is the force pushing down on a handles rather than twisting a knob. The spring-action levers used on Dutch elbow locks were decorated in a number of ways. Spoon-top levers, whose handle resemble a bent spoon, were the most common variety surveyed. Mushroom-capped levers were also plentiful. These locks had dome-topped handles that turn upward. A few houses near Charles Town, such as STRAITHMORE, RICHWOOD FARM, and LITTLE ELMINGTON utilized elbow locks with brass knobs, but these were not found in other parts of the county. Roughly half of the Dutch elbow locks had slide bolts that were used to lock an interior door from keyed entry.

Decorative nut filings on Dutch elbow locks can be used to identify locks made by the same artisan or shop. These filings could be done quickly and may have served as a trademark of sorts. A few locks were signed with the tradesman's name. Examples include a rim lock at SCOLLAY HALL stamped "John Post," and a wooden lock at BELVEDERE stamped "Vansands."

Some interesting escutcheon plates were found during the survey, likely executed by local blacksmiths. These decorative covers protected the keyhole and door from wear. The most

Rim lock, reverse side showing handle and escutcheon plate, Grantham-Stone House

Rim lock with brass mushroom-capped lever, Grantham-Stone House

Carpenter lock, ca. 1835, stamped "WR," Piedmont

Wooden stock lock, Belvedere

Wooden stock lock, Happy Retreat kitchen

unusual type, the double-turtle escutcheon, was used on the exterior doors of four houses: HAZELFIELD, THE ROCKS, WOODBYRNE, and PROSPECT HALL. Some of the earliest locks and hardware found during the survey were those at NEW HOPEWELL. The closet rim locks have filed corners and were engraved with bars resembling the British Union Jack flag. The handsome escutcheon plates with these locks were detailed with points and balls.

Keepers for box locks held the operative latch closed against the opening. A variety of keeper types were found including those that were driven into the frame like a pintle. Others were screwed in place, requiring modifications to the door casing in order for the plate to rest flat.

Imported Carpenter rim locks, named for English inventor James Carpenter, were used widely between 1830 and 1850. The lock's brass-edged keeper has the initials of the contemporary British ruler under Carpenter's name and, therefore, can be dated. Most of the Carpenter locks found locally are stamped "WR" for William Rex, King William IV who ruled from 1830 to 1837. A few "VR" keepers were found dating to Queen Victoria's reign. Many older local houses were updated with Carpenter locks during the 1830s and 1840s. American-made knockoffs of the Carpenter lock were also used widely in Jefferson County. These smaller pieces used less brass and therefore would probably have been less expensive. Wooden locks, called stock locks, were installed in basements and outbuildings where there was more moisture and rust was an issue. In addition, the pretense of a fine lock was unnecessary in these storage spaces.

Mortised locks, those with the lock mechanism hidden within the door stile, required thicker doors, like those found locally after 1840, to install the locking mechanisms. These locks were exceedingly rare in Jefferson County, with only BEALLAIR, WILD GOOSE, and BOIDESTONE'S PLACE having original sets. Remodeled by R. D. Shepherd in the 1840s, Boidestone's Place utilized brass mortised locks, likely made in Philadelphia or Boston. These locksets had a swinging brass keyhole cover and a delicate night-latch knob that activated a deadbolt.

Many houses were equipped with firetool hooks to the side of the firebox opening. Almost all of these delicate pieces have been lost. The fine brass hooks at FERTILE PLAIN and SPRINGLAND are rare survivors of a once standard detail.

"Union Jack" incised rim lock,
New Hopewell

Butterfly latch with exposed workings,
Henry Strider House

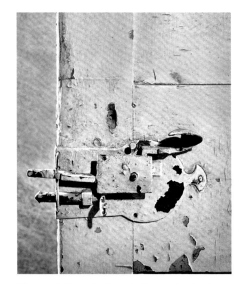

Unusual elbow lock with decorative back
plate, Adam Link House

Dutch elbow lock and striker, Woodbyrne

Dutch elbow lock with decorative nut filings
and end profile, Prospect Hall

Dutch elbow lock and striker, Fertile Plain

Decorative escutcheon plate, New Hopewell

Double-turtle escutcheon plate, Woodbyrne

Double-turtle escutcheon plate on exterior
door, Prospect Hall

Brass mortise lockset with night-latch knob and decorative eschutcheon cover, Boidestone's Place

Decorative thumb latch, Wynkoop Tavern

Spade-topped thumb latch, Grantham-Stone House

Bean-topped thumb latch, Rosemont

Moravian-type screw-off handle, or "coffee-grinder" lock, with decorative escutcheon plate, Adam Link House

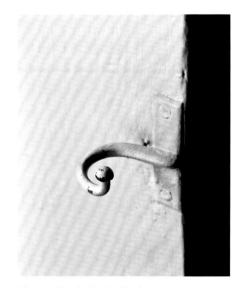

Firetool hook, Springland

Backplate to missing firetool hook, Henry Strider House

Simple wooden door latch, Elmwood quarter

Rudimentary wooden door latch with locking spring action, Springdale barn

Windows

Large twelve-over-twelve window, second-floor bedroom, Mountain View

Natural light was an essential resource to the county's early residents in their domestic affairs and the production of household goods. Window glass was an expensive material, so most houses had a limited number of windows. Houses generously endowed with large windows signaled the owners' wealth, as "light became a sensory metaphor for genteel society."[6]

The early houses of Jefferson County used double-hung sash windows to light and ventilate the rooms. Window sashes are held in place by stops, interior wooden pieces covering the sides and top of the sashes. In the oldest houses the stops were ornamented with molded backbands, but generally they were simply beaded. The window jambs of masonry houses were usually splayed, or angled, to allow more light into the room through the thick exterior walls. Jambs were paneled in more formal homes and left flat in others.

In a few early houses, such as the Daniel Bedinger House and Harewood, paneled jambs operated as interior shutters. These shutters could be unfolded and extended across the window and retracted and pocketed into the jamb cavity when not needed.

In some masonry buildings, like Harewood, Linden Spring, Glenburnie, and Fertile Plain, window seats were placed under the windowsill. The area under the sill was sometimes decorated with an underpanel, as at Riverside, Woodlawn, Rion Hall, and Belvedere. Muntins, or sash bars, held the glazing in place. These molded wooden bars were wider in the earliest houses and then became thinner and more delicate thereafter, even after the pane size became significantly larger. Interior windowsills were often molded and decorative. In many houses predating 1820, the windowsill was integrated with the chair rail wrapping the room. A few early houses did not have cased window openings, such as Prato Rio, the Peter and Jacob Williamson House, and the McPherson Mill House. In these houses a backband was applied to the window stop. A plaster bead at the intersecting jamb corner marked the transition plane of the wall.

Several of the county's transverse-hall houses, and some later houses, were built with windows that also functioned as access portals to porches. In these houses the lower window sash rested on a pair of low jib doors. These doors could open when the sash was raised, allowing access to first- or second-floor porches. Houses like Western View, Woodbury, Ripon Lodge, and Barleywood utilized these windows.

Developed window casing with paneled wainscot, The Hill

Central window with sidelights and operable jib doors, Woodbury

Six-over-six window with splayed and paneled jambs, seatback, and undersill, Harewood

Nine-over-six window with flat-paneled jamb, Rockland

Decorative arched-top closet, Mount Ellen

Panel-doored bedroom closet, Piedmont

Chimney cupboard, Beallair

Glass-doored cupboard with radiused top and butterfly shelving, Elmwood

Cupboards and Closets

Many of the surveyed houses had built-in closets and cupboards. These storage areas were placed beside chimneys, an arrangement that made good use of the recesses to either side of the chimney mass. As with other design elements, closets ranged greatly in sophistication. Glass-doored china cupboards were found at Taylor's Meadow, Elmwood, and Woodbyrne. These cupboards have radiused tops and concave profiled shelves, known as butterfly shelving. The shell motifs applied below the keystone detail of the Taylor's Meadow cupboards are unusually decorative for the area. More typical cupboards were rectangular and utilized flat-panel doors, like those at Rock Spring, Retirement, and the John Kearsley House. These solid-door cupboards used plain shelving and were usually found in dining rooms and bed chambers. Utilitarian plank-doored storage closets were common in work areas such as kitchens and basements, like those found at the Toole-Van Sant House.

A few houses like Beverly, Harewood, and the John Ware House had closets with windows. These storage areas were lit by thin gable-end windows. Only the most stylish local houses had this type of closet.

Shallow storage closets were sometimes worked into the space at the edge of the chimney perpendicular to the wall. These chimney cupboards may have been designed to store fire materials such as kindling. Others were intended for clothes storage, as they were fitted with pegboards for hanging garments.

Pair of flat-panel bedchamber cupboards, Glenburnie

Standard mantel-wall closet, Grantham-Stone House

Glass-doored cupboard with unusual shell appliqué, paneled end wall, Taylor's Meadow

Pair of plank-door kitchen cupboards, Toole-Van Sant House

Mantels

Mantels are major interior features of Jefferson County's early houses and their detailing showcases the palette of local millwork. As we have seen in other interior elements, design preferences changed over time. For the purpose of organizing the hundreds of different mantels into categories, the discussion will be chronological, beginning with the earliest extant examples.

In the period before 1790, many chimney walls did not have mantels—instead using paneling that covered the end wall and surrounded the firebox. Corner fireplaces were also generally paneled, as at the Richard Morgan House and the Nathan Haines House, unless they were located in bedchambers. In secondary rooms without paneling, mantels with raised-panel friezes and shallow shelves were common. By the end of the colonial period, as paneling became less common, mantels replaced paneling as the significant chimney-wall feature. Early mantels, like those at the Wynkoop Tavern and Mount Misery, mimicked the raised panels of their predecessors. As evidence of the emerging preference for flat panels, the Dr. Nicholas Schell House and Piedmont used both raised- and flat-panel mantels in various rooms.

Mantel wall, Cold Spring, ca. 1800

Radiused panel bedroom mantel, Harewood, 1770

Paneled harp mantel, Dr. Nicholas Schell House, 1787

Console-bracket with guttae, John Rion House, ca. 1785

Flat-panel mantel with dentil band, Happy Retreat, ca. 1785

During the 1790s, paneled walls would only be seen in the last hall-and-parlor houses; other houses of the period used mantels. Some of the early mantels combined unique features as the local joiners developed Jefferson County's vernacular forms. The Dr. Nicholas Schell House, Wynkoop Tavern, and William Chapline House in Shepherdstown featured raised-panel harp mantels in which the frieze ends are curved. Console brackets, dentil bands, and end blocks all provided areas for experimentation during this decade, though the resulting pieces were quite restrained. As with doors of the county, houses utilized flat-panel mantels more during this last decade of the eighteenth century.

Flat-panel mantel with end block fluting, Piedmont, ca. 1790

Paneled harp mantel, William Chapline House, 1795

Fluted console bracket mantel, George Tate House, 1800

Decorative punch band, George Tate House, 1800

Paneled frieze mantel, Wynkoop Tavern, ca. 1790

The first two decades of the nineteenth century were a golden age for Jefferson County's interior detailing. Mantels became more interesting and diverse during this period, incorporating features like dentil bands that refined chimney pieces. Excellent examples can be seen at Hazelfield, Hopewell, Rock Springs, Richwood Hall, George Tate House, and The Rocks. Decorative medallions were also used in great numbers on end blocks and occasionally on frieze blocks. The mantels at Glenburnie, George Weis House, John Motter House, Casper Walper House, Hopewell, Prospect Hall, Linden Spring, William Burr House, Belvedere, and Hazelfield had these decorative flourishes. Other mantels were adorned with console brackets, like those at Simeon Shunk House, Springwood, Cold Spring, Piedmont, and others. Mantel reeding was another popular design element of the 1810s, especially in the areas near Middleway and Leetown. Houses such as the Michael Shaull House, Frederick Rosenberger House, Peter Sharff House, Medley Springs, Vinemont, Grantham-Stone House, and William Stephenson House have at least one reeded mantel. Interesting gouge-work designs, where decorative geometric designs were cut into the millwork, were used frequently and added to the growing vocabulary of local detailing. Gouge-work detailing is found in the mantels of the George Tate House, William McSherry House, The Hill, Daniel Haines House, Mount Ellen, Richwood Hall, and Conrad Kounslar House—all located in the area from Charles Town to Middleway. These houses share similarities in masonry and massing, and evidence suggests that the builders of these houses did not stray to other parts of the county. Few examples of truly national designs from this period were found in the county. Only the parlor mantels at Linden Spring and Swearingen-Baker House approach national styles. During this period, buildings in Jefferson County were still subject to the designs of local interpretation, not imported urban styles or strict copying from plan books.

Mantel center block with decorative star appliqué below clipped punch-and-key band, Hopewell, ca. 1810

Mantel center block with decorative sunburst appliqué, Belvedere, ca. 1818

Opposite: Sunburst frieze and end block mantel, Linden Spring, ca. 1818

Medallion end block with fan frieze appliqués, Casper Walper House, 1805

Medallion end block with clipped and punched band, Hopewell, ca. 1810

Reeded end block with clipped punch band, Rock Springs, ca. 1810

Flat-panel end block and reeded columnette, Grantham-Stone House, ca. 1810

Flat-panel end block and fluted columnette, George Reynolds House, 1812

Console-bracket mantel, Simeon Shunk House, ca. 1813

Fluted end block with decorative punch band over crossette casing, Snow Hill, 1813

Detail of paneled frieze, Mountain View, ca. 1813

Reeded end block with gauged frieze band, Mountain View, ca. 1813

Medallion with gouge-work band,
Hazelfield, 1815

Fluted end block with Wall-of-Troy band,
Hazelfield, 1815

Medallion frieze with punch-and-dentil
band, Glenburnie, ca. 1815

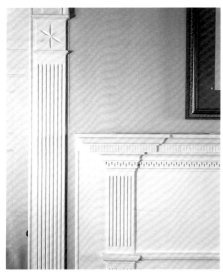

Fluted end block with Wall-of-Troy band,
Richwood Hall, ca. 1815

Paired columnette mantel,
Swearingen-Baker House, 1815

Gouge-band decorated mantel,
Frederick Rosenberger House, ca. 1815

Gouge-band and inlaid end block mantel,
Caledonia, 1816

Gouge-band decorated mantel,
Henry Boteler House, 1817

Projecting molding end block,
Belvedere, ca. 1818

Through the 1820s, mantels began to lose the flourishes of the previous decades. Plain end blocks and friezes typify this period. Geometric motifs like those at RIVERSIDE and CASSILIS were restrained compared to the busy gauge-work and dentils of the previous decades. Symmetrical moldings were being used now on mantels, replacing stepped pieces. This occurrence coincides with that trend in casings locally. The Greek Revival influence slowly crept into local mantel designs, so that by the 1830s, mantels boasted great finned friezes and freestanding columns. The mantels at SOUTHWOOD, WOODBURY,

SNIVELY TAVERN, COOL SPRING, JACOB MOLER HOUSE, and ROSE-MONT typify these bold features. Knife-shelf mantels, popularized in Winchester, became common in Jefferson County during this decade.[7] The deeply recessed bands below the shelves of these mantels give them an unmistakable profile. Popular frieze designs, like hipped panels and convex scallops, made mantels of the 1830s striking and complex by local standards. Mantels at BOIDESTONE'S PLACE, CLAY HILL, SCOLLAY HALL, MANTIPIKE, the WILLIAM B. WILLIS HOUSE, and COOL SPRING have these interesting frieze designs.

Reeded columnette and end block, Sharff-Homar House, ca. 1820

Finned frieze mantel, Clay Hill, 1835

Reeded end block and columnette,
York Hill, ca. 1825

Knife-shelf mantel,
Dr. John R. Hayden House, 1826

Finned frieze detail,
Daniel Bedinger House, added ca. 1830

Paneled columnette mantel with projecting
end block, Rosemont, 1830

Bull's-eye end block with scallop frieze,
Jacob Moler House, 1834

Knife-shelf mantel,
Jacob Moler House, 1834

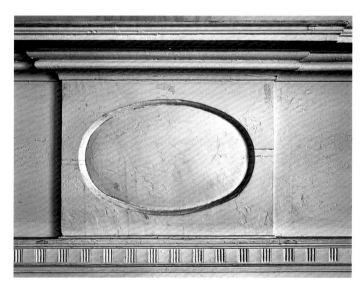

Mantel center block with incised oval above gouge band,
Riverside, ca. 1822

Knife-shelf mantel, Woodbury, 1833

1835–1850

As if in reaction to the busy detailing in the local mantels of the 1830s, simplicity again pared the millwork of the following decade to its essential elements. The thin and sinuous forms of local late-Federal mantel detailing gave way to the plain friezes, thick pilasters, and dense projecting shelves of the Greek Revival. These mantels differ little from those of the same period in other parts of the eastern United States. With the ease of communication to urban areas, Baltimore via train and Washington by canal, national details had finally subdued the vernacular Jefferson County style. By this time, even marble mantels were being imported and used in fine local houses such as Happy Retreat, Beallair, Ripon Lodge, Glenwood, and Vinton.

The progression of interior details in the early houses of Jefferson County reflects the changing tastes of its citizenry, as well as the culture and prosperity of the county over time. During the earliest years of settlement through the Revolution, details were slow to change, but the economic upswing in the 1790s through 1820 fostered greater diversity of ornament. Transportation developments in the 1830s allowed wider access to the materials and designs of urban areas. In this way, the interior details of the surveyed houses encapsulate Jefferson County's history.

Pair of scallop frieze mantels, Boidestone's Place, 1835

Hipped frieze panel detail,
Ripon Lodge, ca. 1835

Hipped frieze panel, Springland, 1835

Decorative oval end block,
Isaac Clymer House, 1835

Greek Revival marble mantel,
Happy Retreat, 1842

Hipped frieze paneled mantel,
Boidestone's Place, ca. 1850s

Gothic-inspired marble mantel, Ripon Lodge, ca. 1850s

Chapter Nine

The End of Local

Arrival of the Railroad and Canal, 1835–1850

Shenandoah Street, Harpers Ferry

New Transportation Systems

Beginning in the late 1820s through the 1830s, protracted battles between the Chesapeake and Ohio Canal and Baltimore and Ohio Railroad caused delays to both projects. These competing interests were on a collision course, in a race to reach the narrow strip of land across the Potomac River from Harpers Ferry. At this location, the railroad would have to pass over the canal in order to bridge the river and reach the Virginia shore. Positive leadership changes, direct orders from the Maryland legislature, and skilled negotiations with landowners had been necessary to achieve such a complicated intersection. And yet, in 1835, just as the Baltimore and Ohio Railroad sat poised to cross the Potomac at Harpers Ferry and push west, it faltered. A malaise had settled over the company as it dealt with the

mounting costs of the project. It would take a new voice to focus investors on the urgency of the matter.

Into the breach stepped an erudite Baltimore lawyer, John Pendleton Kennedy. Kennedy had strong ties to Jefferson County, which was home to his family. His parents and brothers had moved to a farm near Charles Town in 1820. Brother Andrew Kennedy built Cassilis in 1834, while another brother, Philip, lived at The Bower. In addition to being an attorney, Kennedy was also a writer and had based his popular novel, *Swallow Barn*, on his memories of summers in Jefferson County.[1]

In a speech given in the fall of 1835, Kennedy urged the board of directors and shareholders of the Baltimore and Ohio Railroad, and the Maryland government to forge ahead. The

Baltimore and Ohio needed an infusion of new capital in order to accomplish its mission. As a strong supporter of the railroad, Kennedy inspired public confidence in the need for progress, which in turn helped raise additional funds from the Maryland legislature. With his persuasive speech and published letters, Kennedy changed public opinion and reenergized the railroad's push for the Ohio River.[2] The railroad's arrival and progress would have broad effects on the culture and architecture of Jefferson County.

The people of the county understood that changes were coming via the railroad. As resident John Yates wrote in 1831, "An event of great magnitude is coming home to us and is being constructed to unite Baltimore with the Ohio River."[3]

Finally, the railroad—after enduring nagging problems with its bridge over the Potomac and the transfer from horse-drawn to locomotive power—offered regular service to Jefferson County in 1835. Meanwhile, the Chesapeake and Ohio Canal had skirted the county border on the Maryland side of the Potomac River and made its way past Shepherdstown. At this same time, another rail line, the Winchester and Potomac Railroad, crossed the county, connecting Harpers Ferry to Winchester in 1836. The arrival of these two new transportation systems, along with the new National Turnpike in Maryland, brought profound changes to the local economy and culture that can be clearly seen in the residential and commercial architecture of that time.

John Pendleton Kennedy by Matthew Wilson, collection of the Maryland State Archives

Harper's Ferry, Va. Lithograph showing the Baltimore and Ohio Railroad bridge crossing over the Chesapeake and Ohio Canal, ca. 1850, author's collection

George Zurger House, ca. 1840, Washington Street, Bolivar, built with pressed brick

Henry Gannon House, ca. 1846, Union Street, Bolivar, west elevation

Armory worker Charles Hoddinott House, 1846, 103 Gilbert Street, Bolivar

Armory worker Joshua Cavalier House, 1850, Rowles Street, Bolivar

Armory worker William Wentzell House, 1852, Rowles Street, Bolivar

Armory worker Joseph Wentzell House, 1852, Rowles Street, Bolivar

As one might expect, the rate of building in the county increased around the time of the arrival of the railroad and canal. Nowhere in Jefferson County can this be seen more dramatically than in the towns of Harpers Ferry and Bolivar. The National Armory had been the major employer in Harpers Ferry during the early years of the nineteenth century. However, it was the anticipation of and, finally, the arrival of these transportation systems that launched a building boom there. Most of the existing buildings in the lower town of Harpers Ferry date from this period. By 1830, the population of Harpers Ferry caught up to Shepherdstown, which had previously been the county's most populous town. At mid-century, Harpers Ferry was by far the largest settlement in the county, with over fifteen hundred inhabitants.[4] Neighboring Bolivar also experienced population growth through the 1840s and 1850s.

Though the ravages of the Civil War and frequent flooding destroyed scores of buildings in the two towns, many mid-nineteenth-century houses remain. Generally constructed of hard brick not found in the rest of the county, the houses of Harpers Ferry and Bolivar tend to be smaller than the farmhouses of the era. Features such as corbeled and sawtooth brick cornices typify these buildings. House plans were similar to those in the surrounding area, though some of the housing built by and for the armory workers utilized the old hall-and-parlor plan. The use of this antiquated plan had more to do with economy of space than an aesthetic preference for the arrangement.

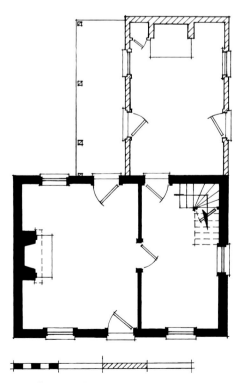

Joseph Wentzell House, first-floor plan

The plans of the large commercial buildings of Harpers Ferry broke ranks with contemporary domestic templates in the area. In Shepherdstown and Charles Town, former houses were retrofitted for commercial uses. Where new stores were built, house forms were employed. In Harpers Ferry, the gable-fronted White Hall Tavern of Potomac Street and the six-bay three-story Marmion-Graco Building on Shenandoah Street are examples of the divergent designs of commercial architecture.

Since shale is the dominant stone strata near the meeting of the Shenandoah and Potomac rivers—exposed shale outcroppings and cliffs can be seen all around the lower town in Harpers Ferry—it was used extensively in the two proximate towns. This material fractures into small, thin pieces and must be densely packed into fine layers as masonry. This signature stonework distinguishes Harpers Ferry and Bolivar structures from the limestone ones in the rest of the county.

Much of the brick employed in the two towns during this period also differed from what was typical locally. Harder pressed brick was used widely in residential construction in Harpers Ferry and Bolivar. The regular shape and color of this material gave the houses a contemporary look. Pressed brick was often used just for the front elevation and laid in common bond. In contrast, none of Shepherdstown's or Middleway's houses and only one house in Charles Town was found to have used pressed brick. Later in the 1840s, machine-made brick fired in the industrial kilns of Baltimore brickyards was brought in to Harpers Ferry aboard trains and canal boats.[5]

Another foreign influence at work on the local architecture came to Harpers Ferry by way of the National Armory. Armory employment increased steadily in this period, with the number of workers doubling from 1821 to 1847.[6] The government had difficulty keeping up with the expanding housing requirements of both laborers and officers. Over the years, an assortment of small and large houses were designed for the armory personnel by nonlocal architects and builders. Armory superintendents George Rust and John Symington brought new ideas about building into the county. Superintendent Rust built a number of houses in Harpers Ferry for armory workers. His design called for a twenty-eight-by-twenty-two-foot house, one-and-a-half stories with a rear kitchen wing. In 1833, Rust sent drawings for these houses for approval from the U.S. Department of Ordnance in Washington.[7] These small brick houses became the templates for armory worker housing built in Harpers Ferry and Bolivar. Among other improvements, Superintendent Symington directed the construction of the Paymaster's Quarters on Camp Hill.[8] With its interior chimneys and a shallow pyramidal roof, this house shares few similarities with the local houses of the time.

Along with the railroad, the canal hastened the transformation of the local architecture by importing urban-made goods to Jefferson County. The Chesapeake and Ohio Canal's predecessor, the Potomac Company, shipped materials downriver, but rarely up. The Potomac Company relied on in-river channels and sluices to move Shenandoah Valley produce to market, so it was almost exclusively exporting materials downstream. Many of the early boats used to deliver products to Georgetown were dismantled once they had reached the city.[9] With the development of the the still-water Chesapeake and Ohio Canal, this trade became a two-way enterprise. By the 1830s, valley flour was sent to Georgetown on boats that returned with loads of urban materials.

The introduction of distant building materials reflected changes that were occurring nationally. As transportation systems rapidly improved and expanded, building goods traveled from urban markets to more rural areas. Items such as bricks, lath, window sashes, hinges, locks, nails, roofing slate, flooring, and even framing members could be delivered to places like Jefferson County in a cost-effective manner.[10] Trains would unload materials in Harpers Ferry, Duffields, Halltown, Kearneysville, Charles Town, Summit Point, or Rippon. Canals could off-load near Harpers Ferry, Shepherdstown, or at various ferries along the two rivers. The availability of these imported materials fueled a slow progression from a local vernacular style into a more regional style. The continuing presence of the railroad and canal connecting those areas ensured they would share more and more stylistic similarities. For example, the local ascendancy of the Greek Revival style paralleled its trajectory in other rural areas in America.

Marmion-Graco Building, 1845, Shenandoah Street, Harpers Ferry, east gable with shale outcroppings behind

Opposite: Paymaster's Quarters (Lockwood House), 1848, Fillmore Street, Harpers Ferry

Thin shale coursing typifies the stonework in Harpers Ferry

George Sappington House, 1843, East Washington Street, Charles Town, west elevation laid in common bond with pressed brick

Later Farmhouses

The post-1835 farmhouses of the county were different from those that had come before in two significant ways—detailing and scale. With immediate access to the Baltimore market via the new train, and cheap transportation by way of the canal to Georgetown, both builders and owners were given new freedom to expand the detailing available locally. Marble and decorative plaster pieces were brought in from Baltimore along with contemporary urban millwork. These stylistic touches broke with the local tradition of conservative, restrained interior detailing. Exterior detailing, however, remained understated, with the exception of molded brick cornices. Molded bricks may also have been produced in Baltimore and sold to masons by local suppliers. Houses such as VINTON and HAPPY RETREAT showcased new features like marble mantels, decorative plaster, and operable interior transoms. FRUIT HILL, built in 1842 for Baltimore native Archibald Robinson, hid its ornate Greek Revival interior behind a reserved facade. Only the finely detailed entry would

hint at the high level of development inside. ROSE BRAKE, along with many other houses of the 1850s, utilized narrow paired windows. This new feature was especially popular in the areas in and around Charles Town.

The other significant change to Jefferson County houses coinciding with the arrival of the railroad, turnpike, and canal was that of scale. Vinton, Happy Retreat, and many later Jefferson County houses are larger than those of the pre-railroad era. Mammoth houses such as EASTWOOD, GLENWOOD, and WALNUT HILL included expansive double-parlors and large bedchambers. In 1842, R. D. Shepherd completed his country estate WILD GOOSE near Shepherdstown. After completion, Shepherd's house boasted more than nine thousand square feet of finished space. The house used a unique side-hall plan tucked behind the main building mass, interior chimneys, and unbalanced elevations. In this way, the amorphous plan of Wild Goose was a harbinger of what would become popular locally in the Victorian era.

Walnut Hill (Humphreys–Alexander House), ca. 1845, Halltown vicinity, Historic American Buildings Survey photograph, 1937

Fruit Hill (Archibald Robinson House), 1842, Shepherdstown vicinity, oblique view

R. D. Shepherd of Wild Goose, 1860, carte de visite, courtesy of the Massachussetts Historical Society

Wild Goose (R. D. Shepherd House), 1842, Terrapin Neck area, east elevation

Westwood (Hugh Nelson Pendleton House), 1848, Summit Point vicinity, east elevation oblique view

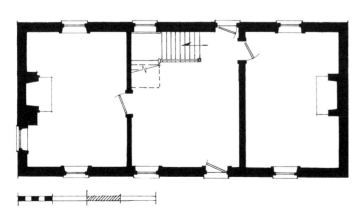

Wayside (Daniel Hefflebower Jr. House), 1844, Rippon vicinity, first-floor plan

Detail of window casing corner block, Westwood

Other novel plans were emerging in the county, such as the tripartite arrangement of WESTWOOD, built in 1848 by Hugh Nelson Pendleton. This house broke with local tradition by having a two-bay main block with flanking wings. The intricately carved corner blocks on the exterior casings of the house were almost certainly imported from one of the coastal cities. The triparte house type was popular in parts of eastern Virginia and North Carolina in the nineteenth century but never caught on in Jefferson County.[11] WAYSIDE, built in 1844 for Daniel Hefflebower Jr., used the locally rare four-bay front to develop a plan with an unusually wide entry hall that served as a parlor. By the mid-nineteenth century, houses like FEDERAL HILL, LOST DRAKE, and the YATES-BEALL HOUSE showcased asymmetrical floorplans and alternating wall planes. These buildings along with others in the county show the influence of imported national trends.

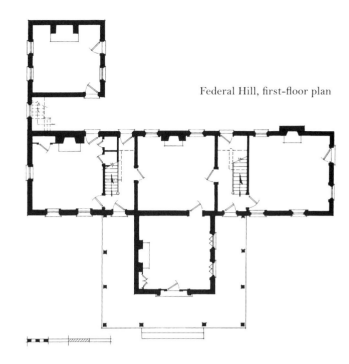

Federal Hill, first-floor plan

Federal Hill (George W. Eichelberger Jr. House), 1850, Bloomery vicinity

Of course, not all houses built after 1835 challenged local traditions. Five-bay center-hall houses were still constructed, though fewer than before. Late examples of five-bay center-hall houses include Bear Garden (1836), William S. Kerney House (1837), Shannon Hill (1840), Windward (1842), La Grange (1845), and Rose Hill (1850).

After 1835, side-hall farmhouses were also less popular than they had been earlier in the century. Examples of post-1835 side-hall houses include Ore Banks (1838), Head Spring (1840), Martin Miller House (1841), Elmwood-on-Opequon (1842), Fruit Hill (1842), and the George Eichelberger Sr. House (1849). The vertical design of Barleywood, however, does not share the squarish orientation of most local Greek Revival houses. Though built in 1842, Barleywood has details that typify houses of an earlier era, such as its Flemish bond front and tall jack arches. False chimneys placed on the hall side of the building balance the facade. Like most of the earlier plans, the side-entry began to lose favor locally by midcentury.

William S. Kerney House, 1837, Shepherdstown vicinity, south elevation

Windward (James Marshall House), 1842, Shepherdstown vicinity, south elevation

Ore Banks (John Brien Heirs House), 1838, Bakerton vicinity, east elevation

Martin Miller House, 1841, Shepherdstown vicinity, oblique view

George Eichelberger Sr. House, 1849, Bloomery vicinity, north elevation, oblique view

Opposite: Barleywood (Robert McPherson House), 1842, Leetown vicinity, oblique view

Eastwood (John Humphreys House), 1841, Kabletown vicinity, east elevation

The transverse hall plan also began to decline in popularity after 1835. Only three pure examples, EASTWOOD (1841), WILLIAM B. WILLIS HOUSE (1841), and HAPPY RETREAT (1842), were built after 1835. The large house near Rippon now known as GLENWOOD was constructed with a modified transverse-hall plan in 1845 for wealthy planter, Charles S. Taylor. Meanwhile, the earlier RICHARD MORGAN HOUSE was changed from hall-and-parlor plan to transverse-hall in the 1840s by new owner John McEndree. CLAYMONT COURT, having burned, was rebuilt by Bushrod C. Washington in 1838. Though the wings of the house were enlarged, the original plan of the 1822 main block remained. These six residences were the last in the county to utilize the distinctive transverse-hall arrangement.

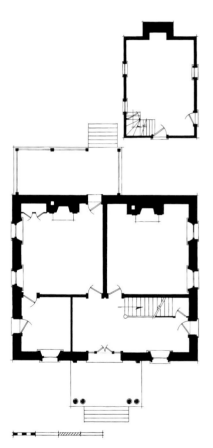

William B. Willis House (Locust Grove), 1841, Summit Point vicinity, north elevation

William B. Willis House (Locust Grove), first-floor plan

Happy Retreat (Isaac Douglas House), 1842, Charles Town, north elevation

Rion Hall (William Lucas House), 1836, Halltown vicinity, oblique view

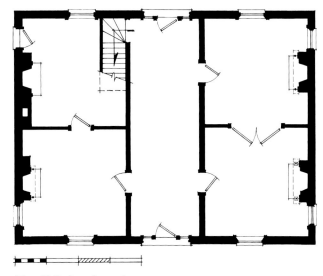

Rion Hall, first-floor plan

Uriah Kerney House (Rose Lawn), 1840, Kearneysville vicinity

In Jefferson County, the only house type to retain its prevalence after 1835 was the three-bay center-entry house. The continued popularity of this house form can be explained by the plan's versatility. Elevationally, the three-bay arrangement worked well with the Greek Revival vocabulary of details, as it was symmetrical and could accommodate hipped or gable roofs. And, as discussed in previous chapters, improvements had been made by the 1830s to introduce more light to the central hall, making these houses more inviting. Formal three-bay examples include RION HALL (1836), STONE FELS (1836), BYRDLAND (1836), ROCK HALL (1837), URIAH KERNEY HOUSE (1840), JOHN SNYDER SR. STOREHOUSE (1843), RANSON HOUSE (ca. 1845), ASPEN HILL (1846), VINTON (1848), MICHAEL FOLEY HOUSE (1848), MAPLE TREE FARM (ca. 1850), WOODLAWN (1850), BEALLAIR (1850), ROBERT ENGLISH HOUSE (1850), and GAP VIEW. Less formal examples of the three-bay form include JAMES WALKER HOUSE (1839), MARY NOLAND HOUSE (ca. 1845), and TULIP HILL (1847).

Square in form like many transverse-hall houses, VINTON retains the standard center-hall plan. The stair hall in this house, however, is divided into two chambers, front and back. This broken hall arrangement is the only known example in the county, though this plan was popular in areas of Virginia and North Carolina. Vinton has four finished floors with kitchen and dining room in the basement. The expanded scale of the house, at nearly eight thousand square feet, contrasts with the compact early houses in the area.

The John B. Packett House, known to locals as LOCUST HILL, was one of Jefferson County's great antebellum homes until it was destroyed by fire in 1973. This square brick structure had interior chimneys and a hipped roof like neighboring Springland and Cassilis. And like the latter house, Locust Hill had a modified center-hall plan with two large parlors at the rear.

John Snyder Sr. Storehouse, 1843, Duffields

Ranson House, ca. 1845, Ranson vicinity,
Historic American Buildings Survey photograph, 1937, demolished

Aspen Hill (James G. Hurst House), 1846, Ranson vicinity

Michael Foley House, 1848, Reedson vicinity, south elevation

Entry hall with stair in rear, Vinton (Jacks-Manning House),
1848, Charles Town vicinity

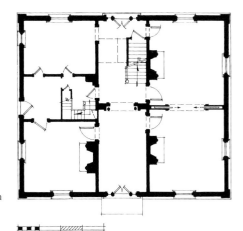

Vinton (Jacks-Manning House), first-floor plan

Robert English House, 1850, Halltown vicinity

Gap View, altered ca. 1845, Bardane vicinity, east elevation

Locust Hill (John B. Packett House), 1844, Charles Town vicinity, photograph courtesy of Robert Orndorff

One of the last large center-hall houses to be built during this period is Beallair. Additions were begun in 1850 by Lewis Washington to the early hall-and-parlor house. Washington's building campaign lasted for six years resulting in a patchwork of attached structures. The main block of the building, however, is a three-bay center-hall form. This brick section also utilizes a transverse-hall at the rear to house the stair. Freight logs detail building materials that Washington imported by way of the Winchester and Potomac Railroad that included lath, planking, stone, lyme, and doors.[12] The building presents details like stepped gables, shallow-pitched roof, and projecting end pilasters that would be favored features of the local architecture until the Civil War.

Of the post-1835 houses surveyed, the three-bay center-entry house was the most common type. These houses make up more than a third of the existing 1835–1850 farmhouses. Even after mid-century, the three-bay arrangement would be used to fashion hundreds of small tenant houses on farms throughout the county. Thus, the center-hall house remained a favored plan from the 1770s, when it was introduced to the area by Harewood, to the end of the nineteenth century—a testament to its functionality and the enduring appeal of the familiar.

The houses of Jefferson County built after 1835 until the middle of the century embody a shift in the local culture and architecture. The arrival of the railroad and canal not only

Beallair (Crow-Washington House), 1850–1855, Halltown vicinity

introduced imported materials to the county, but also new national ideas and fashions. The Greek Revival style reached its apex locally after the railroad and canal entered the county, availing foreign building and decorative materials to local craftsmen. Previously, the expense of moving such products from the coastal cities could only be borne by the wealthiest residents. With the canal and railroad in direct competition for cargo, the price of moving freight became reasonable. The escalating production of urban industry further lowered the costs of architectural items and other desired materials. The new transportation systems also brought the towns of Harpers Ferry and Bolivar increased population and wealth. These towns developed their own building vocabulary during this era, distinguishing them from the county's other population centers. The National Armory brought regional influences to the county in the form of formal house designs for officers and vernacular types for the armory workforce. Outside the county's crowded towns, more experimental plans were developed in response to the new access Jefferson County had to the outside world. These new house types, introduced locally in the 1840s and 1850s, would evolve into the county's Victorian houses of subsequent decades.

Entry hall with stair hall behind, Beallair (Crow-Washington House)

Andrew Hunter House, 1842, Charles Town, side-hall house with shallow roof and later round turret

Lane-Cordell House, 1850, Charles Town, two-bay front elevation with interior chimneys and shallow-hipped roof

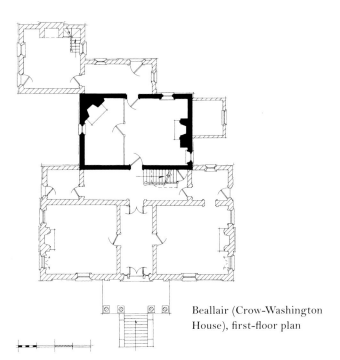

Beallair (Crow-Washington House), first-floor plan

337

Conclusion

Parlor at Clay Hill with detailing of the 1830s

The Survey Reviewed

The Shindler Family Bible, printed in German and used by the family through the nineteenth century. Their brick hall-and-parlor home stands in Shepherdstown. Courtesy of Historic Shepherdstown and Museum.

Prospect Hall mantel detail, from the brick center-hall house built for the Hunsikers, who were of German ancestry

Before documenting the two-hundred and fifty houses included in this book, I was already familiar with many of the historic resources in Jefferson County. I had visited a number of its celebrated houses and working farms during my decade of residence in the area. Unlike Henry Glassie, who compiled his landmark work *Folk Housing in Middle Virginia* as an outsider, I knew my way around the survey area.[1] But because of this familiarity, I held preconceived notions about the county's early buildings, and expected the survey to reaffirm those ideas. There were surprising discoveries, however, that caused me to reassess this peculiar architecture and what has long been believed about it.

From the 1730s to the end of the American Revolution, the houses in what is now Jefferson County varied significantly in plan, scale, and formality. Most of the extant houses from this period do not conform to the prevailing house types used in later decades. Early surveys and documents confirm this observation by describing numerous unusual dwellings from the colonial era. At this time, the county was sparsely populated with families of differing cultural backgrounds, so a degree of architectural divergence would be expected. What was startling to find was that within a decade nonconforming houses almost ceased to be built. Beginning in the 1790s, a narrow range of residential architecture took shape. A handful of established house types would dominate the county's landscape for more than four decades. The desire of varying cultures to assimilate after the Revolution may have contributed to the reduction of house forms. Still, the rate of conformity during this period is astonishing, with 96 percent of the houses fitting neatly into the four dominant house categories.

The survey also documents the material preferences of the county's early residents, and there is no indication that ethnicity dictated choice of building material. This evidence should lay to rest the local belief that settlers of German ancestry favored stone, while those of English lineage used brick. The same lack of cultural bias held for plan types. Trends of material and plan usage seem to be equally distributed among the county's European ethnic groups during the study period.

Surprising, too, was the degree to which Jefferson County's pre-1835 residential architecture differed from neighboring counties. Though certain facets of the local vernacular can be found in other counties, the unique complement of building materials, forms, and details are indigenous only to this small area. Certain house types such as the flurküchenhaus and the two-door house, seen in adjacent Washington County, Maryland, and Frederick County, Virginia, were not found at all in Jefferson. Likewise, the transverse-hall plan, popular in Jefferson, is not present in those counties. Though different from its neighbors, the survey findings point to a remarkably consistent building culture countywide. However, this architectural equilibrium ended in

Nathan Haines House, hall-and-parlor house built of stone for English Quakers, photograph courtesy of Robert Orndorff

Beverly (Beverly Whiting House), center-hall brick house and stone outbuildings built for family of English heritage, photograph courtesy of Robert Orndorff

the 1830s when new transportation systems brought economic and cultural change to the area.

The people of Jefferson County would be transformed by the developments of the mid-1830s, and that transition is embedded in the architecture of the period. Railways cut their way through the county, linking the residents with the goods, markets, and ideas of distant places. The easy flow of foreign materials through the county changed the complexion of the local economy and society. By the following decade, the same phenomenon was happening across the eastern seaboard. In a few short years, the eyes of the country turned from the eastern cities to the western plains in search of the nation's future. It was clear that new opportunities for economic prosperity lay in that direction. Architectural historian, Richard Guy Wilson, writes that the architecture of Virginia's Tidewater and Piedmont regions stagnated at this very moment, losing "self-confidence."[2] Wilson concludes that the energy and vitality of the state's architecture

left during the 1840s and 1850s with the outflow of youthful talent to points west and south. Certainly the economic hardships presented by the recession of 1837 and poor crop years in the intervening decade could have caused a loss of faith in those tobacco-dependent areas. However, in the Shenandoah Valley, and in Jefferson County in particular, building continued at a steady pace, indicating that the residents remained confident in the local economy. The Baltimore and Ohio Railroad and Chesapeake and Ohio Canal provided easy access to urban markets for farmers, merchants, and tradespeople. In addition, the United States Armory in Harpers Ferry was a major economic engine, a source of jobs and cash for the immediate area. The people of the county also knew that the local land was still among the most fertile and productive in the country. In 1840, Jefferson County had the second highest wheat yield of all Virginia counties. Other major wheat producing counties of the antebellum period were Rockingham and Loudoun, both of which are

Piedmont and its springhouse

significantly larger in area than Jefferson. Despite its small size, Jefferson County became Virginia's top wheat producer by 1860.[3] New agricultural practices and the rapid expansion of slave labor on the county's farms during this period help to explain the mounting crop yields. The burgeoning prosperity is evidenced in the large houses built in the county from 1835 to 1850, but more interestingly, in the more substantial construction of the average farmhouse. Brick became a standard building material, not just for wealthy residents, and was even used to construct common outbuildings. Yes, the local architecture changed during the 1830s and 1840s, but it did not lose its energy. If anything, the ambition and scale of local residences were heightened. What was lost in the buildings of that period was a measure of the local accent, as the county was absorbed into the larger region. The major trends of this era—mass production, technological innovation, population growth and westward expansion—worked in tandem to dilute the local vernacular.

Portico with Greek Revival elements such as octagonal columns, Hefflebower Mill House

William Norris House (Riggs-Stiles) features Greek Revival detailing

The catalog of existing structures assembled for this book tells a story of the first one hundred years of development of the lower Shenandoah Valley. The survey data clearly show the prevailing house types used by the early residents and builders, identifying common house forms, but few outlying plans. The construction materials and techniques used in these buildings was also highly standardized, and the similarities held for interior and exterior detailing. So, after answering the question of what was built, we must now ask why were the houses so similar. Why wasn't there more variation? To answer that question, more work must be done in neighboring counties. Many of these counties in West Virginia, Maryland, Virginia, and Pennsylvania have made cursory surveys of their historic resources. These records indicate significant differences in residential forms from those standing in Jefferson County. The books now available on the local architecture of Berkeley County, West Virginia, Washington County, Maryland, Frederick County, Virginia, and Clarke County, Virginia, provide a good starting place for comparison. However, comprehensive studies of these areas, with full documentation of all early buildings, would allow for a much better understanding of how and why the buildings of these areas developed, and how and why they differ from those distilled forms in Jefferson County. Even studies of noncontiguous counties, if comprehensive in nature, would open up rich areas for comparative study and exploration.

The historic houses of Jefferson County hold stores of information about previous residents and builders. The distinctive group of houses documented in this study, however, tells a unique story of this area's settlement, innovation, cultural assimilation, and integration into the larger region. Single buildings, no matter how wonderful, cannot fully impart this rich heritage. Only the group as a whole can tell the nuanced history of our shared home. We are very fortunate to have so many beautiful and useful artifacts of our early history remaining in the county. These houses contain details of the everyday lives of those who settled the land and forged our history. The early houses of Jefferson County represent an uncommon vernacular and are truly treasures worth celebrating and preserving.

Woodlawn, built for John C. Wiltshire in 1850

Opposite: View to the water gap in the Blue Ridge Mountains from the porch of Elmwood

List of Surveyed Houses

William Green House
Archaeological Site
Terrapin Neck area
ca. 1740

Hyatt's House
Kearneysville vicinity
ca. 1760

Hopewell
(Jacob Hite House)
Leetown
ca. 1760

White House Tavern
(Dr. John McCormick House)
Summit Point vicinity
ca. 1760

Reginal Green House
Archaeological Site
Terrapin Neck area
ca. 1765

Richard Morgan House
(Springdale)
Shepherdstown vicinity
ca. 1765

Peter Burr House
Bardane vicinity
ca. 1765

Harewood
(Samuel Washington House)
Charles Town vicinity
1770

Nathan Haines House
(Fairfax Grant Stock Farm)
Summit Point vicinity
ca. 1770

Thornborough House
(Millbrook)
Shepherdstown vicinity
ca. 1770

Michael Burkett House
(Fruit Hill Stone House)
Shepherdstown vicinity
ca. 1770

Avon Hill
(Wormley-Gantt House)
Kabletown vicinity
ca. 1770

Traveler's Rest
(Gen. Horatio Gates House)
Kearneysville vicinity
1773

New Hopewell
(Thomas Hite House)
Leetown vicinity
1774

Prato Rio
(Hite-Lee House)
Leetown
ca. 1775

Rees-Daniels House
Middleway vicinity
ca. 1775

James Keith House
(Mount Eary)
Wheatland vicinity
ca. 1775

Van Deever-Orndorff House
Shepherdstown vicinity
ca. 1775

Taylor's Meadow
(John Taylor House)
Moler's Crossroads vicinity
ca. 1780

Bellevue
(Joseph Van Swearingen
House)
Shepherdstown vicinity
ca. 1780

Ralph Wormley House
(The Rocks kitchen)
Long Marsh Run
ca. 1780

Josiah Swearingen House
(Willowdale)
Shepherdstown vicinity
ca. 1780

Morgan's Spring
(Abel Morgan House)
Shepherdstown vicinity
ca. 1780

Robert Harper House
Harpers Ferry
ca. 1780

Fenton Hill
(William Little House)
Bloomery vicinity
ca. 1780

Traveler's Rest
(Ariss Addition)
Kearneysville vicinity
1781

Peter and Jacob Williamson
House
Shepherdstown vicinity
1782

John Rion House
(Henkle House)
Halltown vicinity
ca. 1785

McPherson Mill House
(John McPherson House)
Rippon vicinity
ca. 1785

Thomas Campbell House
Middleway vicinity
ca. 1785

Cato Moore House
(Crooked House)
Shepherdstown
1786

Christian Clise House
Shepherdstown
1786

Dr. Nicholas Schell House
Shepherdstown
1787

Philip Sheetz House
Shepherdstown
1790

Piedmont
(Dr. John Briscoe House)
Charles Town vicinity
ca. 1790

Wynkoop Tavern
(Selby-Hamtramck House)
Shepherdstown
ca. 1790

Mount Hammond
(James Hammond House)
Kabletown vicinity
ca. 1790

Van Swearingen House
(Springwood)
Terrapin Neck area
ca. 1790

Sojourner's Inn
(William Buckles House)
Ridge Road vicinity
ca. 1790

Daniel Bedinger House
Shepherdstown
ca. 1790

Thomas Crow House
(Beallair)
Halltown vicinity
ca. 1790

Jacob Staley House
(Parran House)
Shepherdstown
1791

Philip Shutt House
Shepherdstown
1792

Spaulding-Baker House
Shepherdstown
1793

William Hendricks House
(Quinn House)
Moler's Crossroads vicinity
1794

William Chapline House
(Chapline-Shenton House)
Shepherdstown
1795

Fouke-Shindler House
Shepherdstown
ca. 1795

Hurston
(James Hurst House)
Bardane vicinity
ca. 1795

Boggess-Moore House
Harpers Ferry vicinity
ca. 1795

The Rocks
(Ferdinando Fairfax House)
Long Marsh Run
ca. 1795

Altona
(Abraham Davenport House)
Charles Town vicinity
ca. 1795

Adam Wever House
(Vinemont)
Leetown vicinity
ca. 1795

Opposite: William Hendricks House interior

Richard McSherry House
(Retirement)
Leetown vicinity
ca. 1795

John Cowan House
Cat-Tail Run
ca. 1795

Henry Fizer House
Shepherdstown
ca. 1795

Adam Link House
Uvilla vicinity
ca. 1795

John Locke House
(Star Lodge)
Charles Town
1796

Elmwood
(Edward Lucas III House)
Shepherdstown vicinity
1797

Caty Hill House
Shepherdstown
ca. 1797

Joseph McMurran House
(Hill Building)
Shepherdstown
1798

Michael Cookus House
Shepherdstown
1798

York Hill
(John Snyder House)
Ridge Road
ca. 1798

Abraham Merchant House
Middleway
ca. 1798

George Tate House
(Tate-Fairfax-Muse House)
Charles Town
1800

Beverly
(Beverly Whiting House)
Charles Town vicinity
ca. 1800

Rankin-Hammond-Lee House
Charles Town
ca. 1800

Hezakiah Swearingen House
(Lost Drake)
Terrapin Neck area
ca. 1800

John Peyton House
(Aspen Hill)
Ranson vicinity
ca. 1800

White House Tavern
(Andrew McCormick addition)
Summit Point vicinity
ca. 1800

Vanderveer-Butler House
Kearneysville vicinity
ca. 1800

Cold Spring
(Robert Lucas III House)
Shepherdstown vicinity
ca. 1800

Abraham Shepherd Jr. House
(Neck Farm)
Terrapin Neck
ca. 1800

Riverside
(Nathaniel Craighill House)
Bloomery vicinity
ca. 1800

John Eckhart House
(Scollay Hall)
Middleway
ca. 1800

Melvin Hill
(Thomas Melvin House)
Duffields vicinity
ca. 1805

Weltzheimer Tavern
Shepherdstown
ca. 1805

David Hestant House
(Snively Tavern)
Shepherdstown
ca. 1805

Elizabeth Strider House
Middleway
ca. 1805

Moses Smith House
Middleway vicinity
ca. 1805

Casper Walper House
(Pleasance)
Walper's Crossroads
1805

The Bower
(Adam Stephen Dandridge
House)
Opequon Creek
1806

Willoughby W. Lane House
Charles Town
1808

William Tate House
Charles Town
1808

Jacob Haines House
Shepherdstown
ca. 1808

William McSherry House
(Siebert House)
Middleway
ca. 1810

William Stephenson House
(Ramsey Tavern)
Middleway
ca. 1810

Daniel Fry House
Middleway
ca. 1810

Shaull-Smith House
Middleway
ca. 1810

Bell-Fry House
Middleway
ca. 1810

Woodbyrne
(George Muse House)
Long Marsh Run
ca. 1810

Prospect Hall
(Peter Hunsiker House)
Opequon Creek
ca. 1810

Lansdale
(Thomas Lafferty House)
Ridge Road
ca. 1810

Samuel Mendenhall House
(Aylmere)
Summit point vicinity
ca. 1810

Reichstine-McElroy House
Shepherdstown
ca. 1810

Burr-McGarry House
Ridge Road
ca. 1810

John Motter House
Shepherdstown
ca. 1810

Hopewell
(William Little Jr. House)
Bloomery vicinity
ca. 1810

Michael Dorsey Mill House
(Viand Cottage)
Bloomery vicinity
ca. 1810

Rock Springs
(Hendricks-Snyder House)
Ridge Road
ca. 1810

Henry Strider House
(Strider House)
Harpers Ferry vicinity
ca. 1810

Grantham-Stone House
(Virginia Inn)
Middleway
ca. 1810/1828

Fair View
(Rees-Daniels-Flood House)
Middleway vicinity
ca. 1810

John Line Building
Shepherdstown
ca. 1810

Medley Springs
(Carver Willis House)
Middleway vicinity
ca. 1810

George Reynolds House
Moler's Crossroads vicinity
1812

Rockland
(James Verdier House)
Walpers Crossroads vicinity
1812

Snow Hill
(John Hurst House)
Leetown vicinity
1813

Simeon Shunk House
(Calico Cottage)
Kearneysville vicinity
ca. 1813

Mountain View
(James W. McCurdy House)
Kabletown vicinity
ca. 1813

Swearingen-Baker House
Shepherdstown
1815

Hazelfield
(Ann Stephen Dandridge
Hunter House)
Bardane vicinity
1815

The Hill
(Matthew Frame House)
Charles Town vicinity
ca. 1815

Thornborough-Billmyer House
(Millbrook)
Shepherdstown vicinity
ca. 1815

Richwood Hall
(Smith Slaughter House)
Charles Town vicinity
ca. 1815

The Hermitage
(Fairfax-Ranson House)
Kabletown vicinity
ca. 1815

William Burr House
Bardane vicinity
ca. 1815

Glenburnie
(James Glenn House)
Ridge Road
ca. 1815

Valentine Dust House
Bolivar
ca. 1815

Vinemont
(Wever-Beall House)
Leetown vicinity
ca. 1815

Frederick Rosenberger House
(Round Top)
Middleway vicinity
ca. 1815

Michael Shaull House
(Green Spring)
Middleway vicinity
ca. 1815

Nicholas Shaull House
(Thorn Hill)
Middleway vicinity
1816

John Kearsley House
(The Manse)
Shepherdstown
1816

Caledonia
(William Cameron Sr. House)
Cameron's Depot
1816

Hammond-Lee House
Charles Town
ca. 1816

Henry Boteler House
Shepherdstown
1817

Merchant-Janney House
Middleway
1817

Retirement
(Richard McSherry House)
Middleway vicinity
ca. 1817

Henry Garnhart House
Schaeffer's Crossroads
ca. 1817

Gap View
(Walter Baker Jr. House)
Bardane vicinity
ca. 1817

Catherine Weltzheimer House
Shepherdstown
ca. 1817

Claremont
(Thomas Beall House)
Halltown
ca. 1818

Daniel Haines House
Summit Point vicinity
ca. 1818

John Moyer House
Middleway
ca. 1818

Linden Spring
(Michael Moler House)
Moler's Crossroads vicinity
ca. 1818

Fertile Plain
(Samuel Harris House)
Moler's Crossroads vicinity
ca. 1818

Mount Ellen
(Benjamin Davenport House)
Summit Point vicinity
ca. 1818

Belvedere
(William Tate Heirs House)
Charles Town vicinity
ca. 1818

George Weis House
Shepherdstown
1819

Clise-McCauley House
Shepherdstown
1819

Shenstone
(Harfield Timberlake)
Summit Point vicinity
1820

Fouke-Shindler House
(Conrad Shindler House)
Shepherdstown
ca. 1820

Peter Sharff House
(Sharff-Homar House)
Leetown vicinity
ca. 1820

Jacob Allstadt House
Harpers Ferry vicinity
ca. 1820

Feagan's Mill House
Wheatland vicinity
ca. 1820

Mount Eary
(Dr. Alexander Straith House)
Wheatland vicinity
ca. 1820

Swearingen-Shepherd House
(Springwood)
Terrapin Neck area
ca. 1820

Hiser-Shugart House
Shepherdstown
ca. 1820

David Keplinger House
Shepherdstown
ca. 1820

John Graham Tavern
Bolivar
1821

Blakeley
(John Augustine Washington II
House)
Charles Town vicinity
1821

Claymont Court
(Bushrod Corbin Washington
House)
Charles Town vicinity
1822

Marcus Alder House
(Boidestone's Place)
Terrapin Neck area
ca. 1822

Riverside
(Samuel Lackland House)
Bloomery vicinity
1822

Reverend James Black House
Moler's Crossroads vicinity
1823

Willoughby W. Lane House II
Charles Town
1824

Pleasant Valley
(Abraham Snyder House)
Duffields vicinity
1825

York Hill II
(John Snyder, Jr. House)
Ridge Road
ca. 1825

George Fulk House
Shepherdstown vicinity
ca. 1825

Yates-Beall House
Ranson vicinity
ca. 1825

Mount Pleasant
(Charles Yates-Aglionby
House)
Bardane vicinity
ca. 1825

Fizer-Morrow House
(Tabler Store)
Shepherdstown
ca. 1825

William Smallwood House
Harpers Ferry
ca. 1825

Allemont
(William Craighill House)
Bloomery vicinity
ca. 1825

Abraham Hefflebower House
Kabletown vicinity
1826

William Grove House
Duffields vicinity
1826

Hefflebower Mill House
Kabletown vicinity
1826

Dr. John R. Hayden House
(Lee-Longsworth House)
Bolivar
1826

Aspen Pool
(John Unseld House)
Moler's Crossroads vicinity
1827

Daniel Hefflebower Jr. House
Kabletown vicinity
1828

Daniel Morgan House
(Rose Brake)
Shepherdstown vicinity
1828

Samuel Cameron House
Cameron's Depot
1829

Cedar Lawn
(John T. A. Washington House)
Charles Town vicinity
1829

Thomas Campbell Jr. House
Middleway vicinity
1829

Clearland
(Thomas Abell House)
Duffields vicinity
1829

Straithmore
(John Myers House)
Wheatland vicinity
1830

Little Elmington
(Samuel Howell House)
Charles Town vicinity
1830

Rosemont
(James Wysong House)
Charles Town vicinity
1830

Conrad Kounslar House
Middleway
1830

James Webb House
Charles Town
1830

Isabella Engle House
(Terrace Lawn)
Duffields vicinity
ca. 1830

Toole-Van Sant House
Terrapin Neck vicinity
ca. 1830

Sharff-Homar House
Leetown vicinity
ca. 1830

Dust-Downey House
Bolivar
ca. 1830

Western View
(James Hite House)
Kearneysville vicinity
1831

Richwood Farm
(Thomas B. Washington
House)
Charles Town vicinity
1831

Snively Tavern
(Hestant-Snively House)
Shepherdstown
1832

Cool Spring
(Thomas Griggs Jr. House)
Summit Point vicinity
1832

Sharff Storehouse
(Jefferson John House)
Leetown vicinity
1832

Warner Briscoe House
Shepherdstown
1832

Hawthorne
(John Thomson House)
Summit Point vicinity
1832

Mantipike
(Thomas G. Baylor House)
Leetown vicinity
1833

Rawleigh Moler House
Bakerton vicinity
1833

Southwood
(Edward Southwood House)
Kearneysville vicinity
1833

Woodbury
(Henry St. George Tucker
House)
Leetown vicinity
1833

Jacob Moler House
(Bel-Mar)
Zoar vicinity
1834

Cassilis
(Andrew Kennedy House)
Charles Town vicinity
1834

George W. Moler House
Bakerton vicinity
1834

Falling Spring
(Jacob Morgan House)
Shepherdstown vicinity
1834

Altona II
(Braxton Davenport House)
Charles Town vicinity
1834

Sallie Melvin House
Bakerton vicinity
1834

Clay Hill
(John Hurst II House)
Ranson vicinity
1835

Springland
(Samuel Lackland House)
Charles Town vicinity
1835

Boidestone's Place
(Alder-Shepherd House)
Terrapin Neck area
1835

Staley Heirs House
Shepherdstown
1835

William Orndorff House
(Staub's Cottage)
Shepherdstown vicinity
ca. 1835

Ripon Lodge
(William F. Turner House)
Rippon vicinity
ca. 1835

Isaac Clymer House
Bakerton vicinity
1835

Beeler's Mill House
Kabletown vicinity
ca. 1835

Rion Hall
(William Lucas House)
Halltown vicinity
1836

William Burr House II
Bardane vicinity
1836

William S. Kerney House
Shepherdstown vicinity
1837

Ore Banks
(John Brien Heirs House)
Bakerton vicinity
1838

Claymont Court
(rebuild and expansion)
Charles Town vicinity
1838

James Walker House
(Lemen Cabin)
Shepherdstown vicinity
1839

Allstadt Ordinary
Harpers Ferry vicinity
1839

James A. Kerney House
Kearneysville
1840

Uriah Kerney House
(Rose Lawn)
Kearneysville vicinity
1840

Lost Drake
(Kennedy-Shepherd House)
Terrapin Neck area
ca. 1840

Michael Cookus House II
Shepherdstown
ca. 1840

Swearingen-Quigley House
(Willowdale)
Shepherdstown vicinity
ca. 1840

Cowan-Roper House
Cat-Tail Run
ca. 1840

The Hermitage II
(Fairfax-Ranson-Chew House)
Kabletown vicinity
ca. 1840

Eastwood
(John Humphreys House)
Kabletown vicinity
1841

William B. Willis House
(Locust Grove-Shirley Farm)
Summit Point vicinity
1841

Martin Miller House
(Old Walper Place)
Shepherdstown vicinity
1841

John Stephens House
Shepherdstown
1841

Wild Goose
(R. D. Shepherd House)
Terrapin Neck area
1842

Happy Retreat
(Isaac Douglas House)
Charles Town
1842

Fruit Hill
(Archibald Robinson House)
Shepherdstown vicinity
1842

Windward
(Marshall Hall)
Shepherdstown vicnity
1842

Barleywood
(Robert McPherson House)
Leetown vicnity
1842

Elmwood-on-Opequon
(Anthony Kennedy House)
Leetown vicinity
1842

John Snyder Sr. Storehouse
Duffields
1843

George Sappington House
Charles Town
1843

Scollay Hall
(Eckhart-Scollay House)
Middleway
1843

Wayside
(Daniel Hefflebower Jr. House)
Rippon vicinity
1844

Dr. Thomas Hammond House
Shepherdstown
1844

Andrew Hunter House
Charles Town
1845

La Grange
(John Hurst IV House)
Ranson vicinity
1845

David Keplinger House II
Shepherdstown
ca. 1845

Walnut Hill
(Humphreys-Alexander House)
Halltown vicinity
ca. 1845

George Fulk House II
(George Fulk Heirs)
Shepherdstown vicinity
ca. 1845

Gap View
(James L. Ranson House)
Bardane vicinity
ca. 1845

Rock Springs II
(John Snyder Jr. House)
Ridge Road
ca. 1845

Yates-Beall House II
Ranson vicnity
ca. 1845

Mary Noland House
Shepherdstown vicinity
ca. 1845

Aspen Hill
(James G. Hurst House)
Ranson vicinity
1846

Springdale
(John H. McEndree House)
Shepherdstown vicinity
ca. 1846

Tulip Hill
(Humfrey Keyes House)
Bloomery vicinity
1847

Westwood
(Hugh Nelson Pendleton
House)
Summit Point vicinity
1848

Vinton
(Jacks-Manning House)
Charles Town vicinity
1848

Ripon Lodge II
(William F. Turner House)
Rippon vicinity
1848/1852

Michael Foley House
Reedson vicinity
1848

Paymaster's Quarters
(Lockwood House)
Harpers Ferry
1849

George Eichelberger Sr. House
(Willowdale)
Mechanicstown vicinity
1849

Rose Hill
(John Marshall House)
Kearneysville vicinity
1850

Federal Hill
(George W. Eichelberger Jr.
House)
Mechanicstown vicinity
1850

Robert English House
Halltown vicinity
1850

Woodlawn
(John C. Wiltshire House)
Bardane vicinity
1850

Strider-Harley House
Middleway
1850

Beallair
(Crow-Washington House)
Halltown vicinity
1850–1855

Green Hill
(George B. Beall House)
Zoar vicinity
ca. 1850

Notes

Chapter One
From Settlement to Refinement: Houses in Context

1. Warren Hofstra, *The Planting of New Virginia: Settlement and Landscape in the Shenandoah Valley*. (Baltimore and London: The Johns Hopkins University Press, 2004), 5, 7–8.
2. Hofstra, *The Planting of New Virginia*, 86.
3. Warren Hofstra, *The Great Valley Road of Virginia*. (Charlottesville and London: University of Virginia Press, 2010), 67.
4. Hofstra, *The Planting of New Virginia*, 101, 174.
5. Otis K. Rice, *The Allegheny Frontier: West Virginia Beginnings, 1730–1830*. (Lexington: University of Kentucky Press, 1970), 20.
6. David Hackett Fischer, *Albion's Seed: Four British Folkways in America*. (Oxford and New York: Oxford University Press, 1989), 567.
7. Charles A. Hulse, "The William and Reginal Green Sites: The Archaeology of Two Mid-18th Century Farms in the Lower Shenandoah Valley." (Shepherdstown, WV: Shepherd University Cultural Resource Management Report #59, 2009), 8, 12, 15.
8. Hofstra, *The Planting of New Virginia*, 142, 159.
9. "The Jonathan Clark Notebook, July–Aug. 1786," transcription in Peggy S. Joyner, *Northern Neck Warrants and Surveys*, 4:171–173; original document located in the Manuscripts Division, Clark-Hite Papers, The Filson Historical Society, Louisville, KY, 168–69.
10. Rice, *The Allegheny Frontier*, 22.
11. Hofstra, *The Planting of New Virginia*, 274, 284.
12. *The Journal of Nicholas Cresswell, 1774–1777*. (New York: The Dial Press, 1924), 49.
13. *The Journal of Nicholas Cresswell*, 47.
14. Hofstra, *The Planting of New Virginia*, 276.
15. "The Jonathan Clark Notebook," 171.
16. Robert J. Kapsch, *The Potomac Canal: George Washington and the Waterway West*. (Morgantown: West Virginia University Press, 2007), 47.
17. Christ Reformed Church records, Shepherdstown, WV, microfilm collection Scarborough Library, Shepherd University, BX9567.S5 C4.
18. James D. Dilts, *The Great Road: The Building of the Baltimore & Ohio, The Nation's First Railroad, 1828–1853*. (Stanford: Stanford University Press, 1993), 218.

Chapter Two
Early Farmhouses, 1735–1815

1. "United States House Tax Book for the District of Berkeley County for 1798," transcribed by Don C. Wood. (Martinsburg, WV: Berkeley County Historical Society, 2003), 1–24.
2. David Hackett Fischer and James C. Kelly, *Bound Away: Virginia and the Westward Movement*. (Charlottesville: University of Virginia Press, 2000), 49–50.
3. Richard L. Bushman, *The Refinement of America: Persons, Houses, Cities*. (New York: Vintage Books, 1993), 105.
4. David Hackett Fischer, *Albion's Seed: Four British Folkways in America*. (Oxford and New York: Oxford University Press, 1989), 477.
5. Mills Lane, *Architecture of the Old South, North Carolina*. (Savannah: Beehive Press, 1997), 20. Thomas T. Waterman, *Dwellings of Colonial America*. (Chapel Hill: University of North Carolina Press, 1950), 4.
6. R. W. Brunskill, *Vernacular Architecture: An Illustrated Handbook*. (London: Faber and Faber, 2000), 112.
7. Mutual Assurance Society of Virginia. Declarations and Revaluations, 1796–1966, Accession 30177. Business records collection, The Library of Virginia, Richmond.

8. Carolyn Murray-Wooley, *Early Stone Houses of Kentucky*. (Lexington: University of Kentucky Press, 2008), 66, 72, 96, 110, 124, 150, 162.
9. Gabrielle M. Lanier and Bernard L. Herman, *Everyday Architecture of the Mid-Atlantic: Looking at Buildings and Landscapes*. (Baltimore and London: The Johns Hopkins University Press, 1997), 16–21.
10. Sydney George Fischer, *The Struggle for Independence*. (Philadelphia: J. B. Lippincott & Co., 1908), 2:194.
11. Fischer and Kelly, *Bound Away*, 260.
12. Berkeley County Historical Society, *Architectural and Pictorial History of Berkeley County*. (Martinsburg, WV: Berkeley County Historical Society, 1991), 1:291–92.
    Maral S. Kalbian, *Frederick County, Virginia: History Through Architecture*. (Winchester, VA: Winchester–Frederick County Historical Society, 1999), 13.
13. "The Jonathan Clark Notebook, July–Aug. 1786," transcription in Peggy S. Joyner, *Northern Neck Warrants and Surveys*, 4:163–85. Original document located in the Manuscripts Division, Clark-Hite Papers, The Filson Historical Society, Louisville, KY.
14. Donald Jackson and Dorothy Twohig, ed., *The Diaries of George Washington*, vol. 2, 1766–1770. (Charlottesville: University of Virginia Press, 1976), 271.
15. Mutual Assurance Society of Virginia. Declarations and Revaluations, 1796–1966, Accession 30177. Business records collection, The Library of Virginia, Richmond.
16. William Salmon, *Palladio Londinensis: or The London Art of Building*, (London, 1738), plate XXVII.
17. Clay Lancaster, *Antebellum Architecture of Kentucky*. (Lexington: University Press of Kentucky, 1991), 13–15.
18. Mills Lane, *Architecture of the Old South, Maryland*. (Savannah: Beehive Press, 1996), 63–64.
19. United States House Tax for the District of Berkeley County for 1798, 2.
20. *Virginia Gazette*, Rind (publisher), June 16, 1774, 3. Colonial Williamsburg collections.
21. John Ariss to Horatio Gates, August 21, 1773. Emmet Collection, New York City Historical Society, NY.
22. Ariss to Gates, June 21, 1783. Emmet Collection, New York City Historical Society, NY.

Chapter Three
Later Farmhouses, 1815–1835

1. Henry St. George Tucker to his father, St. George Tucker, January 8, 1814. Tucker-Coleman Papers, Correspondence, Item J902, Earl Gregg Swem Library, Special Collections, College of William and Mary, Williamsburg, VA.
2. Mills Lane, *Architecture of the Old South, North Carolina*. (Savannah: Beehive Press, 1997), 99–109.
3. Kimberly Prothro Williams, ed., *A Pride of Place: Rural Residences of Fauquier County, Virginia*. (Charlottesville and London: University of Virginia Press, 2003), 37, 64.
4. Williams, *Pride of Place*, 37–40.
5. Catherine W. Bishir and Michael T. Southern, *A Guide to the Historic Architecture of Piedmont North Carolina*. (Chapel Hill and London: University of North Carolina Press, 2003), 226.
6. Bishir and Southern, *Historic Architecture of Piedmont North Carolina*. 154–55, 226.

Bishir and Southern, *A Guide to the Historic Architecture of Eastern North Carolina.* (Chapel Hill and London: University of North Carolina Press, 1996), 303.

7. William Howard Adams, "Hazelfield: a note on its early history," *Magazine of the Jefferson County Historical Society*, 40 (December 1974), (Charles Town, WV: Jefferson County Historical Society, 1974), 47.

8. Charlotte Judd Fairbairn, "Claymont Court," *Magazine of the Jefferson County Historical Society*, 15 (December 1949), (Charles Town: Jefferson County Historical Society, 1949), 26.

9. Samuel Kercheval, *A History of the Valley of Virginia* (reprint of original). (Harrisonburg, VA: C. J. Carrier Company, 1994), 357.

10. 1830 Jefferson County Land Tax, microfilm collection, Berkeley County Historical Society archives, Martinsburg, WV.

11. *Martinsburg Gazette* (newspaper), October 15, 1829.

12. Kercheval, *Valley of Virginia*, 357.

13. Richard L. Bushman, *The Refinement of America.* (New York: Vintage Books, 1993), 17–20, 120–21, 273.

14. Henry Glassie, *Folk Housing in Middle Virginia.* (Knoxville: University of Tennessee Press, 1975), 78–81.

Chapter Four. Outbuildings
Farm Structures Serve the House

1. John Michael Vlach, *Back of the Big House: the Architecture of Plantation Slavery.* (Chapel Hill and London: The University of North Carolina Press, 1993), 43.

2. Lydia Henderson to Samuel Russell, 1812, Jefferson County Deed Book 37, page 328.

3. Michael Olmert, *Kitchens, Smokehouses, and Privies: Outbuildings and the Architecture of Daily Life in the Eighteenth-Century Mid-Atlantic.* (Ithaca and London: Cornell University Press, 2009), 42.

4. Amos Long Jr., *The Pennsylvania German Family Farm.* (Breinigsville, PA: The Pennsylvania German Society, 1972), 187.

5. Mary Randolph, *The Virginia Housewife or, Methodical Cook.* (New York: Dover Publications, 1993, first edition 1824), 48–50.

6. 1830 U.S. Census for Jefferson County, Virginia, 1850 U.S. Census for Jefferson County, Virginia; and *The Magazine of the Jefferson County Historical Society*, 56, 61. Data compiled by Donald E. Watts for the author.

7. Long, *Pennsylvania German Family Farm*, 252–55.

8. George Washington Papers, Library of Congress, Series 5, Ledger Bk 1, 131 (image 326).

9. David Hackett Fischer, *Albion's Seed: Four British Folkways in America.* (New York and Oxford: Oxford University Press, 1989), 535.

10. Robert F. Ensminger, *The Pennsylvania Barn*, 2nd ed. (Baltimore and London: The Johns Hopkins University Press, 1992), 21–37, 202–11.

11. R. W. Brunskill, *Traditional Buildings of Cumbria: The County of Lakes.* (London: Cassell, 2002), 105–12.
R. W. Brunskill, *Vernacular Architecture: An Illustrated Handbook.* (London: Faber and Faber, 2000, fourth edition), 154–57.

12. "The Jonathan Clark Notebook, July–Aug. 1786," transcription in Peggy S. Joyner, Northern Neck Warrants and Surveys, vol. 4; original document located in the Manuscripts Division, Clark-Hite Papers, The Filson Historical Society, Louisville, KY. 171–73.

13. Long, *Pennsylvania German Family Farm*, 455.

Chapter Five
Town Houses, 1780–1835

1. Clifford Musser, *History of Shepherdstown.* (Shepherdstown: The Independent, 1931), 7.

2. 1840 U.S. Census for Jefferson County, Virginia, from digitized original records.

3. Mabel Henshaw Gardiner and Ann Henshaw Gardiner, *Chronicles of Old Berkeley.* (Durham, NC: The Seeman Press, 1938), 53–54.

4. Thomas Kemp Cartmell, *Shenandoah Valley Pioneers and Their Descendants.* (Winchester, VA: published by author, 1909), 240.

5. Dell Upton, *Urban Life and Urban Spaces in the New American Republic.* (New Haven & London: Yale University Press, 2008), 4.

6. A. D. Kenamond, *Prominent Men of Shepherdstown* (Charles Town: Jefferson County Historical Society, 1963), 96.

7. A. D. Kenamond, "The Franks' Baker House," *Magazine of the Jefferson County Historical Society*, 27 (December 1962) (Charles Town: Jefferson County Historical Society, 1962), 21.

Chapter Six
Siting and Construction

1. 1810 U.S. Census for Jefferson County, Virginia, Prepared by Thomas Smallwood, first day of September 1810, transcribed from the original by John Vogt. 1830 U.S. Census for Jefferson County, Virginia, from original digitized records. 1850 U.S. Census and the *Magazine of the Jefferson County Historical Society*, 56, 61. Prepared by Donald E. Watts for the author, 2009.

2. David Hackett Fischer and James C. Kelly, *Bound Away: Virginia and the Westward Movement.* (Charlottesville: University of Virginia Press, 2000), 137.

3. Warren Hofstra, *The Planting of New Virginia: Settlement and Landscape in the Shenandoah Valley.* (Baltimore and London: The Johns Hopkins University Press, 2004), 98–102, 141.

4. David Hackett Fischer, *Albion's Seed: Four British Folkways in America.* (New York and Oxford: Oxford University Press, 1989), 655.

5. Alan B. Chance, "The Surveyor's Rod: A Value Expressed in Wood," *Point of Beginning.* (www.pobonline.com), November 25, 2002.

6. Hofstra, *The Planting of New Virginia.* 219–21.

7. Clay Lancaster, *Antebellum Architecture of Kentucky.* (Lexington, KY: University Press of Kentucky, 1991), 45–62.

8. "The Jonathan Clark Notebook, July–Aug. 1786," transcription in Peggy S. Joyner, Northern Neck Warrants and Surveys, vol. 4; original document located in the Manuscripts Division, Clark-Hite Papers, The Filson Historical Society, Louisville, KY. 168–69, 171–73. "United States House Tax Book for the District of Berkeley County for 1798." Transcribed by Don C. Wood, (Martinsburg, WV: Berkeley County Historical Society, 2003), 1–24.

9. Oral history: discussions with county residents and contractors, Michael Taylor and Joe Wimer with the author.

10. *The Potomac Guardian*, August 7, 1799.

11. *Berkeley and Jefferson County Intelligencer*, July 8, 1803.

12. U.S. House Tax of 1798, 1–24.

13. Clifford S. Musser, *History of Shepherdstown, 1730–1931.* (Shepherdstown, WV: The Independent, 1931, reprint edition, 1981), 13, 28.

14. Carl R. Lounsbury, *An Illustrated Glossary of Early Southern Architecture and Landscape.* (Charlottesville and London: University of Virginia Press, 1999), 379.

15. Lounsbury, *Glossary of Early Southern Architecture and Landscape*, 87.

16. J. Richard Rivoire, *Homeplaces: Traditional Domestic Architecture of Charles County, Maryland.* (La Plata, MD: Southern Maryland Studies Center, Charles County Community College, 1990), 12.

17. *Martinsburg Gazette*, January 9, 1824.

Chapter Seven
Exterior Features

1. William Salmon, *The London Art of Building.* (London: Second Edition, 1748), 104.

William Pain, *The Builder's Companion.* (London: Third Edition, 1769), 12.

2. *Potomac Guardian and Berkeley Advertiser*, November 14, 1791, and the Shepherdstown Board of Trustees minutes, July 1794, 10–11.

3. Danske Dandridge, *Historic Shepherdstown.* (Charlottesville, VA: The Mitchie Company Printers, 1910), 286.

4. Calder Loth, "Notes on the Evolution of Virginia Brickwork from the Seventeenth Century to the Late Nineteenth Century," *Bulletin of the Association for Preservation Technology*, 6, no. 2. (Springfield, IL: Association for Preservation Technology International, 1974), 95.

5. Loth, "Notes on the Evolution of Virginia Brickwork," 112.

6. Historic Preservation Trust of Lancaster County, *Lancaster County Architecture, 1700–1850.* (Lancaster, PA: HPTLC, 1992), viii, 53–169.

7. "The Jonathan Clark Notebook, July–Aug. 1786," transcription in Peggy S. Joyner, Northern Neck Warrants and Surveys, vol. 4; original document located in the Manuscripts Division, Clark-Hite Papers, The Filson Historical Society, Louisville, KY. 168–69, 171–73.

8. Richard Bushman, *The Refinement of America: Persons, Houses, Cities.* (New York: Vintage Books, 1992), 125.

9. Freight shipment bills and receipts 1836, Virginia Misc. Reel 54, Godfrey Miller Papers, Thornton Perry Collection, Charles Town Library, Charles Town, WV.

10. Carl R. Lounsbury, *An Illustrated Glossary of Early Southern Architecture and Landscape.* (Charlottesville and London: University Press of Virginia), 181–82.

11. Pamela H. Simpson, "The Molded Brick Cornice in the Valley of Virginia." *Bulletin of the Association of Preservation Technology*, 12, no. 4. (Springfield, IL: Association for Preservation Technology International,1980), 29–33.

12. "The Jonathan Clark Notebook, July–Aug. 1786," 171.

13. Mutual Assurance Society of Virginia. Declarations and Revaluations, 1796–1966, Accession 30177. Business records collection, The Library of Virginia, Richmond.

Chapter Eight
Interior Detailing

1. *The Berkeley and Jefferson Intelligencer*, January 13, 1814.

2. Owen Biddle, *The Young Carpenter's Assistant; or, a System of Architecture, Adapted to the Style of Building in the United States.* (Lancaster, PA: Benjamin Warner, publisher, 1806), plate 31.

3. Virginia Lindsay Miller and John G. Lewis, *Interior Woodwork of Winchester, Virginia: 1750–1850.* (Winchester, VA: Published by the author, 1994), 64.

4. Will of Battaile Muse, 1803, Jefferson County Will Book 1, page 49.

5. David G. Allen, "Jefferson County Ironworks." *Magazine of the Jefferson County Historical Society*, 70 (December 2004), 94–102.

6. Richard L. Bushman, *The Refinement of America: Persons, Houses, Cities.* (New York: Vintage Books, 1993), 126.

7. Miller and Lewis, *Interior Woodwork of Winchester, Virginia.* 120–27.

Chapter Nine
The End of Local: Arrival of the Railroad and Canal, 1835–1850

1. Charles H. Bohner, *John Pendleton Kennedy, Gentleman from Baltimore.* (Baltimore: The Johns Hopkins Press, 1961), 74–79.

2. James D. Dilts, *The Great Road: The Building of the Baltimore and Ohio, the Nation's First Railroad, 1828–1853.* (Stanford: Stanford University Press, 1993), 209.

3. Elizabeth Daniel, "Walnut Grove," *Magazine of the Jefferson County Historical Society*, 13 (December 1947). (Charles Town: Jefferson County Historical Society, 1947), 16.

4. 1830 U.S. Population Census for Jefferson County, VA, and 1850 U.S. Population Census for Jefferson County, VA, from digitized original documents.

5. *Annual Report of the Baltimore and Ohio Railroad*, 1847, 1848 and 1849, CSX Collection, Hays T. Watkins Research Library, Baltimore and Ohio Railroad Museum, Baltimore, MD.

Virginia Free Press, May 22, 1845 and June 5, 1845, microfilm collection, Harpers Ferry National Historical Park (HAFE) archives, Harpers Ferry, WV.

6. Paula Reed and Associates, "Lockwood House" Historic Structure Report, GWWO, Inc./Architects, Harpers Ferry National Historical Park. (June, 2006), 25.

7. Charles W. Snell, *A Comprehensive History of Armory Dwelling Houses of the U. S. Armory at Harper's Ferry, Virginia, 1798–1884.* (Denver: United States Department of Interior, 1981), 105–12.

8. Robert J. Kapsch, Historic American Buildings Survey, addendum to report on Paymaster's Quarters, HABS WV-179, National Park Service, U.S. Department of Interior, 1994–1995, 4–12.

9. Robert J. Kapsch, *The Potomac Canal: George Washington and the Waterway West.* (Morgantown: West Virginia University Press, 2007), 242, 253–56, 263.

10. "Register of Tolls Collected at Georgetown, compiled 1845–1854," MLR #P-315 and "Returns of Manifests Given at Lock 37, compiled 1851–1868," MLR #P-321, NARA RG 79, Textual Records of the Chesapeake and Ohio Canal Company (1828–1924), Archives II, College Park, MD.

11. Mills Lane, *Architecture of the Old South, North Carolina.* (Savannah: Beehive Press, 1997), 99–108.

Catherine W. Bishir and Michael T. Southern, *A Guide to the Historic Architecture of Eastern North Carolina.* (Chapel Hill and London: University of North Carolina Press, 1996), 295.

12. Winchester and Potomac Railroad Halltown Depot Ledger, October 1849 through September 1850, Handley Regional Library, Stewart Bell Jr. Archives.

Conclusion

1. Henry Glassie, *Folk Housing in Middle Virginia.* (Knoxville: University of Tennessee Press, 1975), 15.

2. Richard Guy Wilson and contributors, *Buildings of Virginia: Tidewater and Piedmont*, Society of Architectural Historians, Buildings of the United States. (Oxford: Oxford University Press, 2002), 25.

3. U.S. Department of Agriculture, *The Census of Agriculture, 1840* and. *The Census of Agriculture, 1860.* United States Department of State, *Compendium of the Enumeration of the Inhabitants and Statistics of the United States, 1841.* US Census Bureau, *1850 Census of Agriculture and Housing.* Compiled for author by Donald E. Watts.

Acknowledgments

I would like to thank the people who made significant contributions to this book: Lyle Rush, my assistant throughout the project, for his patience, humor, and willingness to work in driving snow, pouring rain, bitter cold, sweltering attics, dark basements, and poison ivy; Walter Smalling for his artistic vision, good company, and remarkable endurance throughout the entire project; Andy Lewis for teaching me new ways of looking at buildings and especially for sharing his many talents in this book; Edie Wallace for her careful research and enthusiasm for the project; Paula Reed for giving me much-needed perspective; Jenny Cooper for her beautiful pen work in inking the plans; Min Enghauser for her stunning scans of the scores of images in this book; Libby Howard for her keen eye and ear in editing the manuscript; Judd Stitziel for helping me to find my voice; Don Watts for digging deep into the record to find the information I needed; Bill Howard for his invaluable assistance with ever-frustrating computer systems; the staff at Black & White for their amazing film processing; Mehrdad Rahbar for his flawless scans of the plans and illustrations; Deborah Patton for the index; Robert Wiser for the design of the book; and finally, to the good people at WVU Press for bringing this project to life.

My thanks also go to the families of those individuals who worked on this book as they all sacrificed in order that their loved ones could help me meet schedules and deadlines. In particular Theresa Rush, Vicky and Eli Lewis, Ray Rhinehart, and the Howard family were selfless in their contributions. Of course my family had to sacrifice so that I could make this book, so my deepest gratitude goes to Jenny and Grady; my mom and dad; Heather, Ted, and Angie. Your love and support during this project means the world to me.

I would like to acknowledge those preservationists and historians who inspired me to take on this project: Catherine Bishir, John Cuthbert, David Hackett Fischer, Warren Hofstra, Clay Lancaster, W. Brown Morton, Thomas T. Waterman, and Don Wood. Thank you for sharing your passion for history with me.

Finally, I could not have made this book without the cooperation and assistance of the more than two hundred property owners throughout Jefferson County who allowed me to study their houses. These gracious people welcomed me into their homes and businesses with an openness I could not have foreseen. For their generosity and hospitality, I will always be grateful.

Research Information and Other Assistance

W. Howard Adams

Barbara Adamson

David G. Allen

American Institute of Architects

Berkeley County Historical Society

Catherine Bishir

Kip Campbell

S. Allen Chambers

Rodney Collins

Carmen Creamer

John Cuthbert

Alexandra di Valmarana

Curt Gaul

Galtjo Geerstsuma

Mary Glendinning

James Grantham

Bill Grantham

Kristine Gray

Hager House Museum: John Bryan

Harpers Ferry National Historical Park: Cathy Boyer, Peter Dessauer, Dennis Fry, Michelle Hammer, Rebecca Harriett, Mia Parsons, and Richard Raymond

Historic Shepherdstown and Museum

Warren Hofstra

Holy Cross Abbey: Robert Barnes and Carole Hensley

Greg Huber

Chuck Hulse

Jay Hurley

Jefferson County Historical Society

Jefferson County Museum: Jim Glymph and Sue Collins

David A. Kemnitzer

Chris Knorr

Library of Congress

Library of Virginia

Tom McGarry

Martha Ann McIntosh

Curt Mason

Michael Musick

Neumann Lewis Buchanan Architects

New York City Historical Society

Robert Orndorff

Susan Pierce

Jim Price

Doug Perks

Martin Perschler

Thomas Quick

Barbara Rasmussen

Doug Reed

Sarah J. Reed

Meghan Reed

John Restaino

Bill Rice

Erin Riebe

Cynthia Schott

Mark Schiavone

Victora Seibert

Shepherdstown Men's Club

Shenandoah County Historical Society

Beverly Sherrid

Vickie Smith

Michael Southern

Jim Surkamp

Bill Theriault

Cam Tabb

Virginia Tabb

Dan Tokar

Virginia Historical Society

John A. Washington

Walter Washington

Don Watts

Matt Webster

Joe Wimer

Don Wood

Rebekah Wood

Tony Wrenn

Artwork

The Colonial Williamsburg Foundation

Corcoran Gallery of Art

Godel & Co. Fine Art

Historic Shepherdstown and Museum

Maryland Historical Society

Maryland State Archives

Massachussetts Historical Society

Metropolitan Museum of Art

Museum of Early Southern Decorative Arts

Virginia Historical Society

West Virginia and Regional Collection

Survey Facilitators

Harry and Bernadine Barr

Brenda Burlin

Jody Carter

Linda Case

Nigel Casserley

Peter Corum

John Cowan

Carmen Creamer

Paul Davis

Phil Dietrich

Jim and Barbara Gibson

Pat Fiori and Bill Jackson

Denver Hipp

Nancy Hockensmith

Mary Frances Hockman

Jay Hurley

Chipp Huyette

Earl and Rita Jones

Marty and Carol Kable

Ann Knode

Jackie Lewis

Betty Lowe

Nancy Lutz

Bill Marshall

Curt Mason

Sarah Mathias

Kit McGinnis

Delores Milstead

Rusty and Cricket Morgan

Brucie Moulton

Carlos Niederhouser

John and Sylvie O'Brien

Roger and Wanda Perry

Paul Pritchard

Bob and Marty Putz

Jane Rissler

Lyle and Theresa Rush

George Rutherford

Scooter Scudieri

Henry Shepherd

Carolyn Snyder

Fred Soltow

Virginia Tabb

Michael Taylor

Walter Washington

Margaret Welling

Hank Willard

Creighton Workman

Ian Workman

Readers and Reviewers

Keith Alexander

Joan Brierton

Heather Ewing

Andy Lewis

Brown Morton

Paula Reed

Walter Smalling

Judd Stitziel

Bill Theriault

Edie Wallace

Plans

Historic American
Buildings Survey

David A. Kemnitzer

Alan Levitan

Andrew Lewis

Michael Mills

Gavin Perry

Lyle Rush

Walton "Kip" Stowell

Thomas Waterman

Jill Ziegler

WVU Press

Patrick Conner

Floann Downey

Abby Freeland

Carrie Mullen

Than Saffel

Property Owners

Charles and Elizabeth Adams

Lynn Adams

W. Howard Adams

AF and AM Star Lodge #1

David and Bea Aguilar

Tom and Janet Aitchson

Michael and Rene Arant

Pat and Dave Arnaudo

George and Catherine Athey

John Bane

Harry and Bernadine Barr

Mary Bell and Sandy Jenkins

Dow and Linda Benedict

Barbara Bratino

Wayne Bronson
and Brenda Thorne

Ronald Brown

Frank Buckles

John Buckley
and Patricia Weaver

Caleb Burns

David Burns

Jimmy Burns

John Porter Burns

Richard Burns

Harry and Barbara Byrd

Catherine Byron

Jamie and Snowden Byron

Mary Ann Cage

Lou Sullivan Carter

Woodbury and Patricia Carter

Linda Case

Jim Casey

Dabney Chapman

John Christman

Ann Christy

Claymont Society
for Continuous Education

David Coleman

David Collins

Ora Cooper

Ellen Corbin and Phil Falzgraf

Peter and Andrea Corum

Tom Coyle

Julia Shirley Creamer

Carmen and John Creamer

Bruce Dahlin

Henry and Faye Davenport

Blackie and Eileen Davis

Paul and Laura Davis

Pat and Jean Denny

Rodney and Lynn Dias

Maureen DiLella

Sam and Lane Donley

Tom and Sandy D'Onofrio

Duffields Station Inc.:
Jack Snyder

Sinclair Dunlop

Stanley and Kitty Dunn

Tom Farndon

Susannah Flanagan

Anita and Bruce Fleshman

Mark Folk

Guy Frank

Robert French

Charles French

Nick Frobouck

Mrs. Funkhouser

Randy and Sissy Funkhouser

Pat Gageby

Bill and Mary Gavin

George Tyler Moore Center
for the Study of the Civil War:
Mark Snell and Tom White

Dr. Jim and Barbara Gibson

Margery Gifford

Marshall and Laura Glenn

Bill White and Kerry
Grantham

William Grantham

Patricia and Russell Graves

George and Robin Greenhalgh

Jeff Grier

Deborah and Philip Hale

Chris and Maura Halverson

Thomas and Elise Hastry

Randolph and Betty Hayes

Bernard Heiler

Gay and Mike Henderson

Hazel Hendricks

Jesse Hendrix

Mary Hendrix

Bill Hewitt

Frank Hill

Russell and Louise Hobson

Nancy Hockensmith

Gordon Hockman

Jerry Hockman

Mary Frances Hockman

Ruth Hoxton

Arthur and Sally Hurme

Tom and Barbara Ingersoll

Mike and Jane Ishman

Jefferson County Historic
Landmarks Commission

Eric and Catharine Johnson

Ernest and Joan Johnston

Lee and Katie Jones

Marty and Carol Kable

James Keaton
and Mark Reinhart

Jim Keel

Bob and Cindy Keller

David, Sue, and Alex
Kemnitzer

Kent Cartridge:
Linda Barnhart and
Tony Jameson

Suzette Kimball
and Curt Mason

Ann Knode

Cris Kwisella

Jim Leathers

Jim and Kate Lehrer

Eric and Joy Lewis

Jackie Lewis

Andy Link

Eric and Stacy Lindbergh

Philip Lowe

John and Renee Lowe

Kim Lowery and Bill Neufeld

Bill Lukens

Daniel Lutz

Nancy Lutz

J. Davitt and Kathryn
MacAteer

Martha Ann MacIntosh

Jake McFarlaine

Louise McDonald

Suzanne Leland McKenzie

Cooper McQuilken

Sen. Charles "Mac" Mathias

Joe Matthews and John Shank

Ellen and Bill May

Brian and Allison Meley

Millville Quarries: Greg Barr

Delores and Wayne Milstead

Roger Munro

Bob Moore

Elizabeth Moores

Frances Morgan

Rusty and Cricket Morgan

Bucky Morrow

Sally Moulton

Annette Murphy

Michael Musick

Suellen Myers

Carlos Niederhouser

Abbie Northrup

John and Sylvie O'Brien

Sandra and Kenneth Osbourn

Mark Outhier

Alfred Owens

Michele Palencar

Christine Parfitt

William and Diana Penrod

Roger and Wanda Perry

Paige Pfifer

Ray and Barbara Pichot

Tony Price

Grant and Lillian Prillaman

Charles and Beth Prinz

Paul Pritchard

Prospect Hall Shooting Club:
Phil Dietrich

Harry and Linda Puster

Bob and Marty Putz

Jack and Dottie Quinn

Toby Raphael and Hali Taylor

Turner Ramey

Ionna Ramsay

Neal Randella

Mrs. Renaud

John Restaino and Mark
Schiavone

Alice Reynolds

Charles Rocheleau

Eleanor Rodman

Craig and Terri Rosenthal

George Rutherford

Robert and Jo Anne Scharmer

GT and Susie Schramm

Laury Scott

Guy and Gwen Shelton

Henry Shepherd

Shepherd University

Mike Shepp and Janet Olcott

Frances Shirley

Cindy Shomo-gatto

Cricky and Michele Shultz

Stephen Skinner

Elizabeth Smith

Matt and Donna Smith

Henry and Edna Snyder

John and Hope Snyder

Kevin Snyder

Mac and Helen Snyder

Nick and Mimi Snyder

Joe and Barbara Sobol

Mary and Ron Sosnicki

Stanley and Barbara Stiles

Oscar and Janet Stine

Thomas and Judy Stokes

Bill Strider

Becky and Allen Sullivan

Dianna Suttenfield

Howard Tabb

Virginia Tabb

Yves and Giulia Tencalla

Michael and Anne Taylor

Leah Taylor

Mary Toborg

Seldon Todd

David and Nancy Trail

USDA Experimental
Fruit Tree Farm

Annette and Frank Van Hilst

Charles Via

Esther Via

Evelyn Lucile Waltz

Burwell Ware

Joe and Heidi Ware

Walter Washington

Paul and Lisa Welch

Tammy Wells-Cato

Wesley and Kathy Wendell

Ron and Lynn Widmyer

DeMariss and
Van Court Wilkins

Hank Willard

Nancy Wilson

Virginia Winston

Ed Wormald

Carissa and Christopher Zane

Linda Zangla

Contributors

JOHN C. ALLEN, JR., is an architectural historian in Jefferson County, West Virginia, where he lives with his family. A graduate of Tulane University, Allen is a member of the Society of Architectural Historians and the Vernacular Architecture Forum. He serves as the chairman of the Jefferson County Historic Landmarks Commission and consults on preservation projects in the area. *Uncommon Vernacular* is his first book.

ANDREW LEWIS, AIA, is a principal at the architectural firm Neumann Lewis Buchanan Architects of Washington, D.C., and Middleburg, Virginia. He received his architectural education at Virginia Tech. In addition to his residential and commercial design practice, Lewis also works as an architectural illustrator, and is a member of the Society of Architectural Illustrators.

WALTER SMALLING, JR., has been an architectural photographer in Washington, D.C., for more than thirty years. He began his professional career documenting buildings for the National Park Service. Smalling has worked for the American Institute of Architects, the National Register of Historic Places, and the Historic American Buildings Survey. His photographs have been published in numerous architectural books and magazines.

EDITH WALLACE is senior historian with the cultural resources consulting firm Paula Reed and Associates in Hagerstown, Maryland, where she has worked for twelve years. After receiving her bachelor of arts in anthropology from the University of Delaware, Wallace earned a master of arts in historic preservation from Goucher College.

Index

A Note on the Type

JOHN BELL (1746–1831), an English publisher of newspapers and books, started the British Letter Foundry in 1788. Employing the talented punchcutter Richard Austin (fl. 1788–1830), the foundry produced the notable Bell type, considered today a great English type in the tradition of William Caslon and John Baskerville. Inspired by the work of the Frenchmen Pierre Simon Fournier and Firmin Didot, Bell and Austin created what the renowned typographic scholar Stanley Morison has referred to as the first English modern-style typeface, one whose design is characterized by greater stroke contrast and vertical stress than other English types of the period. American type founders copied the Bell type as early as 1792. In 1864, the American book publisher Henry O. Houghton acquired type cast from the original Bell matrices for use by his Riverside Press, which later employed such typographic luminaries as Daniel Berkeley Updike and Bruce Rogers. Updike liked the Bell type so much he created his own version called Mountjoye and Rogers followed suit with his typeface Brimmer. Stanley Morison supervised a facsimile revival of the Bell type by Monotype, in collaboration with Stephenson-Blake, to celebrate the centenary of John Bell's death in 1931.